BRAGGING RITES

BRAGGING RITES

COLLEGE FOOTBALL'S DISPUTED TITLES

KEITH GÅDDIE

TCU Press

FORT WORTH, TEXAS

Library of Congress Control Number: 2025019026

On the cover: Caricature of Georgia running back Herschel Walker by Jack Davis. For full illustration and caption, see page 22. Printed with permission of the Davis family as rights holder.

TCU
Press

TCU Box 298300
Fort Worth, Texas 76129

www.tcupress.com

Designed by Julie Rushing

For Kim,

the biggest, baddest UGA football

fan in all of Bulldog Nation, or as our good friend

Peay termed her, "Khaleesi of the High Cotton

and Mother of Bulldogs."

CONTENTS

ACKNOWLEDGMENTS

This book has been on my mind for a long time, but it really started in earnest in January 2018, when the University of Central Florida (UCF) decided to claim the Colley Matrix national title. Mind you, the College Football Playoff (CFP) Selection Committee had pitted four storied franchises with some of the best overall records of the 2010s against each other—Alabama, Clemson, Georgia, and Oklahoma—in dramatic matchups that resulted in another Alabama title. UCF, meanwhile, had gone undefeated against the seventy-fifth-toughest schedule in the Football Bowl Subdivision. They ranked tenth in the last regular-season AP poll and then beat Auburn, 34–27, in the Peach Bowl to finish sixth in the final AP rankings. All four CFP teams played far tougher schedules and had higher power ratings. Then I noticed that Oklahoma State had generated a national title from the ether for 1945. And Kentucky had decided to suddenly claim a retrospective title for 1950. USC and Georgia had also claimed historic titles long after they occurred.

Then I reflected on all the times the writers poll and the Coaches Poll disagreed. Like 2003. And 1997. And 1991. And so on. I decided I needed to dig into this puzzle. Toni Morrison said, "If there's a book that you want to read, but it hasn't been written yet, then you must write it." I spent three seasons sitting in "the football chair," that perfectly positioned chair in the living room that affords a view of the TV, quick access to the beer fridge, and a handy place to put a plate with a barbecue sandwich where the dogs can't get it. With all the Saturday games playing, I pored over seasons and champions and metrics, trying to run down, analyze, and understand the disputed national champions of college football and how and why we ended up with this fun, convoluted, and frustrating history of selecting national champs.

Kim was right there, all along the way, as well as our bulldogs Georgia (b. 2013, d. 2021), Rosie, Winston, and Baxter, listening to me recount what I found and encouraging the effort. We also ended a frustrating drought of titles for our beloved UGA with back-to-back CFP championships in 2021–2022 and no dissents. Winston also presided over writing sessions in my study, staring expectantly at whatever snack sat next to my laptop and providing close supervision (Winston in his editorial position appears below).

TCU Press was then good enough to express interest in the book. My thanks to editor Dan Williams for taking a chance on this book and to my dear friend (and now colleague) Jim Riddlesperger for connecting me with Dan. TCU undergraduate Delaney Vega of the Bob Schieffer College of Communication did a great job of copyediting the final manuscript, which is far improved by her efforts. The outstanding work of the copy editors and production team at TCU Press took a typescript and a bundle of pictures and created this wonderful, attractive book: Adrienne Martinez, Kurt Daniels, Alex Gergely, and Julie Rushing.

Any errors of logic, research, or reasoning reside with me and arise from my education at the University of Georgia. Lewis Grizzard (UGA '68) noted, "A lot of people said that if you drove through Athens with your window down, they'd throw a diploma in your car. That ain't true. You've got to stop first." And so I did.

Go Dawgs.

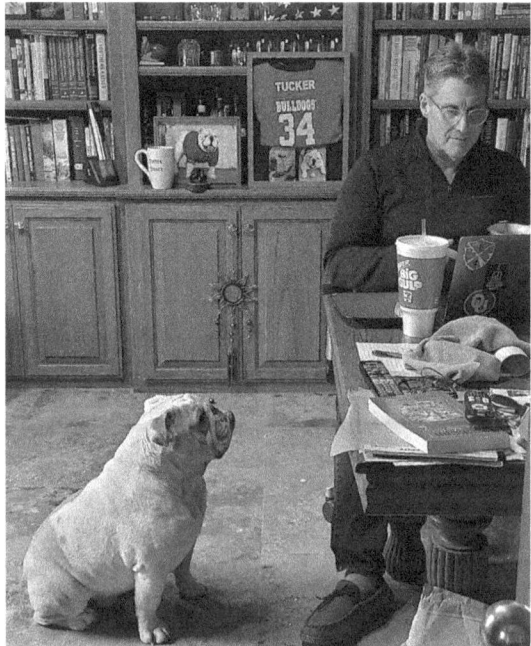

The author at work. AUTHOR IMAGE

BEST PRACTICES FOR CLAIMING A NATIONAL FOOTBALL TITLE

1. Win all the Consensus Major Selector titles for the season.

2. In the event that the Consensus Major Selectors split, be the winner of at least one of those titles.

3. Beat all other claimants to titles for that season.

4. <u>Do not</u> make the sole basis for your title claim an algorithm or other selector who disagrees not just with the Consensus Major Selectors but also with all the participants in the games who determined the title (BCS, CFP, or other one-two matchups in major bowls).

5. <u>Do not</u> accept a title retrospectively, unless you also happen to have defeated one of the Consensus Major Selectors for that season. And even then, don't do it.

6. <u>Definitely do not</u> apply for a retrospective title based on an algorithm, especially one no one has ever heard of.

7. <u>Do not accept</u> a national title from a state legislature.

8. <u>Do not confer a title on yourself</u> with absolutely no other basis for the claim from an external party or authority.

INTRODUCTION

As it was in the beginning
So it is and ever shall be
Bama should win
Amen, amen!

—DOXOLOGY OF THE SEC

On January 20, 2025, history was made. Ohio State won the College Football Playoff (CFP), topping Notre Dame, 34–23, at Mercedes-Benz Stadium in Atlanta. Buckeyes head coach Ryan Day stood in the middle of UGA's second home field and held aloft the greatest prize in college sports, the College Football Playoff National Championship Trophy. Two seasons before, Day had seen a march to the national title come undone in the Peach Bowl against the aforementioned Georgia Bulldogs, when a last-second field goal attempt by OSU's Noah Ruggles missed at the stroke of midnight, handing Georgia a 42–41 win and trip to a second-straight CFP final and title.

The Buckeyes' convincing win over Notre Dame, who had beaten UGA in the quarterfinals, offered Day salvation from a regular season that had ended with a stinging[1] loss at home to Michigan. Ohio State's march through the playoff fundamentally changed Ryan Day's career trajectory in Columbus.

The Buckeyes came into the championship showdown as a nine-point favorite and led from the second quarter forward in a game where they were more dominating than the score indicated. These two teams were nowhere near the favorites, though. At the start of the CFP, the odds said it would be Oregon and Georgia. The Buckeyes were given a one-in-eight chance of winning it all; the Irish one-in-eleven. Earlier that Monday morning, Ralph Russo[2] of *The Athletic* asked the critical question that goes to the heart of this book, "How should the final AP poll handle the twelve-team Playoff? College football history depends on it."

The four-round knockout tournament was intended to end decades of argument and controversy surrounding the choice of a national collegiate football champion. However, the tournament was declared "failed" by the punditry from the moment the seedings were announced. Within minutes of the reveal of CFP participants on December 8, talking heads in sports journalism, partisans of the teams left out of the playoff (especially Alabama), and athletic directors upset with the seedings were all attacking the choices, the criteria, and even the composition of the committee members who selected the final field. The SEC, which was incredibly competitive and had beat up on itself all season, was disappointed at only claiming three of a dozen slots. So as it had been with the four-team CFP, the two-team BCS Bowl, the bowl system before that, the dueling and sometimes incongruent AP and Coaches polls, and the various other mythical championships of the distant past, the process came under fire.

That journalists, pundits, and fans went after the twelve-team format should come as no surprise. They often attacked the old systems. They've argued over the cutoff points for participating in a four-team playoff. Before there was a playoff, they criticized the people who determined champions: writers, coaches, algorithms. To be an American sports fan is to live in a euphoria wrapped up in discontent. To be a sports journalist is to activate euphoria and discontent, raising the stakes of big ol', full-grown men playing games on a cow pasture to a level comparable to the Battle of Stalingrad.[3]

Then the playoff had the audacity to work. The format was designed to resolve a decades-long controversy over picking a consensus national champion while ensuring representation among the conference champions and other outstanding teams. When Ohio State won the CFP, the Coaches Poll was contractually bound to vote them as champion. No such limitation existed for two journalistic Consensus Major Selectors: the Associated Press (AP) writers poll and the Football Writers Association of America. The AP dissented from the BCS result after the 2003 season, and it seemed the possibility of a dissent might loom again in 2024. So where the AP landed mattered. The AP poll is the gold standard, the historic title against which all other comers have been measured.

The writers also anointed the Buckeyes the CFP champion and cemented the legitimacy of the playoff and its result. Stewart Mandel hinted at the direction in his column for *The Athletic*, opining that Ohio State "was always the best" while also noting that OSU had kept it "interesting." When the final poll dropped just after lunch on January 21, Ohio State was the unanimous No. 1 pick, followed by Notre Dame, Oregon, Texas, Penn State, and Georgia.

So there would be no formal controversy with the result of the 2024 CFP. The Playoff, the human beings, and in all likelihood most, if not all, of the algorithms would agree. The benchmark Sagarin rating for top-rated Ohio State (97.21) was well above Notre Dame (92.92) and all others. ESPN's similar Power Index placed the Buckeyes (27.9) first and clearly above Texas (25.3) and Notre Dame (25.2). The Simple Rating System score over at Sports-Reference, a foundational measure to which other algorithms are highly correlated, computed Ohio State as the strongest team in the nation after the Playoff final with a power rating score (25.21) substantially above Notre Dame (21.69), Oregon (20.04), Penn State (19.60), and Texas (19.30). While some algorithm somewhere might have another champion, the Playoff, the writers, and the math all agreed. So for at least one year, controversy could (finally) take a holiday.

This has not always been the case, and that is why I wrote this book. For nearly a century, controversy and also resistance to reform have been the norm in picking major college football champions. This book is the story of the controversies as well as the lurching, flawed consequences of efforts to reform the champion-picking process.

ORGANIZATION OF THE BOOK

This book has seven chapters, and also three short appendices. Chapter 1, "The Ultimate Sports Bar Argument," introduces the controversy that historically surrounded the selection of college football national champions and the kind of reasoning that is used by fans to justify their preferences when there isn't a consensus about who is the best team.

Chapter 2, "Picking National Champions: Creating the Era of Bowls and Polls," describes the initial creation of the concept of "national champions" by lawyer and former Princeton player Parke Davis and the subsequent creation of algorithmic and expert poll championships in the first half of the twentieth century. The section also lays out the fan-centric rationale for the disputed championships examined in the book.

Chapter 3, "Split Consensus Major Selector Champions," examines the cases where the big-time selectors—the AP writers and Coaches—disagreed on who was champion, while chapter 4 looks at "Four Notable Dissents by the Football Writers Association of America," which is deemed a Consensus Major Selector on par with the AP and Coaches polls. Then in chapter 5, we'll take up "The Dissenting Title Claims," where programs that did not win a Consensus Major Selector title still claim one conferred by another NCAA-recognized entity. This chapter also deals with recent retrospective titles claimed by major programs.

The last two chapters of the book delve into the efforts taken to fix the "problem" of disputed collegiate national championships and determine a champion on the field. Chapter 6, "BCS: A Fix as Good as the Problem," explores the creation and clunky evolution of the Bowl Championship Series (BCS), from its inception in the 1990s, through its failure in 2003, until it was supplanted by the College Football Playoff in 2014, which is examined in chapter 7, "The CFP: Fighting over Pecking Order."

The appendices following the main text include my own subjective take on disputed titles, a list of all the Consensus Major Selector winners, and an examination and discussion of college football power ratings that I once wrote up for a sports client and decided to include here as a supplement.

My thanks for your readership and your fandom.

Go Dawgs.

CHAPTER 1

THE ULTIMATE SPORTS BAR ARGUMENT

"If they choose to vote you number one, then you're the national champion. But a national champion is a mythical national champion,[1] and I think you guys ought to know that. It's mythical."
—BO SCHEMBECHLER, 1989

Fans demand championships. Institutions demand championships. Failure in the drive to be at the top has cost even the very best coaches their jobs. Expectations are high at the highest levels of competition. Symbolic of this is the undated national championship trophy presented to Jimbo Fisher upon being named head coach at Texas A&M in 2018. The Aggies have not claimed a title since before World War II and would pay any price to get one. Fisher had been an offensive coordinator for a national champion at Louisiana State University (LSU) in 2003 and won a unanimous national title as the head coach at Florida State (FSU) in 2013. A&M signed Fisher to a record contract, but no title was forthcoming. He was fired before the end of the 2023 season and paid a contract buyout of $77.5 million—the largest in football history.

For a college football fan, there's no better bar argument than, Who is "the best"? Who is the best quarterback? Running back? Defensive back? Offense? Team? Fan base? Tailgate? And in the case of the National Collegiate Athletic Association (NCAA) Division I Football Bowl Subdivision (FBS), Who is the best team in the nation? Is the national champion really the champion?[2]

This last argument is historically tough to resolve in college football because, unlike every other college sport, until recently major college football historically lacked a mechanism to pick a single champion on the field. And the efforts at creating a mechanism have suffered from problems of implementation and legitimacy, requiring incremental efforts over three decades to resolve. As of the completion of this book in 2024, these problems have continued.

For decades, the collegiate powers left the decision to others to pick a champion. By the time the need and public desire to have a singular champion became set in mortar, myriad claims existed based on different authorities or evidence. Rather than sorting the matter out, the NCAA simply recognized all those claims, even if doing so set up conflicts. As the folks over at Bleacher Report noted a few years back, "From polls closing before bowl games were played prior to 1965, to the mess that is the BCS, college football has struggled with one problem more than any others: Deciding who the best team is. In some cases it's clear; in many, many others, it's far from it."[3] Indeed, to this day the NCAA has no formal role in the selection of college athletics' marquee national champion.

Let's cut to the chase. The historic matter of "Who is champion?" is still a mess. In thirty-seven of the eighty-nine seasons since the first Associated Press (AP) poll (1936–2024), there are at least two teams claiming the national championship. These claims are backed by recognition from the NCAA, which can be added to the litany of equivocating failures by that august body. That's 42 percent of all championship seasons. The mess is working itself out. An expanded playoff was pursued and accomplished in the early years of the 2020s, with a twelve-team field being used for the first time in the 2024 season.

The century-long internal conflict in deciding a champion was hard to avoid as the game and media went national. College football grew up and became institutionalized in an environment where rivalries were local or regional, determined by scheduling that was based on limited travel budgets and relied on trains and buses rather than jets to convey teams and fans. Other than those in the stands, no one saw or heard the games. At best, secondhand knowledge conveyed by reporters served to create a body of knowledge that was driven by comparison of reputation and

Walter Cronkite was the original voice of University of Oklahoma football for WKY radio in Oklahoma City. He instead went on to do serious news, eventually becoming "the most trusted man in America" as anchor of the *CBS Evening News* from 1962–80. The fifty-thousand-watt clear-channel radio stations of America broadcast coast to coast, bringing local news and brands to listeners, including updates on local sports. And before nationally televised games came along, it was radio that brought college football to the country. (This image of Cronkite hangs on my office wall because my first regular radio work was for WKY 930 in Oklahoma City.) UNIVERSITY OF OKLAHOMA WESTERN HISTORY COLLECTION

comparison of performance. Results were conveyed through newspapers, sports magazines, or through sports news recaps over the radio as national networks emerged in the 1920s. Radio broadcasts or rebroadcasts of games eventually brought the sport to the masses. (Two of the men who defined the latter twentieth century in the United States, Ronald Reagan and Walter Cronkite, got their starts behind radio microphones calling sports.)

But there was no national championship. The Rose Bowl began its annual run in 1916 with other bowl games emerging in the 1930s. And some experts started declaring champions, largely based on selection criteria or mathematical algorithms. But no one had the authority to organize the sport to determine who was the best. Today's sports fan, constantly bombarded with sports content and complex sports regulatory and economic sources, might find it surprising, but the modern sports championship industry and the idea of the NCAA as a national brand took most of the twentieth century to emerge.

The NCAA was created in 1906—in response to conferences at the White House, sponsored by President Theodore Roosevelt—to curb violence and deaths related to college football (a ban on the game was threatened).[4] Christopher Klein wrote about this intervention and the *Chicago Tribune*'s documentation of the sport's viciousness, noting "that in 1904 alone, there were 18 football deaths and 159 serious injuries, mostly among prep school players. Obituaries of young pigskin players ran on a nearly weekly basis during the football season. The carnage appalled America. Newspaper editorials called on colleges and high schools to banish football outright." Klein also referred to how the *Tribune* described the 1905 season as a "death harvest" following 19 fatalities and 137 serious injuries.

The Intercollegiate Athletic Association of the United States, which eventually evolved into the NCAA, was created therefore to govern the

Teddy Roosevelt was the youngest president in US history and in 1906 won the Nobel Peace Prize for brokering the peaceful end of the Russo-Japanese War. More importantly, he saved college football by helping to institute new rules designed to make the game safer. The magazine *Puck* made good use of the intersection of Roosevelt's "strenuous life" philosophy and football in this 1906 cartoon. FROM *PUCK* MAGAZINE, 1906; IMAGE IN THE PUBLIC DOMAIN

Andy Coats was district attorney of Oklahoma County and later mayor of Oklahoma City. Eventually he was dean of the University of Oklahoma College of Law. Legal history knows him best for representing OU and the University of Georgia in *NCAA v. Board of Regents of the University of Oklahoma*, the case that successfully broke the NCAA's monopoly of college football broadcasting. The head coaches at OU and Georgia, Barry Switzer and Vince Dooley, had collected three national titles in the eight years before the bench trial of the case in 1982. In 2023, Coats would bemoan his role in opening up the coffers of college football TV revenue. The NCAA was represented by Frank Easterbrook, who was later named a federal appeals judge by Ronald Reagan. I enjoyed these nuggets when I found them because I'm acquainted with Andy from when he was dean at OU, and I twice appeared as an expert witness in federal court before Judge Easterbrook. IMAGE IN THE PUBLIC DOMAIN, CITY OF OKLAHOMA CITY

health and safety of collegians and to ensure the maintenance of amateurism and prevent corruption. The organization of the sport through regional conferences managed issues of scheduling and competition and even the declaration of regional champions. Sponsorship of different sports started in the 1920s and expanded through the 1960s. And the NCAA started sponsoring championships and tournaments before World War II, including its crown jewel, the men's college basketball tournament.

Still, the NCAA seemed to be in the business of limiting exposure to football. Until the 1980s, two games were televised in any market on weekends, and radio was the medium through which most football was enjoyed. A team might appear on national television once a season. The NCAA constrained TV broadcasts because of a 1950s study by the National Opinion Research Center at the University of Chicago, which found TV broadcasts hurt game attendance.

All this changed when the "Men Who Invented Saturday," the Board of Regents of the University of Oklahoma and the University of Georgia Athletic Association, sued the NCAA over the organization's stronghold on TV revenue. The case, *NCAA v. Board of Regents of the University of Oklahoma*, 468 U.S. 85 (1984), changed the sports world, breaking the NCAA's monopoly on distribution and revenue and unleashing a torrent of content that would fill the hours of the then-infant sports cable industry. The drumbeat for an on-the-field champion took off soon after, even as the frequency of split championships continued.

The environment for determining a national championship on the field wasn't truly created until the 1990s, after the game went national and the NCAA lost its primacy over major college football once losing control of the money in 1984. In the meantime, what we were left with was championship by bar argument.[5]

Absent an on-the-gridiron system to cull the field and leave a single winner standing, someone, somewhere was going to dig up what's historically called the "Slippery Rock Argument" to justify a champion. It is foundational to the bar-argument approach to determining a college football champion. The Slippery Rock Argument applies what's called transitive logic through chains of matchups in order to land on an ultimate king of the hill.[6]

Here's how: in arguing about "real champs," for one hundred years we've encountered the **superficial transitive property theorem** (STPT). The odds are, if you're a sports fan, you've been in a bar or a chatroom and

The Slippery Rock Argument. The 1936 Slippery Rock football team went 6–3 but owned transitive-property superiority over three teams that had been ranked No. 1 and one that had been ranked No. 3. NCAA-recognized selectors chose four different national champs in 1936, three of whom could trace a loss chain back to someone defeated by the Rockets. PRINTED WITH THE PERMISSION OF SLIPPERY ROCK UNIVERSITY ATHLETICS

someone starts playing the "whatabouta" game. The conversation starts out about a team, a contender. Then a fan of some other contender challenges the conversation, using the "Team A beat Team B, who beat Team C, who in turn beat Team D. Thus, Team A is better than Team D." A > B > C > D, therefore A>D. This is the STPT as applied to sports.[7]

The STPT is arguably the most important tool developed in the history of bar arguments over which team is better. Also called "backtracking arithmetic," the STPT began entering conversations about national championships in 1936 (also the first year the Associated Press would pick a national champion—Minnesota). Six other selectors picked Pittsburgh (Pitt), Duke, or LSU, so sportswriters started having fun trying to figure out if there was a college—any college—that had a series of transitive wins to create a domain over all other purported national champions. This was the first of four Consensus Major Selector titles won by the Gophers.

But if we apply the STPT, we discover that the school then known as Slippery Rock State Teachers College in Western Pennsylvania had a pretty good transitive claim. The Rockets were 6–3 that year but beat Westminster, which had defeated West Virginia Wesleyan, which beat Duquesne, which beat Pitt, which beat Notre Dame, which beat Northwestern, which had beaten Minnesota. The last two teams had been ranked No. 1 in the AP poll at some point during the regular season, and Pitt had been ranked as high as No. 2.

This book informs the bar argument and tries to take it seriously by jumping past superficial transitivity (while also promising to not get lost in stats-speak after this paragraph) to get the conditional tools and subjective and objective proof needed by fans to tease out championship arguments using data, history, bar logic, and other means that extend beyond the STPT framework. The following pages get into expert evaluations, polls by the wire services, committees, and to some extent the blessed but cursed algorithms.

My journey starts with a story of the first crash and burn by the Bowl Championship Series (BCS), which was supposed to render all the other championship mechanisms obsolete. It did not. Come with me to January 4, 2004.

Bob Stoops won a national title in 2000 and went 190-48 in eighteen seasons at OU (1999-2016). He then stepped in as interim coach in 2021 to lead the Sooners to victory in the Alamo Bowl. His teams played for the BCS title or in the CFP in 2000, 2003, 2004, 2008, and 2015. THE UNIVERSITY OF OKLAHOMA

I'm in Atlanta on an election-law consulting job. The clients are suing the state of Georgia. After buying a suit and having it altered because I left mine hanging in my closet back in Norman, Oklahoma, it's dinner with the lawyers and then downtime before the start of the trial the next day. They're not football fans. I excuse myself after dessert and go back to the Four Seasons Hotel to watch the Sugar Bowl. I land in front of the TV in my room just in time for kickoff. The Oklahoma Sooners (OU), coached by Bob Stoops,[8] were taking on the LSU Tigers, coached by Nick Saban, for the BCS title.[9] OU had run the table in the regular season, holding the No. 1 spot in the AP and Coaches polls while going 12–0 to win the Big 12 South. The Sooners were amid an amazing ride that started with the perfect 2000 national championship season. That fall, on October 1, OU had moved into the AP's top ten and had practically stayed there for four years. The Sooners only dropped out of the top four for a total of six weeks over that span, falling below eighth just once, a two-week stretch in 2001. Now in 2003, they were set to go wire-to-wire ranked No. 1, from the preseason to the BCS title game.[10]

In December, the Sooners had gone into the Big 12 title game in Kansas City as a prohibitive favorite against the conference's North winner, Kansas State. Wildcats head coach Bill Snyder, a legend who counted Stoops among his protégés as well as much of the Sooner staff, was still stalking his first national title, having come close in 1998 (until R. C. Slocum's Texas A&M Aggies derailed Kansas State's perfect season with a loss in the Big 12 title game).

A win here, five years later in Kansas City, wouldn't put Snyder's Wildcats back in the national title hunt, but it would return the favor from 2000 when Stoops's Sooners had beaten No. 2 Kansas State, 41–31, on an October afternoon in Manhattan with ESPN's *College GameDay* in town (OU then beat K-State again in the Big 12 title game before going to Miami to destroy Florida State, 13–2, in the January 2001 Orange Bowl).

But this was 2003, December, and a far cry from the mild but windy autumn afternoons found on the Kansas high prairie. The weather at Arrowhead Stadium was bloody cold, mid-twenties, with a severe wind chill. And in those bitter, freezing temperatures, the great team from the Little Apple came through and upset the Sooners, 35–7.[11] The Wildcats decimated OU's fifth-ranked team defense, coordinated by Mike Stoops (the brother of head coach Bob) and Brent Venables.[12] Oklahoma finished the regular season ranked No. 3 in the AP and Coaches polls but persisted as the top seed for the BCS title game thanks to additional factors in the ranking formula.

The other championship bracket slot was filled by the Tigers of LSU, ranked No. 2 in the AP poll, the Coaches poll, and by the BCS. The Tigers had gone 12–1, took the SEC Western division, and decisively won the SEC title game in Atlanta, 34–13, over No. 5 Georgia.[13] The only blemish on LSU's record was a loss to head coach Ron Zook and his Florida Gators.[14]

Saban's Tigers scored first, led 14–7 at the half, and then opened up a 21–7 lead when defensive end Marcus Spears ran back an interception of a Jason White throw. The Sooners then scored with eleven minutes left in the game on running back Kejuan Jones's second goal-line touchdown rush to cut the score to 21–14, but LSU's defense held from there to win by a touchdown. The LSU Tigers were BCS champions. And consistent with the agreement between the Coaches Poll and the BCS, they were named the No. 1 team.

The BCS was supposed to resolve the matter of "Who is champion?" on the field. It used a combination of human polls, computer algorithms, and other contextual factors to rank teams. The top two schools then met for

Geaux Tigers. The LSU Tigers have won all of their national titles in New Orleans. And they have amazing, enthusiastic fans. This was my view of the 2019 SEC title game between LSU and Georgia at Mercedes-Benz Stadium in Atlanta. The Tigers rolled all over UGA, 37–10, before inflicting even more suffering on Oklahoma and then Clemson in the College Football Playoff. AUTHOR IMAGE

a title game. This was the sixth BCS championship game and the twelfth straight effort to create a one versus two matchup from either the BCS or the previous bowl alliance that preceded it. However, this was the first time the No. 1 team in both the AP and Coaches polls was excluded from the championship game.

The excluded team? USC, under third-year head coach Pete Carroll.[15] The Trojans had opened the 2003 season with a 23–0 road win over Auburn (a common opponent shared with LSU). Ranked No. 3 by AP after four weeks, USC lost on the road to unranked Cal, tumbling to No. 10 in the polls. They then ran off eight straight wins to win the PAC-10 behind the leadership of sophomore quarterback Matt Leinart. Denied a spot in the BCS title game, the Trojans beat Michigan, 28–14, in the Rose Bowl on New Year's Day and were voted national champions by the AP poll and also the Football Writers Association of America. The Coaches Poll was contractually obliged to name the winner of the BCS game (LSU) as champion. Nonetheless, three coaches ranked the Trojans at the top of their ballots. Coaches do this sometimes.

So the BCS, designed to choose a champion on the field, instead produced a split championship in year six. Algorithms and humans had disagreed on ranking the best teams in the nation. The humans lost to the algorithms. This clearly would not do, and we're going to come back to the matter later in the book.[16] The difficulty that the media and some in sports fandom had with exclusion is at the heart of the puzzle here. We want a champ decided on the field, rather than depending on subjective expert judgment. But when the result of the math and other objective criteria choose participants, and those choices conflict with subjective experts—writers and coaches—the math loses. The math is the problem, rather than the possibility that the subjective experts might be missing some important data or might fail to recognize their own prejudices.

USC got half a title; this happens to the Trojans a lot, just so you know (read on). But in the 2004 regular season, an echo of justice was realized after a sort.[17] USC would run the table, defeating No. 2 Oklahoma in the BCS title game, 55–19, behind the play of Leinart, that season's Heisman Trophy winner. The Trojans later vacated their final regular season win over the University of California, Los Angeles (UCLA) as well as their postseason BCS bowl win and the BCS-mandated

Broken Trojans. Pete Carroll's Trojans won back-to-back national titles in 2003 and 2004 and nearly took a third in 2005. They also had two Heisman winners during that stretch, quarterback Matt Leinart and running back Reggie Bush. Carroll left after the 2009 season for the NFL. However, NCAA sanctions marred the era, leading to the vacating of the 2004 national title. CREATIVE COMMONS

Coaches Poll title. An NCAA investigation of gifts made to running back Reggie Bush by sports agent Lloyd Lake and his business partner Michael Michaels led to the sanctions. The AP allowed USC to keep its title.[18] Bush would win the Heisman the following year when USC would again go to the BCS title game but lose this time to head coach Mack Brown's Texas Longhorns. His trophy was subsequently stripped following the NCAA investigation.

Anyhow, after the Atlanta trial and the Sugar Bowl loss to Saban, I returned to Norman and OU. It was a sad situation. The first loss of the season brings with it an appreciable despair on the old North Campus. A pall falls across the fanbase and student body. The chatter on talk radio and the internet evolves from desperation, to a search for explanation, to blame, which inevitably leads to the officiating.[19] Occasionally, some fool would demand the firing of Bob Stoops.[20] This was worse in many ways. The start of spring term was tempered by an understandable letdown, as a previously undefeated team closed out with back-to-back losses.

If you've ever been to Norman, or the Cotton Bowl in October, or for that matter just been a fan of teams in the old Big Eight or Big 12, you know there's a swagger to Oklahoma football, a swagger to compensate for the tragedy and trauma of life on the plains. Oklahoma is a tough place sometimes, what with the burning summers, freezing winters, perpetual wind, and periodic oil busts. Ten years after the end of the Dust Bowl decade, the pains of the plains became a lot easier to bear for football fans. The reason? With the end of World War II, a bunch of fine young coaches came home and took up coaching major college football, and the best of those was Bud Wilkinson.

From the moment Wilkinson set foot on the campus of OU as an assistant

George Lynn Cross was president of OU for a quarter-century (1943–68). His 1977 memoir, *Presidents Can't Punt*, sits on my desk and is one of the best practical works ever on university leadership and especially dealing with college athletics. PUBLIC DOMAIN

Bud Wilkinson played for three straight national champions at Minnesota under Bernie Bierman and won three national titles, thirteen straight conference titles, and at one point forty-seven consecutive games as head coach of the Oklahoma Sooners. He also ran for the US Senate in 1964, losing to Fred Harris. WESTERN HISTORY COLLECTION, THE UNIVERSITY OF OKLAHOMA

coach in 1946, Sooners football was the successful exception to a place punished by the weather, climate, energy economies, and the haughty burnt-umber specter of Texas to the south.[21] George Lynn Cross, Oklahoma's legendary president who served in the job for a quarter century, once appeared before a state legislative appropriation committee to discuss the budget. When asked what he would do if appropriated more legislative money, he responded, "I would like to build a university of which the football team could be proud." Between 1947 and 2000, OU football would garner seven Consensus Major Selector titles and more conference crowns than everyone else in the Big Eight or Big 12 conferences *combined*. Dr. Cross set his sights high, as did Sooner Nation.

The situation in 2004 was doubly damning since not only had the Sooners lost to LSU, but their presence in the BCS title game was called into question because of USC's Rose Bowl win.[22] And all the arguments in the legacy media, the internet, on sports radio, and in the bars ran in circles. So I thought to myself, *Why not dig up all the potential bar arguments about who was the best team in college football? Go take a look at those contested titles, where the writers and the coaches disagreed. Go look at all the made-up titles some people say Alabama has built their reputation upon.*[23] *Go look. I mean, how hard could it be?*

I started digging, got curious about the split championships in college football history, why the splits happened, wondering, *Who is really the champion?* It was harder than I thought. There were a lot of split titles and contentious claims. You don't really think about this as a fan because you usually reflect back to a recent or relevant case. Or you make fun of Alabama, who seem to have a title for every occasion, much like Bama sorority girls and social events.

Going back and looking systematically also involved understanding how the information we use to pick champions had changed, how the standards had changed, and indeed how the game and the sports culture it fueled had changed. The national champion debate used to be one of either fighting over who was the better champion when the AP writers poll and the United Press International coaches poll disagreed at the end of the season or fighting about the worthiness of an also-ran who came up short in the polls.

A good example would be Auburn in 1993, who went 11–0 but was banned from postseason play.[24] With the advent first of the BCS and later the CFP, the fight has been over how to objectively select either of the two teams for a championship game or four teams for a championship playoff.[25] The primary effect of these systems has been to shift the argument to a discussion of who got left out of the playoff and whether they were better than who got in. Examples include USC missing the 2003 BCS game, Ohio State missing the 2017 CFP, Georgia missing the 2018 CFP, or Florida State missing the 2023 playoff. Now that we are in a twelve-team playoff, I have no doubt we will fight about whether the thirteenth-ranked team should have been let in.

I picked the introduction of the AP poll (1936) as a starting point for analysis, as it is the longest-running, continuous method used in ranking football teams. The AP draws on "the wisdom of crowds" through the opinions of the writers who follow the sport. The poll was founded in the 1930s when the modern game had matured, and it provided a national forum for assessing the quality of teams that had, up to that point, been dominated by legitimate but arcane mathematical selectors.[26] It is also important to remember that the AP, in business since 1846, had national and global reach to both seek opinion and to disseminate results. They could articulate a truly *national* championship.

Then there's another issue, that of popular legitimacy. The NCAA recognizes a variety of major selectors, including several of the historic mathematical selectors who predate both the AP poll and the initial United Press Coaches Poll, which started in 1950. The primary criterion to be a major selector was to produce rankings and have a presence "national in scope either through distribution in newspaper, television, radio, and/ or computer online." The AP writers poll always enjoyed a powerful PR advantage. The writers wrote about the champion picked by the writers or by the poll the wire service used (such as the UP Coaches Poll). The AP poll was the definitive championship because the writers and editors set the standard.[27] As a kid growing up, the AP poll was the Cadillac standard in my dad's eyes, the real rankings and the real champion. Of course, growing up in Kentucky in the 1970s, winning college football was a distant and hypothetical exercise. But the old man thought the Coaches Poll had deeper biases with coaches voting for their buddies and to strategically rank their opponents. As it turns out, the old man was right. Systematic quantitative analysis by sports economists shows that coaches are more likely to rank recent opponents and their alma maters significantly higher. Coaches also puff up teams from their own state and teams from the SEC and Big Ten.

So I went to look at the splits between the historic major selectors and how often there were dissenting college football national champions. *If a program claimed a title,* I thought to myself, *just look at some evidence and see who had the best case for being champion. I mean, how many dissents could there have been?* As it turns out, there were *a lot* of dissents. Going beyond those numerous, acknowledged major selectors like the AP and the Coaches polls, I looked at any *claimed* title, even if it came from an obscure, NCCA-recognized selector, such as the Nutshell Sports Football

Ratings (Oklahoma A&M in 1945) or was self-bestowed (like Boston College in 1940 or, for about five minutes, Auburn in 2004).

There are so many split titles even among the Consensus Major Selectors (including twelve splits just among the two major wire-service polls), and so many other potentially legitimate disputed claims where the math and record on the field could credibly challenge the human polls that I found myself *arguing with myself* about the result.[28] Pandora's box was wide open.[29]

A quick note for the reader who thinks their team is slighted at some point in this book—it's meant to be fun. Sport requires some trash talk. I've got massive SEC blinders that I wear as a fan and a regional partisan. But for the colleges that claim titles, they are almost always teams that, in fact, performed at very high levels. They would have to in order to even be in these arguments over who was the best.[30]

CHAPTER 2

PICKING NATIONAL CHAMPIONS: CREATING THE ERA OF BOWLS AND POLLS

The history of picking national champions starts in New Jersey,[1] specifically in the expert imagination of former player, coach, and lawyer Parke Davis (1871–1934). Davis was the first authoritative historian of the game. He played line at Princeton in 1889, then coached for six years at Wisconsin (1893), Lehigh (1894), and Lafayette College (1895–97) compiling a 37–11–3 record. He was also athletic director at Lafayette College. In 1898, he left coaching and teaching at Lafayette and took up the practice of law in Easton, Pennsylvania; he later became district attorney of Northampton County.

Davis documented the evolution of the sport and sought to secure its history. Author of *Football—The American Intercollegiate Game* (1911, New York, Charles Scribner's Sons), he made the humorous and dubious claim of biblical origins to the sport, noting that in Isaiah 22:18 it is observed, "He will turn and toss thee like a ball" (sort of like Buck Belue to Herschel Walker in 1980).[2] Davis served on the American Intercollegiate Football Rules Committee, helping to shape both the playing field and the structure and rules of the game itself, including the adoption of uniform numbers. Davis also helped select the 1913 All-America team.

THE COMMITTEE OF ONE: PARKE DAVIS CHAMPIONS

Sports Illustrated's Dan Jenkins observed that, later in life, Davis was suffering some irritation over the emergence of numerous "experts" of the

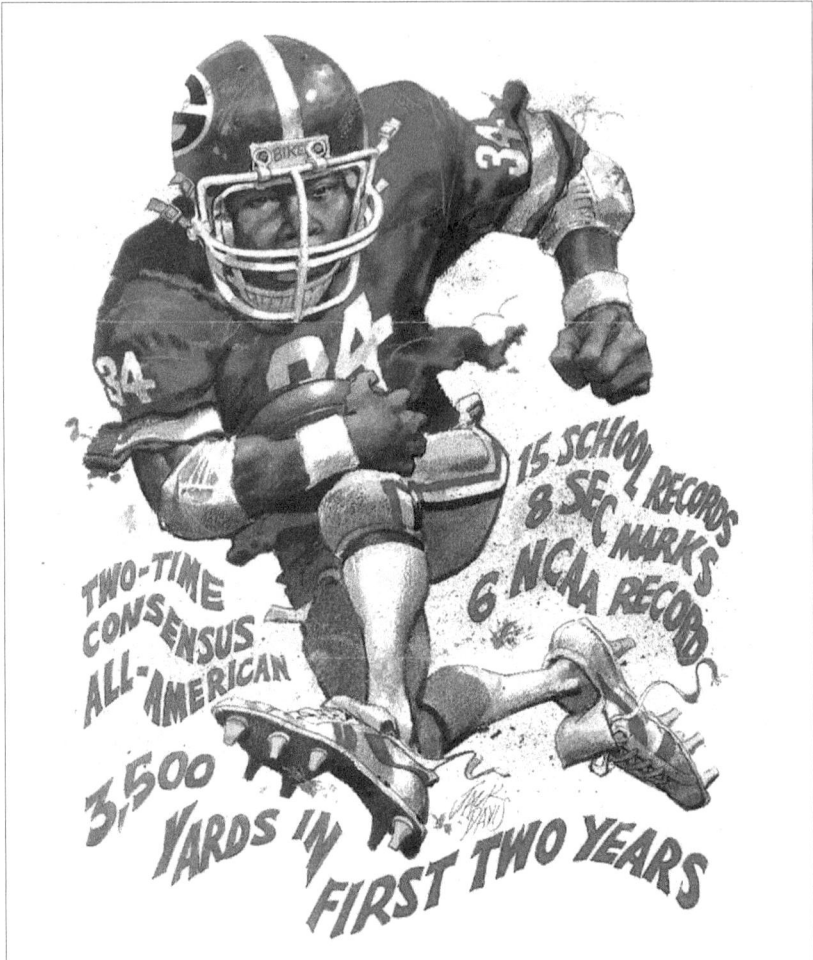

Herschel Walker was a three-time Heisman finalist while at Georgia and won the 1982 trophy. A prolific and powerful rusher, when asked if he got tired running the ball thirty or forty times a game, he replied, "The ball ain't heavy." I suspect he should have stopped there. Jack Davis, who drew this great cartoon, was an internationally known cartoonist for *Mad* magazine and also a UGA alum who crafted outstanding Georgia sports caricatures, often featuring Hairy Dawg. PRINTED WITH PERMISSION OF THE DAVIS FAMILY AS RIGHTS HOLDER

game.[3] He published a 1933 article in *Spalding's Foot Ball Guide* that named champions for every season from 1869 to 1932. He then selected the 1933 team for the 1934 edition but died soon after. Spalding republished his list the next two years as well under the title "Outstanding Nationwide and

Parke Davis is one of the founding fathers of organized modern college football. He played at Princeton, coached, shaped the rules of the modern game, served as a historian of the sport, and was the first authority to declare historic champions. PUBLIC DOMAIN

Sectional Teams." Among Davis's champions was the Lafayette team he coached to a scoreless tie against his alma mater, Princeton, in 1896. The Leopards went 11–0–1 and outscored their opponents, 240–10, for the season.[4]

These titles are considered "canon" in college football, official championships there for the claiming. And some programs have done ample harvesting. For example, of Princeton's twenty-eight national titles, twenty-three were designated by alumnus Davis. But to be fair, the Tigers really were that good. Arguments of implicit bias toward those schools that would eventually form the Ivy League are probably misplaced—most other retroactive selectors using different methodologies confirm many of Parke Davis's selections as being the premier teams of their seasons.

Davis has also been accused of an eastern bias, and this accusation has some merit. Table 1 lists Davis's ninety-four champions or cochampions from 1869 to 1933; it includes just two teams from west of the Mississippi River (Iowa, 1921 and USC, 1932), two from the South (Georgia Tech, 1928 and Alabama, 1930), and fourteen from the industrial Midwest between the Allegheny Mountains and the Mississippi. Most of the champions he named then are today considered Ivy League universities.

To draw distinctions between Davis's selections and the broader field of schools, we're going to turn to some math, specifically a replicable, consistent measure of team strength, the Simple Rating System (SRS) power ratings at Sports-Reference.com.[5] These ratings measure the "power" of a team based on wins, losses, scoring margin, and opponent's power (strength of schedule).[6] Higher (positive) scores are better teams, lower (negative) scores are worse, and a team that is completely average or mediocre will score a zero. A good team will score around plus-eight, and an outstanding team will score over plus-twenty. Conversely, awful programs like Kansas will score below minus-ten. Sports-Reference also does not confer a title, so there's less conflict in baselining from their data rather than using a preferred, better-known source that does pick champs, such as Jeff Sagarin, whom I hold in high regard.

Looking to the SRS power rankings for the period 1869–1933 shows the distribution of "best" teams from year to year (see Table 2). In the nineteenth century, when the number of teams playing organized football was relatively small and the game had been played longer in the East,

TABLE 1: **PARKE DAVIS CHAMPIONS BY SCHOOL AND YEAR**

Alabama	1930*
Army	1914* 1916*
Chicago	1913*
Colgate	1932*
Columbia	1875*
Cornell	1915* 1921* 1922*
Dartmouth	1925
Detroit Mercy	1928*
Georgia Tech	1928*
Harvard	1874* 1875* 1890 1901 1912 1913* 1919*
Illinois	1914* 1919* 1923 1927
Iowa	1921*
Lafayette	1896* 1921* 1926
Michigan	1902* 1932* 1933*
Notre Dame	1919* 1920* 1930*
Penn	1894* 1895* 1897* 1904 1908 1924
Pitt	1915* 1916* 1929 1931*
Princeton	1869* 1870 1872* 1873 1874* 1875*1877* 1878 1879* 1880* 1881* 1884* 1885 1886* 1889 1896* 1898 1899 1903 1911 1920* 1922* 1933*
Purdue	1931*
Rutgers	1869*
USC	1932
Yale	1872* 1874* 1876 1877*1879* 1880* 1881* 1882 1883 1884* 1886* 1887 1888 1891 1892 1893 1894* 1895* 1897* 1900 1902* 1905 1906 1907 1909

*CO-CHAMPION

Davis's best picks and the SRS mathematic selections are highly correlated (**bolded** teams are Davis selections that contradict the top power rankings for that year.) As the game grew in popularity and migrated to the South and West, and Davis moved away from coaching, his expert assessments disagree more often with other authorities.

From 1901 to 1933, in twenty-two of the thirty instances where Davis picked best teams, the math of power ratings disagrees. Of those disagreements, twelve involved teams from the West (defined as every school from west of the Alleghenies, north of the Ohio River, and west of Texas and Oklahoma) while nine were from the South (defined as everything south of the Ohio River and east of New Mexico.) Davis's eastern bias grows evident. In seventeen seasons, at least one of his disagreements with the power ratings involved a team from east of the Alleghenies, most typically an Ivy League team. On two occasions, the dispute involved his hometown Lafayette Leopards.[7]

Clearly something better than the opinion of one knowledgeable, albeit aging lawyer was called for. Enter science. Moving beyond the application of the baseline SRS power rankings used in this study, science—the math of the game—as applied by established selectors generally disagrees with Parke Davis. For the sixty seasons between 1870 and 1933 when Davis picked a title, most or all retrospective or Contemporary Selectors dispute Davis's picks. In twenty of the instances, none of the algorithms or historic research titles agree with Davis. In another eleven, just one selector agrees, and in four other occasions, two agree. In only twenty-five of the sixty years do most of the mathematic selectors agree with Davis's expert evaluations. His post–World War I choices are far less accepted. From 1920 to 1933, Davis has support in just four seasons from most of the algorithms, including his contemporary mathematic selectors.[8] Davis was a historian of the game, and his impact on football's rules and development cannot be disputed. But his expert opinion of evaluating teams suffers outside his prime as a player and coach.

THE BEGINNINGS OF SCIENCE: ALGORITHMS AND POLLS

The college football championship debate is a story about science and how science informs judgment. Why? How?

TABLE 2: **POWER RANKINGS VS. PARKE DAVIS**

YEAR	TOP POWER RANKING*	DAVIS PICK(S)	YEAR	TOP POWER RANKING*	DAVIS PICK(S)
1869	Princeton [†] Rutgers [†]		1905	Yale [†]	
			1906	Vanderbilt	**Yale**
1870	Princeton [†]		1907	Sewanee	**Yale**
1871	*No pick*	*No pick*	1908	Chicago	**Penn**
1872	Princeton [†]	**Yale**	1909	Minnesota	**Yale**
1873	Princeton [†]		1910	Auburn	*No pick*
1874	Yale [†]	**Princeton Harvard**	1911	Minnesota	**Princeton**
			1912	Wisconsin	**Harvard**
1875	Princeton [†]	**Columbia Harvard**	1913	Auburn	**Chicago Harvard**
1876	Yale [†]		1914	Illinois	**Army**
1877	Princeton [†]	**Yale**	1915	Georgia Tech	**Pitt Cornell**
1878	Princeton [†]				
1879	Princeton [†]	**Yale**	1916	Georgia Tech	**Pitt Army**
1880	Yale [†]	**Princeton**			
1881	Yale [†]	**Princeton**	1917	Georgia Tech	*No pick*
1882	Yale [†]		1918	Great Lakes Navy	*No pick*
1883	Yale [†]		1919	Alabama	**Notre Dame Illinois Harvard**
1884	Yale [†]	**Princeton**			
1885	Princeton [†]				
1886	Yale	**Princeton**	1920	Georgia Tech	**Notre Dame Princeton**
1887	Yale [†]				
1888	Yale [†]		1921	Vanderbilt	**Iowa Cornell Lafayette**
1889	Princeton [†]				
1890	Harvard [†]				
1891	Yale [†]		1922	Nebraska	**Princeton Cornell**
1892	Yale [†]		1923	Yale	**Illinois**
1893	Yale [†]		1924	Notre Dame	**Penn**
1894	Yale	**Penn**	1925	Michigan	**Dartmouth**
1895	Penn [†]	**Yale**	1926	Michigan	**Lafayette**
1896	Princeton [†]	**Lafayette**	1927	Georgia	**Illinois**
1897	Penn [†]	**Yale**	1928	Georgia Tech [†]	**Detroit**
1898	Harvard	**Princeton**	1929	USC	**Pitt**
1899	Harvard	**Princeton**	1930	Notre Dame [†]	**Alabama**
1900	Yale [†]		1931	USC	**Purdue Pitt**
1901	Michigan	**Harvard**			
1902	Yale [†]	**Michigan**	1932	USC [†]	**Michigan Colgate**
1903	Princeton [†]				
1904	Penn [†]		1933	Michigan [†]	**Princeton**

*SIMPLE RATING SYSTEM (SRS) SCORE LEADER; VALUES NOT INDICATED.
[†] ALSO PARKE DAVIS CHAMPION SELECTION.

The Parke Davis rankings were the most expansive and the first authoritative measurement. But these rankings, as noted above, were not without criticism and sometimes were a departure from empirical reality. At the same time that Davis is crowning champions, there is a broader "championship rush" occuring in college football. Numerous selectors emerged, usually offering either judgment (expert opinion) or mathematical formula-based champions and rankings. The rise of the AP poll of the mid-1930s and the UP Coaches Poll in 1950 caused the mathematical selectors to recede into the background. Nonetheless, even with the emergence of the polls as championship selectors generally accepted as authoritative, the NCAA continued (continues) to recognize a dizzying number of championships in their records, including post hoc retrospective selections made by expert panels, research panels, algorithms, or even people who just asked for one.[9]

But in almost risible fashion, the one source of championships not recognized by the NCAA are the BCS and CFP championships, which actually resolve the matter on the playing field and have what logicians and scientists call "face validity." The BCS and CFP instead indirectly bootstrap their way into the title count through a contractual tie-in with the Coaches Poll.

The major selector criteria sort into four categories, all of which inform the disputed championship problem. These criteria also inform the selection of teams to compete in the BCS and the CFP: math, including computers; polls of experts such as writers and coaches; research by historical organizations or individuals that grant post hoc and (sometimes) contemporary titles; and on-the-field playoffs (the BCS and CFP). This little project makes use of information from each or several sorts as appropriate.

Below is a brief description of the selectors from which information is drawn at some point or another throughout the book. Descriptions are divided into three categories for the purpose of description: Consensus Major Selectors, Contemporary Selectors, and Retrospective (After-the-Fact) Selectors.

CONSENSUS MAJOR SELECTORS

Of the many major selectors recognized and distinguished by the NCAA, there are four that stand out as "consensus" major selectors:

the Associated Press, the Coaches Poll (UP, UPI, USA Today/CNN, USA Today/ESPN and US LBM Coaches Poll), the Football Writers Association of America, and the National Football Foundation. The first, lone wire service selector was the Associated Press, which started picking champions via a poll of writers in 1936. The United Press joined the club in 1950 with a Coaches Poll while the Football Writers Association of America (FWAA) started awarding a championship in 1954. The last major selector of note, the National Football Foundation (NFF), came on board with its poll in 1959.

In addition to these four, there really should be a fifth organization recognized as a Consensus Major Selector. The International News Service (INS), owned by the Hearst Syndicate, conducted a writers poll from 1952–57 and is a recognized selector by the NCAA. However, the INS is not a consensus selector, even though it is built upon the same reputational model as the AP. The INS later merged into United Press to create United Press International, whose Coaches Poll is a consensus selector. While consigned to the dustbin of history, I put them here because this is where they ought to be.[10]

The Associated Press[11] started releasing a poll of writers and broadcasters in 1936, although the first **AP poll** was performed two years earlier in 1934. In 1935, the AP's sports editor Alan J. Gould declared the national champ a three-way tie, based on his own opinions. In doing so, he thereby formalized the relationship between expert opinion, fan outrage, and the media as Minnesota followers aimed their ire at the editor in question. This caused Cy Sherman and other sportswriters to suggest an editors' rating and thus was born the AP poll. From 1936 to 1960, the poll ranked the top twenty teams. Then from 1961 to 1967, only a top ten was listed before returning to twenty in 1968. In 1989, the poll expanded to rank the top twenty-five in the country. A preseason poll was introduced in 1950.

So our starting point for intensive analysis is 1936, the first year of the ongoing AP poll. To understand why the AP poll exists, we need to go back to 1934 and an initial effort by the Associated Press to deal with the bar conversation problem. Gould had declared a three-way tie for the 1934 champion between Minnesota, Princeton, and Southern Methodist.

Minnesota was undefeated, 8–0. If we look at various power ratings, the Golden Gophers typically come out on top. As I noted a bit earlier, throughout this book I'll refer to the SRS power rating from Sports-Reference to draw comparisons, for consistency, and also because all of their historical data and methodology are publicly available.[12]

In 1934, Minnesota had the highest power rating (25.15), the top-rated offense, and the eleventh-rated defense in the nation. Princeton (7–1–0) had the No. 10 overall power rating (14.41), the third-rated offense, and No. 49 defense. With an 8–2–2 record, Southern Methodist (SMU) had the No. 12 overall power rating (13.53), No. 21 offense, and No. 7 defense. On the field and by the math, Minnesota was the best team in the nation.

Then there was the team that wasn't mentioned by Gould—Alabama. The Crimson Tide, coached by the legendary Frank Thomas, went 10–0–0 to win the SEC. They had the No. 2 overall power rating in the country (23.10), the fourth-rated offense, and the sixteenth-rated defense. In the postseason, they had traveled to Pasadena and decisively beat the previously undefeated Pacific Coast Conference champion Stanford in the Rose Bowl, 29–13.

Frank Thomas coached Alabama for sixteen seasons, going 115-24-7 with four SEC titles and two national championships: in 1934 and a more dubious one in 1941. He traces the line from Knute Rockne, for whom Thomas played at Notre Dame, to Bear Bryant, who he coached at Alabama. Thomas was also roommates at Notre Dame with George "The Gipper" Gipp (played by Ronald Reagan in the movies) and served as an assistant at Georgia for Notre Dame-system acolyte George Woodruff as well as later under his former Notre Dame teammate, Harry Mehre. IMAGE CREATED BY AUTHOR USING CHATGPT

TABLE 3: AP NO. 1 MEETS AP NO. 2 IN BOWL GAMES PRIOR TO THE BCS/CFP

1963 Rose Bowl		1979 Sugar Bowl		1993 Sugar Bowl	
USC (1)	42	Penn State (1)	7	Miami (1)	13
Wisconsin (2)	37	Alabama (2)	14	Alabama (2)	34
1964 Cotton Bowl		1983 Sugar Bowl		1994 Orange Bowl	
Texas (1)	28	Georgia (1)	23	FSU (1)	18
Navy (2)	6	Penn State (2)	27	Nebraska (2)	16
1969 Rose Bowl		1987 Fiesta Bowl		1996 Fiesta Bowl	
Ohio State (1)	27	Miami (1)	10	Nebraska (1)	62
USC (2)	16	Penn State (2)	14	Florida (2)	24
1972 Orange Bowl		1988 Orange Bowl			
Nebraska (1)	38	Oklahoma (1)	14		
Alabama (2)	6	Miami (2)	20		

The AP poll has had some hiccups, which we'll explore. For several years, the final poll was released between Thanksgiving and Christmas after the last regular season games were played. Bowl results[13] were not a factor in selecting the AP final poll champ and the recipient of the championship trophy.[14]

Meaning, a series of champion selections by both the AP poll and the UPI Coaches Poll in the mid-1950s and early 1960s then lost their postseason bowl game (we look at those cases). It is worth noting that bowls were the exception rather than the rule for many competitive teams prior to the 1970s, and some undefeated champions would forego postseason competition. For example, in 1950 there were only nine bowl games, and just ten of the AP top twenty teams competed in a bowl.

In 1965, the AP delayed its final poll until after the bowls, averting such an outcome again as the regular season's No. 1 (Michigan State) and No. 2 (Arkansas) lost their bowl games, and No. 3 Nebraska was defeated by No. 4 Alabama. The AP permanently moved to a final postseason poll in 1968.

Foundational to the championship bar argument problem is not matching up the No. 1 and No. 2 teams before a last poll is taken. Getting No. 1 and No. 2 together on the field was kind of hard, between scheduling issues and the historic use of conference bowl tie-ins. Through 2023, there had been a total of fifty-four meetings between the No. 1 and No. 2 teams in the AP poll, and the No. 1 team had earned a 31–21–2 record. Of those fifty-four, though, twenty-seven happened in a postseason bowl or title game with the No. 1 team going 14–13. In addition, eleven of those postseason battles happened before the inception of the BCS/CFP regime in 1998 (see Table 3); the top team won six of those. Overall in the BCS/CFP era, sixteen of the twenty-six finales have matched Nos. 1 and 2 from the AP poll with the records even at 8–8. Only once has the AP No. 1 failed to at least qualify for inclusion in the BCS or CFP—USC after the 2003 season.

Similarly, the **Coaches Poll** did not issue a poll following the bowl games for many years, resulting in the crowning of champions who went on to lose their bowl game on several occasions. The UPI changed the timing of the last Coaches Poll, moving it to after the bowl games in 1974. That same year, the Coaches Poll began excluding teams that were on probation. The result in that initial season was the selection of USC as the Coaches Poll champ over undefeated and probation-serving Oklahoma, which won the AP honor. The winner of the BCS and CFP titles have automatically been declared No. 1 and the national champion in the Coaches Poll.

The Waterford Crystal trophy awarded for the Coaches Poll winner has undergone many name changes since being initially awarded in 1986.[15] At various times called the Gerrits Foundation-UPI Coaches Trophy, the UPI Coaches Trophy, or simply the UPI Trophy, the prized possession is now termed the American Football Coaches Association National Championship Trophy.[16]

The **Football Writers Association of America** was founded in 1941 and consists of more than twelve hundred professional sports journalists, member media outlets, and sports publicists. From 1954 until 2013, the FWAA selected a national football champion, waiting until after the end of the season and bowls to make its pick. Selections were made by a five-person panel who represented the nation's football writers, and the winner was given the Grantland Rice Award.

As we will see, this contributed to split choices when compared to the major wire-service selectors. The FWAA still selects an All-America Team

Grantland Rice (1880-1954) was a pioneering sports journalist and broadcaster who played at Vanderbilt. His greatest bit of prose is coining Notre Dame's 1924 backfield the "Four Horsemen" in a game against Army at the historic Polo Grounds in New York City: "Outlined against a blue-gray October sky the Four Horsemen rode again. In dramatic lore they are known as famine, pestilence, destruction and death. These are only aliases. Their real names are: Stuhldreher, Miller, Crowley and Layden. They formed the crest of the South Bend cyclone before which another fighting Army team was swept over the precipice at the Polo Grounds this afternoon as 55,000 spectators peered down upon the bewildering panorama spread out upon the green plain below." Notre Dame won 13-7. The Irish went 10-0 that year and dominated their opponents, outscoring them 285-54. With the exception of Parke Davis, all historic selectors (and the algorithms) agree that the Four Horsemen were the best team in football in 1924. And Grantland Rice had an awesome name, befitting a trophy. PUBLIC DOMAIN

and hands out multiple coaching and player awards.[17] With the advent of the College Football Playoff, the FWAA retired the Grantland Rice Award and instead joined with the National Football Foundation in awarding the MacArthur Bowl to the CFP winner.

Founded in 1947 to create a football hall of fame, the **National Football Foundation** named its first champion in 1959. The organization was promoted and shaped by the efforts of Rice, general of the army Douglas MacArthur (who did not play football at the US Military Academy), and former Army coach Earl Blaik. The collegiate national champion designated after the season by the NFF receives the MacArthur Bowl. Multiple winners have been designated in the past, though since 2014 the winner of the CFP automatically is designated the MacArthur Bowl honoree. Together with the FWAA, the NFF sponsors the Grantland Rice Super 16 poll.

The **International News Service** was created by William Randolph Hearst in 1909 as a response to the United Press, which was created by competitor E. W. Scripps.[18] In May 1958, INS merged with UP to become United Press International. Two years after UP entered the sports poll

Douglas MacArthur (shown here at the Battle of Inchon), five-star general, presidential candidate, Medal of Honor winner, and pain in Harry Truman's ass, was a starting high school quarterback and played tennis at the West Texas Military Academy in San Antonio, and he later played baseball at the US Military Academy. Contrary to a general belief that he played football at West Point, MacArthur never took to the gridiron for the Cadets, but athletics were of great importance to him, a foundational aspect of leadership in his mind. Big Mac noted in his 1964 autobiography, *Reminiscences*, "I have always loved athletics and the spirit of competition moved me to participate in as many sports as possible. I became the quarterback on the eleven, the shortstop on the nine . . . [and] the tennis champion of the campus." (Recounted at https://soldierstosidelines.org/blog/general-macarthur-and-athletics/). PUBLIC DOMAIN

business, INS jumped in as well with a poll. While not a formal consensus selector in the eyes of the NCAA, the INS was a legitimate competitor in business with AP and UP. And its champions during the six seasons it operated are largely consistent with AP or UP selections, although its one exceptional choice, picking Georgia Tech in 1952, stands out.

Consensus Major Selector disagreements are surprisingly common. Since 1950, the AP and UP/UPI have disagreed on a national champion on eleven occasions (1954, 1957, 1965, 1970, 1973, 1974, 1978, 1990, 1991, 1997, 2003). The AP and UP both disagreed with the INS once, in 1952; the INS and UP disagreed in 1954; the AP and the INS disagreed in 1957 (see Table 4).

Earl "Red" Blaik coached at Dartmouth from 1934 to 1940, then took over coaching at Army from 1941 to 1958, fielding some of the greatest college teams in football history. Blaik had played college football at the Cradle of Coaches, Miami University in Ohio, and also two years at West Point, where he was a third-team All-American. After graduation, he served in the US Cavalry. Blaik was 166–48–14 as a head coach and would claim three straight national titles from 1944 to 1946, as well as three Heisman winners. Twenty future head coaches can be found in his coaching tree, including Paul Dietzel (LSU) and Murray Warmath (Minnesota), who both won national titles. The playing field at West Point is named for him. It was Blaik who saw the possibilities of platoon-system football when substitution rules were changed, and he perfected the two-platoon model at Army after World War II. PUBLIC DOMAIN

In addition to the wire-service splits, the other Consensus Major Selectors split with AP and UP/UPI periodically. In four instances, the FWAA split with both wire services in a seven-season stretch from 1958–64 (1958, 1960, 1961, 1964). In 1960 and 1964, the AP and UPI had selected a champion before the bowl games, only to have that champion lose in its postseason matchup. The FWAA, acting after the bowls and therefore possessing complete information, picked what would be the more definitive champion, and we look at these seasons in chapter 4. The AP subsequently started picking champions after the bowls in 1968, and the UPI followed suit in 1974.

How a consensus champion is chosen has been repeatedly tweaked. Ongoing efforts at reform in the past quarter century haven't completely solved the puzzle, though we're getting close by use of the novel notion of deciding the issue on the field. The odds of a split became decidedly lower with the implementation of a four-team playoff in 2014. We engage these reforms and consequences in chapters 6 and 7.

Table 5 shows that in eight of ten CFPs from 2014 to 2023, the top four seeds overlapped with both the AP and Coaches polls' top four. The

TABLE 4: SPLIT CONSENSUS MAJOR SELECTOR TITLES SINCE 1950

Year	AP	Coaches	INS	FWAA	NFF/MacArthur
1952	Michigan State	Michigan State	Georgia Tech		
1954	Ohio State	UCLA	Ohio State	Ohio State	UCLA
1957	Auburn	Ohio State	Ohio State	Ohio State	Ohio State
1958	LSU	LSU		Iowa	
1960	Minnesota	Minnesota		Ole Miss	Minnesota
1961	Alabama	Alabama		Ohio State	Alabama
1964	Alabama	Alabama		Arkansas	Notre Dame
1965	Alabama	Michigan St.		Alabama/ Michigan State	Michigan State
1966	Notre Dame	Notre Dame		Notre Dame	Michigan State/ Notre Dame
1970	Nebraska	Texas		Nebraska	Texas/Ohio State
1973	Notre Dame	Alabama		Notre Dame	Notre Dame
1974	Oklahoma	USC		USC	USC
1978	Alabama	USC		Alabama	Alabama
1990	Colorado	Georgia Tech	Colorado	Colorado	Colorado
1991	Miami	Washington		Washington	Washington
1997	Michigan	Nebraska		Michigan	Michigan
2003	USC	LSU		USC	LSU

first instance where a wire-service top four didn't make the playoff was in the initial 2014 season when AP No. 4 Baylor was left out and Ohio State (AP No. 5, Coaches No. 4) made it in. Ohio State would go on to win the CFP. The second occasion came in the last season of the four-team playoff, 2023, when AP No. 4 Florida State was skipped in favor of Alabama (AP No. 5, Coaches No. 4). Just four No. 1 seeds won in the ten, four-team CFPs (LSU 2019, Alabama 2020, Georgia 2022, and Michigan 2023) while two No. 4 seeds have also prevailed (Ohio State 2014 and Alabama 2017).

Can we do better? The CFP hopes as much with the expansion to a twelve-team playoff in 2024. Through 2023, someone's conference champ (or a couple of conference champs) has been left out in every season of the CFP. Some conferences (looking at you, SEC) are seen by rivals as

TABLE 5: CFP SEEDS AND END-OF-REGULAR-SEASON POLL RANKS (CHAMPION IN BOLD)

SEASON	TEAM	CFP	AP	COACHES
2014	Alabama	1	1	1
	Oregon	2	3	3
	FSU	3	2	2
	Ohio State	4	5	4
2015	Clemson	1	1	1
	Alabama	2	2	2
	Michigan State	3	3	4
	Oklahoma	4	4	3
2016	Alabama	1	1	1
	Clemson	2	3	3
	Ohio State	3	2	2
	Washington	4	4	4
2017	Clemson	1	1	1
	Oklahoma	2	2	2
	Georgia	3	3	3
	Alabama	4	4	4
2018	Alabama	1	1	1
	Clemson	2	2	2
	Notre Dame	3	3	3
	Oklahoma	4	4	4
2019	**LSU**	1	1	1
	Ohio State	2	2	2
	Clemson	3	3	3
	Oklahoma	4	4	4
2020	**Alabama**	1	1	1
	Clemson	2	2	2
	Ohio State	3	3	3
	Notre Dame	4	4	4
2021	Alabama	1	1	1
	Michigan	2	2	2
	Georgia	3	3	3
	Cincinnati	4	4	4
2022	**Georgia**	1	1	1
	Michigan	2	2	2
	TCU	3	3	4
	Ohio State	4	4	3
2023	**Michigan**	1	1	1
	Washington	2	2	2
	Texas	3	3	4
	Alabama	4	5	4

overrepresented.[19] And to be fair, the SEC is omnipresent in the BCS and CFP championships. Of the sixteen BCS title games, ten featured an SEC team, and the 2012 game was an all-SEC matchup between Alabama and LSU. Nine of sixteen BCS championships were won by SEC teams.

The College Football Playoff through the 2023 season featured fifteen different schools in its ten, four-team fields, representing forty opportunities. Three SEC teams made twelve appearances in the playoff, with the conference represented in eight final games, including all-SEC matchups in the 2017 and 2021 seasons. The SEC claimed six CFP titles (Alabama with three, Georgia with two, and LSU with one). Two were claimed by Clemson of the ACC. Ohio State and Michigan have each captured one championship for the Big Ten.

When we abandoned arguing about polls and turned to seeking an on-field solution, we also shifted the argument to determining how many teams get to compete in a playoff (two, four, eight? OK, twelve) and how they will be chosen.[20]

OTHER CHAMPIONS: THE CONTEMPORARY SELECTORS

There are other champions besides those decided by the CFP, the BCS, and the wire services. Most of these are not claimed by the winners unless they've been named by the AP, the Coaches Poll, or won the CFP, though some are, and they are a significant source of the claimed split titles.

These several dozen additional selectors are recognized by the NCAA. By and large, they chose champions contemporary to the season, rather than retroactively, and most of the time they agree with the Consensus Major Selectors. Here, I briefly describe those selectors who designated a championship that some program has claimed, which consequentially sets up a disputed title with a Consensus Major Selector. Some of these other, lesser-known selectors created the "championship rush" that sparked Parke Davis to stake out his turf on who were the champions of college gridiron.[21] So who were they?

The **Dickinson System (1926–40)** was an algorithm created by Illinois economist Frank Dickinson. The system used a mathematic formula that awarded points based on wins, losses, ties, and the strength of the opponent.[22] Dickinson first designed his method to rank the Big Nine

Knute Rockne was the legendary Notre Dame head
coach (105-12-5 lifetime) who made regular use of the
forward pass and was immortalized by actor Pat O'Brien
in the 1940 movie *Knute Rockne, All-American*. The
Irish claim three national titles for Rockne in a career
cut tragically short by his death in the crash of a Fokker
trimotor airplane in 1931. PUBLIC DOMAIN

conference teams (a precursor to the Big
Ten) and then extended it to cover the
nation. The prevailing team under the
Dickinson system received the Rissman
Trophy, paid for by Chicago clothier Jack Rissman. Notre Dame retired
the trophy in 1930 after winning the title three times, and the award was
later rechristened the Knute Rockne Intercollegiate Memorial Trophy
after the legendary Notre Dame coach who died in a Fokker trimotor
airplane crash in March 1931.

There is reason to be skeptical of the Dickinson System as there is
a higher degree of subjectivity in terms of how it deals with schedule
strength. Dickinson does so by awarding different points for wins, ties, and
losses over strong versus weak teams, but it determines "strength" subjec-
tively and imprecisely. The consequence
is a higher degree of disagreement with
most of the other math selectors driven
by less-subjective algorithms.[23]

Glenn Scobey "Pop" Warner, whose legacy lives on in
the youth football league that bears his name, coached
the legendary Jim Thorpe at the Carlisle Indian Industrial
School and then went on to a collegiate career coaching
at Georgia, Iowa State, Cornell, Pitt, Stanford, and
Temple, winning national titles at Pitt and Stanford.
He created the single-wing and double-wing offensive
formations, which were precursors to today's spread and
shotgun offenses. PUBLIC DOMAIN

Less commonly remembered than Knute Rockne or Pop Warner but nonetheless important, Howard Jones coached at Syracuse, Yale, Ohio State, Iowa, Trinity College (now Duke), and USC, and national titles are claimed in his name by Yale, Iowa, and USC. One of his USC players was Marion Robert Morrison, better known as John Wayne. PUBLIC DOMAIN

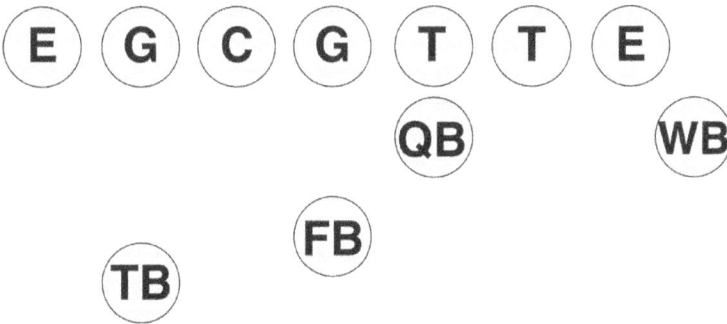

The single-wing offense was invented by Pop Warner while he was coaching Jim Thorpe at the Carlisle Indian Industrial School. The great advantage of the formation over the more common T-formation is the ability to get an additional receiver downfield. IMAGE BY AUTHOR

The **Dunkel System (1929–present)** is a power rating method applied to football and other sports. Originally created by Dick Dunkel Sr., the system has been used since 1929 to rank teams. It was widely broadcast in media outlets and even had its own radio show for nearly thirty years.

After the death of Dunkel, his son, Dick Jr., took over the operation with eventual help from *The Daytona Beach News-Journal*. The operation is now being carried on by a third generation of Dunkels with Dick Jr.'s son, Bob, continuing the tradition. The algorithm is not easily located, but according to Dunkel's website, the point-based metric serves as an absolute indicator of difference of power. Team A with a score on Dunkel ten points higher than Team B should defeat Team B by ten points on a neutral field.

The **Houlgate System (1927–58)** premiered in 1927, the brainchild of Los Angeles publicist and statistician Deke Houlgate and his collaborator and spouse, Dorothy. Like our current twenty-first-century mathematical-ranking algorithms, Houlgate rated teams based on the strength of their opposition to weigh the value of wins or the costs of losses. It considered all games, all teams, in a manner akin to modern power ratings. Houlgate also had the irony and humor required to really work in sports, using his index to create "Futility Bowl" pairings of the two worst college football programs in the United States.

As explained by Deke's grandson, John Houlgate, teams started with an objective letter grade of A and dropped one grade for each loss, down to the lowest ranking of H (seven losses). An A team was worth eight points, an H worth one point. If you beat an A team, it dropped to a B, but you got seven points for the win. If you lost to an A team, it cost you one point, but losing to a D cost you five. Scores were then recalculated each week for all teams and their opponents to retroactively revalue wins and losses. Essentially, Houlgate considered and also revalued quality wins and upset losses.

The **Boand System (1930–60)** was created by William F. Boand of Tucson, Arizona. Boand's algorithm was used to name national champions from 1930 to 1960. He also created retrospective titles for the seasons from 1919 to 1929. Boand, who would move to Chicago in 1932, had his Azzi Ratem[24] rankings published in the *Illustrated Football Annual* from 1932 to 1942, and then they were featured in the weekly *Football News*. Described as using the "best parts of the Dickinson System" (whatever that means), Boand retained legendary coaches Knute Rockne, Pop Warner, and Howard Jones as consultants to assess and improve the system.[25]

Many systems that serve as the basis for dissent title claims are from outside the East. The **Williamson System (1932–63)** is no exception. In 1932, New Orleans geologist Paul Williamson got the idea to create his own ranking method. Also a member of the Sugar Bowl Committee, he generated a power rating of some complexity. His rankings were broadly syndicated across the country, especially in the South. Unlike the polls and some of the other math systems, Williamson did not determine a national champion until after the bowl games had been played, making his system the first to not be flawed by the consequences of postseason play—a flaw that pervaded the wire service polls into the 1960s and 1970s.

Another southern entry in the power ranking game from the 1930s is the **Litkenhous Ratings (1934–84)**, which used a difference-of-scores formula as its backbone. This system is more sensitive to running up scores, less sensitive to singular, close losses, and forgiving of ties (Litkenhous once named the one-loss, two-tie 1968 Georgia team as a national champion).[26] Created by brothers Edward and Frank Litkenhous (the former a Vanderbilt chemical engineering professor) specifically to determine a football national champion, the rankings were initially published and disseminated by the *Courier-Journal* (Louisville). Edward eventually sold the newspaper the rights to the rankings in order to fund his kids' college education.

In 1935, former Ohio Wesleyan football player Richard R. Poling developed his **Poling System (1935–84)**, a mathematical ranking method used for nearly a half century. As was the practice of other rankers, he also rated teams retrospectively back to 1924. His publication, the *Football Review,* was the primary outlet for the rankings, as well as select newspapers that also carried the feature. Poling was a career social correctional counselor for the Ohio State Reformatory, where he worked for many years after World War II. He died in 1994 at age eighty-six.

The **DeVold System (1945–2006)** was developed by Harry DeVold from Minneapolis, who had played football at Cornell. At the end of World War II, he had settled in Detroit and was working in real estate. He went public with his mathematical rating system in 1945 and also crafted retrospective rankings going back to 1939. *The Football News* started publishing the DeVold Rankings in 1962.

What if a bakery could pick a national champion? As it happens, one did: we present to you the **Helms Athletic Foundation (1941–82)**. In 1936, Paul Helms and Bill Schroeder got together in Los Angeles and created the Helms Athletic Foundation as a vehicle to select sporting champions and All-America honorees in several sports, including basketball and football. The foundation, directed by Schroeder, was in fact entirely subsidized by Helms's family business, the Helms Bakery. Using a nonmathematical method with input from the foundation's Hall of Fame Board, Schroeder picked the winners, which were then broadly disseminated. Helms died in 1957, but the bakery's sponsorship continued until its closing in 1969. A savings and loan association then became the benefactor with the foundation eventually changing its name to the Citizens Savings Athletic Foundation and later the First Interstate Bank Athletic Foundation in its final year of 1982. When Schroeder was no longer able to make selections, a committee was formed. Basketball champions were selected starting in 1943 and football in 1941. Retroactive champions, chosen by Schroeder based on impressive individual research, were also released.

The **Colley Matrix (1993–present)** was developed by Virginian Wes Colley and published through *The Atlanta Journal-Constitution*. An astrophysics PhD, Colley's formula was one of the rankings included in the old BCS recipe. His algorithm considers wins and losses rather than scoring margin but does incorporate a strength of schedule component.

Colley was the subject of some notoriety for not considering specific game results, thereby blinding the system to the quality of particular opponents. In 2017, the algorithm had the audacity to contradict the CFP result. Colley's formula ranked a team that didn't make the playoff, undefeated University of Central Florida, as the top team in the nation. Alabama, who beat Georgia and Clemson but had a loss to Auburn, was the choice of the AP and Coaches polls, the CFP, and all other selectors.

Most of Colley's previous heterodoxy was less controversial. The matrix picked Tennessee in 1997 over Nebraska and Michigan; Oklahoma State in 2011 over BCS champion Alabama; Notre Dame in 2012 over Alabama, though Alabama beat the Irish 42–14 in the BCS title game; and Alabama in 2016 over Clemson, when the Tigers had just defeated Bama on the field in the CFP. There's room for dissent, and in these four cases, Colley is the only dissenting selector. Three of his dissents are reasonable, and we'll give them their due. What was different about 2017 was not that Colley was dissenting; it was that UCF actually claimed the title absent any other source of legitimacy.[27]

POST HOC ERGO HOC FUIT[28]

Then there are the **Retrospective (After-the-Fact) Selectors**. As we noted in the previous section, some of the mathematic selectors have declared retroactive champions, as has the research-based Helms foundation. Nearly all the Parke Davis national championships are retroactive and serve as the basis for most of the titles for every school now in the Ivy League and all of Lafayette College's claims. As a general rule, very few programs claim retroactive titles, although it does happen, as we will discuss when we get into the cases. Retroactive claims have been made based on research from three selectors.

To understand retroactive claims and why they are considered, we must visit the AFCA Blue Ribbon Commission. This body (loosely described) was set up to grant official championships for the period 1922–49. In 2016, the **American Football Coaches Association (1922–present)**, at the request of several programs, created the commission to consider potential retrospective titles. These titles, if conferred, would be accompanied by a Coaches Trophy.

The decision to do so elicited some raised eyebrows and some snickers. Both the eyebrows and the snickers were associated with the process and the choices. One gets the idea, if one doesn't read, that the AFCA convened serious sports historians to dig into worthy cases. That's not what happened. They basically put out a "request for proposal" for potential new champions, predated 1949 or earlier, to be voted on by a committee. Multiple champs could be crowned for a single season. There would be no equivalency of method, no discrimination in choosing a champ.

The Oklahoma A&M squad, which was a great team, got the nod because of something called the Nutshell Sports Football Ratings[29] which selected them as the best team in the country for 1945, based on an algorithm that considered the average of opponents' ratings and awarded plus-ten points for a win and minus-ten for a loss. This formulation is not dissimilar to the Dickinson System. And when one digs into that math, the basis for the claim is that Oklahoma A&M had a nominally stronger schedule.

This was the one and (to date) only title that was so conferred. Oklahoma State applied for a title on behalf of its admittedly excellent undefeated 1945 team. Those Aggies did not win the national title at the time because the greatest college football team ever, the Army team from 1944 to 1946, was defeating all comers in resounding fashion. As veteran sportswriter Berry Tramel of *The Oklahoman* newspaper observed, "Army was not just the greatest football team of 1945. That might be the greatest football team of any season."

From the perspective of this writer, following up on going unbeaten against Germany, Italy, and Japan, and then having the season Army did in 1945 trumps winning the Missouri Valley Conference. Unfortunately for Oklahoma State, no other program has come shopping in the attic of history for a title from the AFCA, though Kentucky (Sagarin, 1950) and USC (Sagarin and others, 1939) have in the twenty-first century claimed retrospective titles already recognized by the NCAA.

The **National Championship Foundation (1980–2000)** was founded by Mike Riter of Germantown, New York, in 1980. The NCF issued retroactive titles from 1869–1979 and then contemporary titles from 1980 through 2000. Riter's selections were designated based on research of the season and then placed before a membership committee to vote. NCF titles have sometimes been the subject of criticism and have created curious, though sometimes reasonable, results. The retrospective evaluations done by NCF before the 1970s are good at engaging the problems of the early polls, which picked before the bowls were played.

The **Sagarin Ratings (1978–present)** are a mathematical system developed by Jeff Sagarin of Bloomington, Indiana. A statistician who trained in mathematics at MIT, he is arguably one of the most sophisticated sports ratings thinkers in the business, having developed a portable ranking system that's used across multiple sports. His ratings have appeared in *USA Today* since 1985 and have been used to support both the BCS formula and the NCAA basketball Tournament Selection Committee.

Like all the other algorithm ratings, he doesn't make public his formula. However, one of his techniques is influenced by the Elo rating system, which ranks international chess competitors and only considers wins and losses, not victory margin. Another of his algorithms does use margin of victory, though blowout wins are diminished in terms of relative impact—there's a decay to the margin-of-victory effect. Also, early-season ratings are weighted by a Bayesian[30] network until all teams across the network are generally connected together and not isolated amongst a subset of competitors. Once the network is established, the weights are removed. This is done to prevent early-season bias in the ratings.

When we look at these few claimed, retrospective titles, it's important to be fair. Some retrospective claims might have real merit. And laying snide remarks aside, separating the validity of a claim from a larger, programmatic confidence issue is important. The real question is, do confident programs need to pad their résumés with such titles? Kentucky, Oklahoma State, UCF, and USC remain the only current FBS programs to have claimed a *retrospective* title for a season in the AP poll era (1936 forward).

THE UNCLAIMED

Most possible dissenting titles go unclaimed. Since the wire-service era began in 1936, there are eighty-six unclaimed dissenting titles covering fifty-two seasons and twenty-eight programs (see Table 6). Of the twenty-eight programs not claiming these titles, twenty-two have Consensus Major Selector titles. Of the remaining six (Arizona State, Duke, Missouri, Oklahoma State, Utah, and Wisconsin), only Oklahoma State claims a dissent national title (1945) in the wire-service era as its *only* title. For the teams that are "in the club" with a Consensus Major Selector championship, dissent titles are usually not claimed, especially in the modern era. Of course, there are exceptions. USC making a retrospective claim to the 1939 title in 2004 stands out as the most prominent example.

If we go back in time, back before the wire services, many more titles lie unclaimed. According to the NCAA, the following institutions are eligible to claim a national title from one of the numerous "consensus" selectors but have never claimed *any* national football title: Arizona State, Colgate, Duke, Missouri, Purdue, Utah, Vanderbilt, Washington & Jefferson,[31] and Wisconsin.

TABLE 6: UNCLAIMED DISSENT TITLES (NOT CONSENSUS MAJOR SELECTORS)

Alabama	1945, 1966, 1975, 1977, 2016
Arizona State	1970, 1975
Arkansas	1977
Auburn	1983, 1993
Duke	1936
Florida	1984, 1985
Florida State	1980, 1987, 1989, 1992, 1994, 1996
Georgia	1946, 1968
Georgia Tech	1951, 1956
LSU	1936, 1962, 2011
Maryland	1951
Miami	1986, 1988, 1990, 2000
Michigan	1964, 1973, 1976, 1985
Missouri	1960, 2007
Nebraska	1980, 1981, 1982, 1983, 1984, 1993
Notre Dame	1938, 1953, 1964, 1967, 1970, 1989, 1993, 2012
Ohio State	1944, 1969, 1973, 1974, 1975, 2006
Oklahoma	1949, 1953, 1957, 1967, 1973, 1978, 1980, 1986, 2003
Oklahoma State	2011
Penn State	1969, 1981, 1994
Pitt	1980, 1981
Tennessee	1956
Texas	1941, 1968, 1977, 1981
TCU	2010
USC	1976, 1979, 2002, 2007
Utah	2008
Washington	1984, 1990
Wisconsin	1942

These titles are not claimed by the institution. This list does not include instances where CFP, BCS, or Consensus Major Selector (AP, UP/UPI, FWAA) titles are claimed.

SO DOES IT MATTER WHICH ALGORITHM YOU USE?

Part of the data presented for the reader's consideration relies on a basic power rating algorithm, the **Simple Rating System** (SRS). The SRS is one of over one hundred algorithms out there being used to rank teams and compute schedule strength. As discussed earlier when considering Parke Davis's rankings, this process provides evaluations going back to the origin of the collegiate game, but it also raises the question. Does it matter which algorithm we use? This is because the algorithms don't always agree. After all, everyone has their version of the secret sauce.

The answer is both yes and no.

To make comparisons across time, it does matter that we use one algorithm and that the algorithm we use captures the key hallmarks of performance: wins, losses, margins, and strength of schedule. We need to know the conditions going into the computer so we understand what we're measuring. On the other hand, it doesn't really matter because, as is detailed in the appendix, all the algorithms generally identify the same excellent programs as excellent and generally rank them the same. But different algorithms can make different distinctions at the top of the charts, which means that choice is important. If it didn't matter, all the mathematical selectors would always pick the same champs.

Mathematical measures and the use of statistics are not perfect. There's always error. What is important to understand is when and why we have errors; how much error there probably is; and how to understand the errors when making choices. The data from the computer algorithms don't eliminate error—they reduce it, allowing us to inform our guesses. So the algorithms are often much better than guessing or relying on cherry-picked bits of information.

To study competition across time requires some consistent metrics on team quality, conference quality, and competitiveness. Polling data from AP (writers) and UPI/*USA Today* (coaches) enjoy a high degree of credibility with the public, and these experts rankings are historically recognized as being authoritative indicators of team quality and in choosing champions (even given documented biases of human voters). But those data only rank a select number of teams, leaving the rest of the Division I FBS schools unranked in any given year. And there is no poll data at all for the early years of organized college football. (At the back of this book is a previously unpublished paper on computer rankings, their relative similarity, and the extent to which they conform to, or dissent from, the opinions of the writers and coaches in the major selector polls.)

So why pick the Simple Rating System?[32] As described at Sport-Reference's (SR) website, SRS is "a rating that takes into account average point differential and strength of schedule. The rating is denominated in points above/below average, where zero is average, although it should be noted that margin of victory has been assigned a lower bound of seven points and an upper bound of twenty-four points. Non-major opponents are included as a single team in the ratings."[33]

Rankings from this measure correlate almost perfectly with the average ranking for each team in the 106 other computer ranking models ($r = .987$)[34] and similarly highly with the individual rankings of BCS computer contributors such as Sagarin and Dunkel. Finally, the SRS strongly correlates to the S&P+ ratings ($r = .929$), which is a highly sophisticated measure often brought up in conversations among sports talk, bloggers, fantasy football coaches, and people who bet. (To enhance understanding of some comparisons, Sports-Reference's Strength-of-Schedule (SOS) measure, which contributes to SRS, is also reported.)

IN FANS WE TRUST

The situation was messier than initially thought. Why should anyone trust my picks? The reality is, no one should accept the opinion and judgment of a writer who teaches architecture and election law any more than any other fan.

So let's change the perspective of the problem and how to use the data. Instead of me laying out the case for the singular champion and imposing my judgment, I'll lay out some bar-argument logic for each contender, put out competing proof and evidence, and then turn you loose on the controversies. Fans are smart, insightful, the most important component to the game. We make the big game go. *You decide.*

That's the American way, to argue sports and pluck from history, data, emotion, and authority to make our arguments. College football captures Americans at their analytic best, and when they're most annoying. We argue blown calls, coaching decisions, recruitment decisions, and sched-uling decisions. We argue in family rec rooms, sports bars, coffee shops, airports, and the media. Fans scream from the stands at the coach, con-vinced they know better.[35]

College football fans strongly identify with their teams and sometimes even their conferences. They live and die with every victory and defeat. A philosopher named Noam Chomsky related to me that he listens to sports-talk radio while driving, observing, "I'm quite interested not only in the sophistication and extensive knowledge of the people who call in, but also, even more interestingly, their willingness to challenge authority with great confidence, to tell the coach that he made a mistake when he did so and so. If only those capacities were used in areas that matter."[36]

Sports have easy problems compared to life. The best proof of this is how upset we get when politics, economics, environmental disasters, pandemics, and criminal behavior invade sports and distract us from the games as played.[37] We want sports to be clean and not disrupted by the gritty, difficult parts of life.

CHAPTER 3

SPLIT CONSENSUS MAJOR SELECTOR CHAMPIONS

F rom 1936 to 1949, only the Associated Press conducted and released a college football ranking poll. The United Press then joined the fray with their Coaches Poll in 1950, followed by Hearst's INS writers' poll in 1952. UP would later merge with INS in 1958, creating the UPI and spelling the end of the INS poll. The Football Writers Association of America (FWAA) joined the fray in 1954, setting up the pool of generally recognized Consensus Major Selectors of collegiate football champions.

In twelve seasons the AP, UP/UPI, and INS wire services split over the choice of national champion. Until 1969, the AP and Coaches polls chose their champion before the bowl games. And in several instances, an AP champion or UP/UPI champion was beaten in a bowl game, rendering the title suspect or cheap at best. Since 1974, both major selector polls have picked champions after the bowl games—yet still disagreed on several occasions, including once after the institution of the BCS playoff.

1952: MICHIGAN STATE OR GEORGIA TECH?

From 1936 to 1949, the AP was the only major selector based on polling human experts rather than relying on a competition algorithm. The United Press unveiled the Coaches Poll in 1950 and selected the Oklahoma Sooners as national champion. The AP writers made the same pick. In 1951, both consensus selectors chose undefeated Tennessee as champion at the end of the regular season. The Volunteers would lose to Maryland (No. 3) in the Sugar Bowl, setting up a controversy visited later in this book.

When Hearst International News Service then entered the rankings game in 1952, the result was the first disagreement between major wire-service selectors. The AP and UP both chose the Michigan State Spartans as the No. 1 team at the end of the regular season. The INS, in its first ever poll, selected the 12–0 Georgia Tech Yellow Jackets.

So what's the story?

Michigan State (MSU) spent all but one week ranked at No. 1 in the AP poll. Coach Biggie Munn was in his sixth season with the Spartans. Their offense, led by Don McAuliffe and Billy Wells, averaged 34.7 points per game; McAuliffe scored 7 touchdowns, gained 531 yards on 98 attempts, and finished eighth in the Heisman Trophy balloting. Wells rushed for 585 yards on 118 attempts and scored 6 touchdowns.

The Spartans only had two close games: a one score win, 17–14, on the road against Oregon State in the second game of the season, and a 14–7 win over No. 8 Purdue in West Lafayette, Indiana. Home wins over No. 17 Penn State and No. 6 Notre Dame were not close, while victories over Texas A&M, Syracuse, Indiana, and Marquette were forty-plus point blowouts. The Spartans strength of schedule ranked No. 30.

In addition to winning the final AP and UP polls, Michigan State also ranked at the top of several mathematical selectors of the time (Boand, DeVold, Dunkel, Helms, Litkenhous, Williamson). Only the Poling System dissented, picking Georgia Tech.

Clarence "Biggie" Munn was a longtime assistant coach at Michigan, where he was mentored by the legendary Fritz Crisler, the father of two-platoon football. Munn was named head coach at Syracuse in 1946, where he went 4-5. Coming to Michigan State, Biggie was 54-9-2 in seven seasons, which included a twenty-eight-game winning streak from 1950 to 1953. Among his players was the first Black quarterback in the Big Ten, Willie Thrower, who would also be the first Black QB in the NFL. A sign on the locker room wall in East Lansing read, "Do not cheat your team or your teammates. Know your plays. Block. Protect. Add to what we are trying to do." It was simply signed "Biggie." CREATIVE COMMONS

College Field was completed in 1923 in East Lansing. The original capacity of fourteen thousand was expanded to twenty-six thousand in 1936 as a WPA project under the New Deal program and then to fifty-one thousand in 1948 (now known as Macklin Stadium) when the Spartans entered the Big Ten. It was later expanded to two decks in 1956 with end-zone seating added as well in 1957 to increase the capacity to seventy-six thousand. It was then that the football team's home was renamed Spartan Stadium. AUTHOR-OWNED IMAGE

The Yellow Jackets were the No. 1 team of the INS writers' poll in their inaugural year, giving legendary coach Bobby Dodd, who was in his eighth season, his only national title (the similarly legendary Frank Broyles coordinated the offense). The North Avenue Trade School went 12–0, capturing the SEC title and then taking on conference rival Ole Miss in the Sugar Bowl, winning 24–7. The Yellow Jackets defeated No. 6 Duke and No. 12 Alabama in the regular season and held six opponents to single digits while also shutting out four others. Tech's strength of schedule ranks fortieth and included The Citadel and nonmajor opponent FSU.

Other potential contenders for the national title were Oklahoma (led by running back Billy Vessels) and USC. Both had tougher schedules than Georgia Tech and Michigan State. Oklahoma was indistinguishable from

Grant Field is the oldest on-campus football venue in the South. The game was first played there in 1905, and the first stands were erected by students in 1913, seating fifty-six hundred. The stands were expanded to a thirty-thousand-seat horseshoe in the 1920s and then further expanded to forty-four thousand seats after World War II. The Peach Bowl and also NFL games have been played there. In addition to two Consensus Major Selector titles, Tech also won a mythical title in 1928 and fielded the best college football team in America from 1915 to 1920. AUTHOR-OWNED IMAGE

Bobby Dodd became head coach at Georgia Tech right after World War II and coached the Yellow Jackets until 1966, going 165–64–8. Dodd had played quarterback and tailback at Tennessee under General Bob Neyland, where Volunteers fans hung the catchphrase "In Dodd we trust" on him as he led them to back-to-back 9–0–1 seasons. He then spent fourteen years as an assistant under his predecessor, William

BOBBY DODD *Quarterback*

Alexander, who retired with a mythical national title (1928) and 134 wins on the gridiron. Dodd's teams won SEC titles in 1951 and 1952 and also claimed part of the 1952 national title. He has been admitted to the College Football Hall of Fame as both a player and a coach (only Amos Alonzo Stagg, Bowden Wyatt, and Steve Spurrier have been similarly honored). Dodd's coaching process was built around precision and execution, rather than hard and intensive practices, and he placed substantial control of the games in the hands of his assistants. He is one of the only coaches in college football to own a winning record against Georgia (12–10). Dodd was an early critic of over-recruitment, especially in the SEC, and also set degree completion as a priority for his players. These opinions and some on-the-field issues were at the basis of his ongoing feud with Alabama's Bear Bryant and eventually contributed to the decision by Georgia Tech in 1964 to leave the SEC. PUBLIC DOMAIN

MSU in terms of power rating (25.63 versus 25.65), but the Sooners also had a loss to Notre Dame and a tie to Colorado on their schedule. OU and one-loss USC (24.06) ranked ahead of the Yellow Jackets on the power ranking measure, but none of the other selectors appointed either team as a national champion.

TALE OF THE TAPE FOR 1952

Team (AP)	Power	Schedule	Record	Offense	Defense
Michigan State (1)	25.65 (1)	7.20 (30)	9-0-0	34.7	9.3
Georgia Tech (2)	23.27 (5)	5.52 (40)	12-0-0	27.1	4.9

1954: OHIO STATE OR UCLA?

The Ohio State Buckeyes, under fourth-year head coach Woody Hayes, went 9–0 in the regular season to win the Big Ten before then defeating No. 17 USC in the Rose Bowl. Including the Trojans, six of nine opponents faced by the Buckeyes were ranked by the sportswriters.

The Buckeyes featured Dave Leggett and Howard "Hopalong" Cassady, who would win the Heisman the next year, and started the season ranked at No. 20 before briefly dropping out of the AP top twenty. They

Ohio Stadium opened in the 1922 season with a capacity of more than sixty-six thousand. It was one of the first stadiums to minimize view obstructions due to columns. Architect (and alum) Howard Dwight Smith drew inspiration for the design in part from the Parthenon in Rome. The Shoe currently seats (officially) 102,780, making it the fifth-largest stadium in the world as well as the third largest in the US and also in the Big Ten Conference. AUTHOR-OWNED IMAGE

then held four opponents to single digits and shut out two others in the regular season. The defense was the seventh stingiest in the country, giving up just 6.8 points per game. Ohio State held Wisconsin and its Heisman winner, Alan Ameche, to two scores. The defense totaled thirty-five takeaways on the season, including an eighty-eight-yard pick six against the Badgers.

Meanwhile, out on the West Coast, UCLA and sixth-year coach Red Sanders went 6–0 in the PCC and 9–0 overall.[1] Ranked No. 1 in the UP Coaches Poll and No. 2 in the AP poll. The Bruins' powerful offense was accompanied by the top defense in the country, which gave up just 4.4 points per game, shutting out five opponents and holding three others to seven points or less. Only the Washington Huskies pressed the Bruins, coming up short in a 21–20 duel in Seattle. The Bruins schedule ranked fifty-eighth among major programs for strength.

What could have been an epic fight for national championship bragging rights was averted due to the no-repeat rule, whereby a conference champion could not participate in a bowl game in consecutive years. Thus,

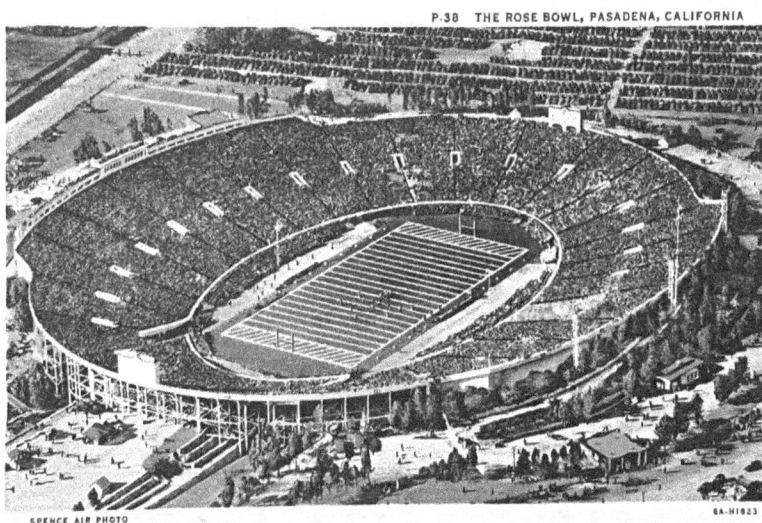

The Rose Bowl was completed in 1922, replacing previous temporary stands used for the Tournament of Roses game. The fully enclosed stand configuration was completed in 1928. The first game played here was between Cal and USC with the Bears winning, 12-0, en route to an undefeated season (Cal claims this as a national title season). UCLA has played their home games in the Rose Bowl since 1982 after playing at the Los Angeles Memorial Coliseum from 1928 to 1981. AUTHOR-OWNED AND IN PUBLIC DOMAIN

On October 30, 1954, No. 3 UCLA beat Cal on the road in Berkeley. The next week they vaulted to No. 1 in the AP poll. The Bruins would slip to No. 2 in the final AP rankings behind Ohio State but retained the top slot in the UP Coaches Poll. PUBLIC DOMAIN

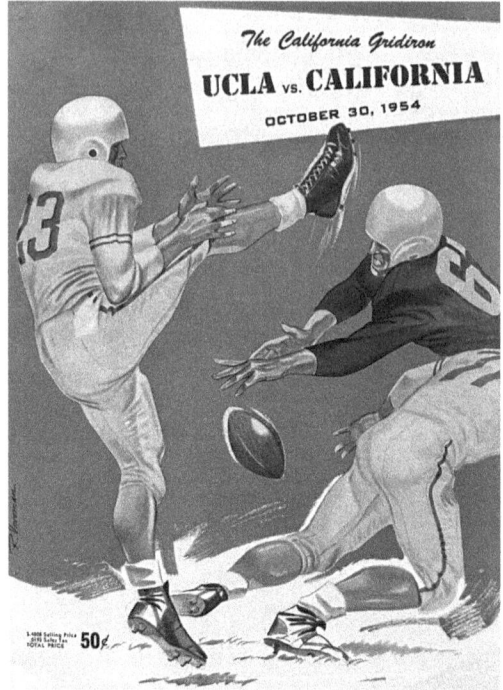

The California Gridiron

UCLA vs. CALIFORNIA

OCTOBER 30, 1954

50¢

the top team in the UP Coaches Poll and FWAA rankings, UCLA, was prevented from returning to the Rose Bowl. Instead, three-loss USC appeared for the PCC and lost, 20–7, in unseasonably rainy conditions. The Trojans were held to six first downs and scored only on a special teams play in falling to the AP's No. 1, Ohio State, in Pasadena.

Notre Dame[2] had briefly made its way to the top spot in the polls before dropping a game to Purdue to finish 9–1 with the second-highest power rating for the season (22.11), just above Wisconsin (20.42) and UCLA but well behind Ohio State. Bud Wilkinson's Oklahoma Sooners spent most of the first half of the season at the top of the AP poll but finished No. 3 after going undefeated against a relatively weak schedule (39th). The Sooners ranked fifth in overall power rating (19.59). None of the non-poll selectors picked either the Irish or the Sooners, removing any potential added claims to the 1954 title.

TALE OF THE TAPE FOR 1954

Team (AP)	Power	Schedule	Record	Offense	Defense
Ohio State (1)	27.08 (1)	11.08 (6)	10-0-0	24.9	7.5
UCLA (2)	19.95 (4)	0.06 (58)	9-0-0	40.8	4.4

1957: AUBURN OR OHIO STATE?

Auburn opened the season with a win over No. 8 Tennessee in Knoxville. The Volunteers, under third-year coach Bowden Wyatt, were the defending SEC champions, had finished 1956 ranked No. 2, and only had a Sugar Bowl loss to Baylor. Shug Jordan, starting his seventh season as the head coach at Auburn, brought back the core of a solid 7–3 team, including 1957 All-Americans Jimmy Phillips and Jerry Wilson, that had finished in the middle of the SEC pack the year before. The Tigers ran the table in the SEC as their top-rated defense gave up just four scores all season and won six games by shutout. Victories over No. 19 Florida and No. 17 Mississippi State also highlighted the schedule, although Auburn did not play in the postseason due to probation banning them from playing in a bowl game.[3]

Woody Hayes, shown here with President Gerald Ford (who played for two national championship teams at Michigan). Hayes coached thirty-three seasons at Denison, Miami of Ohio, and Ohio State, with a record 238–72–10. A Navy veteran who commanded small vessels in the Pacific during World War II, he either won or shared five national titles at Ohio State where he went 205–61–10. His career ended in rather ignominious fashion in 1978 at the Gator Bowl. Trailing Clemson, 17–15, the Buckeyes were in scoring range when Hayes called a pass play that was intercepted by Tigers defensive lineman Charlie Bauman, who proceeded to return the ball up the Ohio State sideline and was run out of bounds. Hayes then slugged the Clemson player in the throat, which resulted in an on-field brawl. After a postgame confrontation with OSU athletic director Hugh Hindman (who had played for Hayes at Miami), the AD met with Ohio State's president at a Jacksonville-area country club. Hayes was fired the next morning. PUBLIC DOMAIN

The Associated Press voted Auburn the top team in the nation, placing them substantially ahead of one-loss Ohio State.

The Buckeyes had started the season in seemingly ignoble fashion, losing at home to the unranked Texas Christian (TCU) Horned Frogs. Ohio State led at halftime but was shutout in the second half while TCU went ahead in the third quarter on a sixteen-yard Jack Spikes rushing touchdown.[4]

Coach Woody Hayes's team would not even break into the AP top twenty until later in October and then found itself behind two other Big Ten schools: Iowa at No. 3 and Michigan State at No. 8. The Big Ten had been tearing itself up all season as MSU was upset by Purdue, Michigan and Iowa tied, and Minnesota lost to Illinois, which helped clear Ohio State's path to the conference title.

Season-finishing victories over No. 5 Iowa and rival Michigan, who ranked nineteenth, put the Buckeyes in the Rose Bowl. They finished the season ranked second in the AP poll and first by the Coaches Poll. The Football Writers Association of America, making its choice after the bowl games, named Ohio State No. 1, accounting for their 10–7 win over Oregon.

The Big Ten was a powerful conference in 1957, led by the Spartans. The SRS power rankings place head coach Duffy Daugherty's Michigan State as the top team. The Spartans went 8–1 and ranked No. 3 in both the AP and UP polls at the end of the season. MSU does claim the national title based on the Dunkel System rankings. Wins over No. 6 Michigan, No. 16 Illinois, and No. 15 Notre Dame bracketed an upset loss to Purdue, which finished 5–4.

Howard "Hopalong" Cassady was born in Columbus and played both ways at Ohio State. He left the Buckeyes with school records in career rushing yards, all-purpose yards, and points scored. PUBLIC DOMAIN

After playing at Tennessee, Bowden Wyatt coached at Wyoming and Arkansas, where he compiled a 50–27–1 record, before then returning to Knoxville in 1955. He was the second straight former Tennessee player to succeed the legendary General Robert Neyland as head coach. Harvey Robinson, who took over in 1953, had gone 6-4-1 in his first year but then suffered a losing season in 1954 at 4-6. Wyatt immediately turned things around and would go 49-29-4 in his eight seasons leading the Volunteers.

PRINTED WITH PERMISSION OF THE UNIVERSITY OF TENNESSEE

Cliff Hare Stadium, circa 1957. Until 1939, Auburn had played most of its "home" games at neutral sites because the campus facility, Drake Field, seated just seven hundred people. In 1939, the school completed Auburn Stadium with a capacity of fifteen thousand, which was expanded to 21,500 in 1949 and renamed for pioneering Auburn football player and chemistry dean Cliff Hare. With head coach Ralph "Shug" Jordan taking over in 1951, the capacity was doubled to 34,500 by 1955. His name was then added to the venue in 1973, now Jordan-Hare Stadium, with the capacity jumping to more than sixty-one thousand by the time he retired in 1975. Auburn would claim the first of its two national titles in 1957. AUTHOR-OWNED IMAGE

It has been speculated that the film *Everybody's All-American*, based on a novel by sportswriter Frank Deford, is based on LSU Heisman Trophy winner Billy Cannon (or University of North Carolina great Charlie "Choo Choo" Justice). Deford denies this is the case, but there are delightful coincidences. The movie was filmed at LSU, including scenes shot at halftime during some Tigers games in 1987. CREATIVE COMMONS

Ralph "Shug" Jordan (JUR-den) coached Auburn from 1951 to 1975, going 176–83–6. An Auburn alumnus, he had served in the European and Pacific theaters of World War II, taking part in four invasions, including Normandy and Okinawa. One of his last quarterbacks, Pat Sullivan, won the Heisman in 1971. Fourteen of his twenty-five teams finished their seasons ranked. Jordan also served as head basketball coach at both Auburn and Georgia. PRINTED WITH PERMISSION OF AUBURN UNIVERSITY

We should also take note of Oklahoma, the defending national champion, who were ranked either No. 1 or No. 2 through the first eight weeks of the season until Notre Dame upset the Sooners, 7–0, breaking the team's forty-seven-game winning streak. The power rating for 1957 places OU behind Michigan State but ahead of Ohio State.

TALE OF THE TAPE FOR 1957

Team (AP)	Power	Schedule	Record	Offense	Defense
Auburn (1)	17.63 (6)	3.33 (49)	10-0-0	20.7	2.8
Ohio State (2)	20.62 (3)	7.62 (17)	9-1-0	26.7	9.2
Michigan State (3)	23.79 (1)	7.46 (20)	8-1-0	29.3	8.3
Oklahoma (4)	21.42 (2)	3.69 (47)	10-1	30.3	8.1

1965: ALABAMA OR MICHIGAN STATE?

Alabama entered the 1965 season as defending national champions (Associated Press) but were coming off a postseason bowl loss that tainted the title. Fifth in the preseason rankings, the Tide then did little to dispel this perception, opening the season with an 18–17 loss to Vince Dooley's Georgia Bulldogs. The defeat came on a controversial (in Alabama) or miraculous (if you are from Georgia) hook-and-lateral play that resulted in a game-winning seventy-three-yard touchdown. Bear Bryant's team tumbled completely out of the top twenty. Three straight conference wins were followed by a tie with Tennessee and then five more victories to close the regular season at No. 4 in the AP and Coaches polls.

Duffy Daugherty became Michigan State's head coach in 1954 after his predecessor, Biggie Munn, was elevated to athletic director. Daugherty had come to MSU from Syracuse with Munn and served on the Spartan's staff throughout Biggie's tenure. Daugherty would spend nineteen seasons leading Michigan State, claiming part or all of four national titles while going 109-69-5. After retiring, Daugherty (shown here with his 1966 All-Americans) started calling college football on ABC with the legendary Chris Schenkel and former Oklahoma football coach Bud Wilkinson. PUBLIC DOMAIN

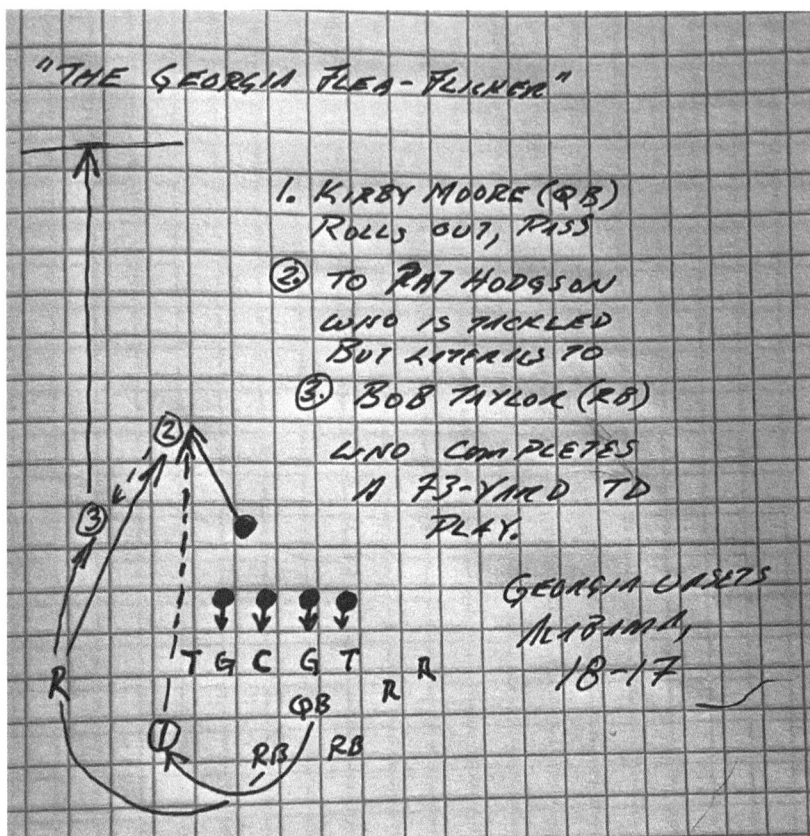

The Georgia Flea-Flicker of 1965. In 1965, Alabama won the AP title despite opening the season with a loss to Georgia and a tie with Tennessee in week five. The defeat was both controversial and epic. The Bulldogs, under second-year coach Vince Dooley, came back from a fourth-quarter, 17-10 deficit when quarterback Kirby Moore rolled out of the pocket and hit wide receiver Pat Hodgson with an eight-yard pass in the left flat. As Hodgson fell under a tackle, he lateraled to halfback Bob Taylor, who scrambled seventy-three yards for a touchdown. Dooley then went for two and beat the Crimson Tide, 18-17. Dooley evidently cribbed the play from Bobby Dodd at Georgia Tech. Was Hodgson down? Depends on whom you ask. AUTHOR-OWNED IMAGE

The previous year's wire-service rankings had both selected a champion before the bowl games. Alabama's loss to Texas in the Orange Bowl led the AP to shift its final poll to after the bowl games. This change would ironically benefit the Tide. On New Year's Day, No. 1 Michigan State and No. 2 Arkansas would lose in the Rose and Cotton Bowls, respectively,

Opened in 1929 with seating for twelve thousand, Denny Stadium (now Bryant-Denny Stadium) was the relocated replacement for Denny Field. Both the field and stadium were named for former Alabama school president George Denny, who also had coached football at Hampden–Sydney College in 1896. Systematic expansion of the facility over the next nine decades provided more than one hundred thousand seats, making it the tenth-largest stadium in the world. The field is one of distinction, as sixteen of Alabama's eighteen claimed national titles were won here, including six each by Bear Bryant and Nick Saban. AUTHOR-OWNED IMAGE

Legion Field in Birmingham opened in 1927 with seating for twenty-one thousand. It was subsequently expanded to forty-five thousand by 1948 and over eighty-three thousand by the 1970s. The enclosed bowl was the effective home field for University of Alabama into the 1990s, and home to the Iron Bowl through the 1990s, when the Alabama vs. Auburn rivalry game moved between Auburn's Jordan-Hare Stadium and Legion Field. The Iron Bowl left Birmingham entirely in 2000 to become a home-at-home series. AUTHOR-OWNED IMAGE

Given that so many books have been written about Bear Bryant, including the one Bryant wrote himself (*Bear: The Hard Life and Good Times of Alabama's Coach Bryant*, written with John Underwood), and his teams show up throughout this book, I'll just focus on some highlights. Bryant, who played football at Alabama, won six national titles as a head coach, all with the Crimson Tide. He won fifteen conference titles—thirteen at Alabama, one at Kentucky, and one at Texas A&M. Bryant was 6-2-1 at Maryland, 60-23-5 at Kentucky, 25-14-2 at Texas A&M, and 232-46-9 at Alabama. In addition, he served as acting head coach in a 7-7 tie against Kentucky during the 1940 season while assisting at Vanderbilt (head coach Red Sanders, who would win the 1954 national title at UCLA, was out from emergency appendectomy surgery). The Bear did suffer one losing season, in 1954, which was his first year at Texas A&M. These Aggies, the legendary Junction Boys, went 1-9 after surviving a hellish ten-day, fifteen-hour-a-day training camp. Two years later, they went 9-0-1 and won the Southwest Conference. CREATIVE COMMONS

while Alabama beat No. 3 Nebraska in the Orange Bowl to claim the No. 1 spot in the last AP poll.

The 1965 Spartans football team defeated four teams ranked in the AP preseason top ten. Undefeated and ranked No. 1 in both the AP and Coaches polls at the end of the regular season, Michigan State lost to No. 5 UCLA in the Rose Bowl, 14–12. The team featured four future College Football Hall of Famers. The UPI Coaches Poll, voting before the bowl games, named MSU the top team in the country, as did the National Football Foundation. The Spartans would slip to No. 2 in the AP poll taken after the New Year's Day bowl games.

The Football Writers Association voting after the end of the season "split the baby" and named Alabama and Michigan State cochampions.[5]

TALE OF THE TAPE FOR 1966

Team (AP)	Power	Schedule	Record	Offense	Defense
Alabama (1)	24.39 (2)	11.02 (12)	9-1-1	23.3	9.7
Michigan State (2)	26.75 (1)	12.66 (3)	10-1-0	23.9	6.9

1966: NOTRE DAME OR MICHIGAN STATE?

The years between head coach Frank Leahy's[6] last season in 1953 and the arrival of Ara Parseghian in 1964 had been difficult ones for the Irish. Under Terry Brennan, Joe Kuharich, and then Hugh Devore, Notre Dame was 51–48, with three losing seasons and three 5–5 seasons in ten years. Parseghian, not a Notre Dame alum nor a Catholic, was a departure. But Father Edmund Joyce, chair of the athletics board, said he was less concerned about religion than winning. Parseghian was coming from a mediocre record at Northwestern, where he was 36–35–1, but he had gone 39–6–1 previously at Miami of Ohio. Notre Dame presented a rebuilding challenge akin to Northwestern, simultaneously tougher yet also holding tremendous prospects. Parseghian's first two Irish teams went 9–1 and 7–2–1, and both were ranked in the top ten at the end of the season.

The Irish had opened their 1966 season at home, ranked eighth, but came away with a 26–14 win over No. 7 Purdue. By the middle of October,

Michigan State's Dick Kenney kicks a field goal against Notre Dame. In 1966, Notre Dame (9-0-1) and Michigan State (9-0-1) finished the season ranked first and second, respectively, in both the AP and Coaches polls after the Irish tied the Spartans in East Lansing on November 19. CREATIVE COMMONS

they had climbed to the top spot of the AP poll when they went to Norman to take on No. 10 Oklahoma, led by new coach Jim Mackenzie. The Irish trounced the Sooners, 38–0. Then in their second to last game of the regular season, they traveled to Lansing to face No. 2 Michigan State. In what was dubbed "the game of the century," the two teams battled to a 10–10 tie. The next week, in the battle for the Jeweled Shillelagh, Notre Dame destroyed No. 10 USC, 51–0. Until 1969, the Irish did not accept bowl-game bids, so here endeth their season.

Before taking on the Irish, Daugherty's thirteenth edition of the Spartans had opened the season at No. 2, then held down the No. 1 spot with blowout wins over North Carolina State, Penn State, Illinois, Michigan, and Ohio State. Notre Dame leap-frogged the Spartans after the Irish decisively beat OU, but Michigan State finished its season with the tie game against Notre Dame. While one would think that MSU, as Big Ten champs, would have gone on to play USC in the Rose Bowl, the use of the "no repeat" rule by the conference meant that Sparty would stay home, having played in Pasadena the previous year. Instead, Purdue went.

The Irish were national champs in the opinion of all the major selectors (AP, UPI Coaches, FWAA, and NFF) though the National Football Foundation recognized Michigan State as cochampion, along with the algorithm Poling System and the bakery/committee Helms Foundation.

The late-season tie between Notre Dame and MSU is one of college football's greatest games. Broadcast on ABC television via tape delay,[7] the game featured Michigan State as a defending national champion and Notre Dame as the current top team. Early in the game, Spartan defensive lineman Bubba Smith had knocked Irish quarterback Terry Hanratty out of the game; two other starters were also lost to sudden injury. At the half, the score was 10–7 with Michigan State leading.

Both defenses completely dominated the third quarter, but then Notre Dame scored on a short Joe Azzaro field goal to start the fourth quarter. Azzaro's forty-one-yard attempt with 4:38 remaining in the game just missed and would have put the Irish ahead for the first time. After a MSU punt, Notre Dame then took over with 1:24 left, but Parseghian, shy of committing a turnover in going for a win, settled for a tie and ran out the clock with six conservative plays, five of them rushes.[8]

Meanwhile, down in Tuscaloosa, the University of Alabama and Bear Bryant went undefeated, won the SEC, and beat No. 6 Nebraska in the Sugar Bowl. The Crimson Tide were captained by Ray Perkins, who would later succeed the Bear as coach at his alma mater and go a "dismal" 32–15–1. The segregated Alabama squad had a perfect record, including six shutouts and three other opponents held to single digits. Their schedule was not weak, even though the first ranked opponent they faced was Bob Devaney's Nebraska Cornhuskers, whom they beat 34–7 in the Sugar Bowl.

It has been argued that the civil rights environment and ongoing segregation in Alabama had muted potential support for the Tide amongst both sportswriters and coaches when voting in the wire-service polls.[9] However, the tale of the tape is pretty convincing—the polls and the analytics put Notre Dame at the top.

TALE OF THE TAPE FOR 1966

Team (AP)	Power	Schedule	Record	Offense	Defense
Notre Dame (1)	26.02 (1)	5.62 (27)	9-0-1	36.2	3.8
Michigan State (2)	21.46 (3)	5.16 (30)	9-0-1	29.3	9.9
Alabama (3)	23.75 (2)	3.85 (37)	11-0-0	27.4	4.0

1970: NEBRASKA OR TEXAS OR OHIO STATE?

Texas came into the 1970 season as the defending national champion, having gone 11–0 in 1969 on the way to taking home all the titles from all the selectors. Darrell Royal, the longtime Texas coach who had now won two national titles in the last seven seasons, then helmed what was one of his greatest Longhorn teams to another undefeated record during the 1970 regular season. That included wins over No. 13 UCLA, No. 4 Arkansas, and a "down" Oklahoma squad, defeating the Sooners, 41–9. Texas, using the popular wishbone offense, had a thirty-game winning streak and were closing in on the forty-seven-straight wins owned by Royal's friend and mentor, Bud Wilkinson of OU. At the end of the regular season, Texas was 10–0, and the UPI Coaches Poll named the Longhorns national champs with the National Football Foundation dubbing them a cochampion.

Just behind them in the Coaches Poll was Ohio State. Woody Hayes had gone 9–0 in the regular season, as the Buckeyes beat No. 20 Northwestern and No. 4 Michigan on the way to a Big Ten title. In the end, Ohio State was named a co–national champion by the NFF. It would be the last national title for Hayes, and it is claimed by Ohio State.

Then came Nebraska. The Huskers went 10–0–1 during the regular season with a September tie at No. 3 USC and wins over No. 16 Missouri, No. 20 Kansas State, and that same Oklahoma team. Coach Bob Devaney and second-year offensive coordinator Tom Osborne had assembled a solid offense that broke fifty points three times (versus Oklahoma State, Iowa State, and Kansas State). Nebraska never got above third in the polls during the regular season, though, their tie with the Trojans keeping them tucked in just behind No. 1 Texas and No. 2 Ohio State.

Ohio State, Notre Dame, and Texas had swapped around the No. 1 spot in the AP poll throughout the season with Texas going into the postseason ranked No. 1, followed by Ohio State, Nebraska, Tennessee, LSU, and Notre Dame.

The Sea of Red. In 1970, Nebraska went 10-0-1, with only a tie versus USC marring its regular-season record, and then beat LSU in the Orange Bowl. When Texas and Ohio State both lost their bowl games, the Cornhuskers were named national champs by the AP. AUTHOR-OWNED IMAGE

Bob Devaney was 101-20 2 in eleven seasons at Nebraska, earning two national titles at the end of his tenure (1970-71). He had started his career as an assistant on the great Michigan State teams coached by Biggie Munn and Duffy Daugherty before going on to lead Wyoming, where he earned a 35-10-5 record. Named head coach at Nebraska in 1962, his teams were consistent winners, as he captured eight Big Eight titles. Devaney's offensive coordinator and successor, Tom Osborne, then coached the Cornhuskers for twenty-five years, going 255-49-3 and winning three national titles in four seasons from 1994-97. Osborne's teams were some of the most dominant in the history of college football, and his rivalry with Barry Switzer of Oklahoma and the 1983 Orange Bowl upset of his Cornhuskers by Miami loom large in college football lore. After retiring from football, Osborne served in the US House of Representatives for a while, then had a failed bid for governor of Nebraska. CREATIVE COMMONS

The wheels came off on New Year's Day. Ohio State lost to No. 12 Stanford, 27–17, in Hayes's fourth coaching appearance in the Rose Bowl. The Cardinal was quarterbacked by the legendary Jim Plunkett.

Texas Memorial Stadium opened in 1924 as a concrete replacement to the old Clark Field. In 1996, the name of legendary head coach Darrell K Royal was added to the stadium. He won three national titles and eleven Southwest Conference championships with the Longhorns. AUTHOR-OWNED IMAGE

Darrell K Royal-Texas Memorial Stadium, as seen at night from the LBJ School of Public Affairs. When they proposed to expand the stadium, former President Lyndon B. Johnson reportedly insisted that only the stands on the west side be double decked so that "everyone can see my school." (Recounted to the author by the late dean of the LBJ School, Elspeth Rostow.) PUBLIC DOMAIN

Down in the Cotton Bowl in Dallas, the Longhorns lost to No. 6 Notre Dame. This marked just the second bowl appearance of the modern era for the Irish and third ever after the 1925 Rose Bowl. Notre Dame's previous modern appearance? The year before in the Cotton Bowl, which was a loss to Texas. In the rematch, Ara Parseghian's Irish held the Longhorns to a field goal and a touchdown (with a two-point conversion) over the first two quarters and led 24–11 at the half. Neither defense budged after that as both offenses were shut down. The Irish upset the back-to-back national champs and also avenged their 21–17 loss from a year earlier.

This only left the Orange Bowl to be decided. Big Eight champ Nebraska, the highest ranked team left standing, faced the SEC champs, 9–2 LSU. Head coach Charles McClendon's Tigers had gone 9–1 the year before but had been ignored by the major bowls. Although LSU had lost to Texas A&M in its 1970 season opener, and then fell to No. 2 Notre Dame in November, the Tigers also had wins over three ranked opponents: No. 6 Auburn, No. 19 Alabama, and No. 16 Ole Miss. Despite the determination to make the most of this opportunity, the defensive battle was won, 17–12, by the Huskers, who held LSU to two field goals and a touchdown.

Darrell Royal is the answer to the question, What Oklahoma Sooners quarterback has a stadium named after him in Texas? Royal, a protégé of Bud Wilkinson, was a player at OU before eventually serving as the head coach at Mississippi State (1954–55) and Washington (1956). Coming to Austin as the thirty-three-year-old head coach of the Longhorns in 1957, he would go 167-47-5 in twenty seasons with Texas, winning eleven Southwest Conference titles and three national championships. CREATIVE COMMONS

The win left Nebraska as the only undefeated team among the AP poll's top three, and they defeated a strong opponent on a neutral field. But what if LSU had won? In all likelihood, given Notre Dame's victory over Texas and also a win over the Tigers (who would have then defeated Nebraska and thereby activated superficial transitivity), the Irish would have been the choice of the writers. The power data still defer to Texas, which has a nominally higher power rating than Nebraska in the SRS. However, nearly all of the algorithms in use at the time, as well as the FWAA, gave the nod to the Cornhuskers.

TALE OF THE TAPE FOR 1970

Team (AP)	Power	Schedule	Record	Offense	Defense
Nebraska (1)	27.63 (2)	10.21 (23)	11-0-1	35.5	15.8
Notre Dame (2)	26.32 (3)	10.41 (19)	10-1-0	32.2	9.8
Texas (3)	28.29 (1)	10.93 (14)	10-1-0	38.5	13.5
Ohio State (5)	24.04 (5)	9.04 (29)	9-1-0	29.0	12.0

1973: NOTRE DAME OR ALABAMA?

The 1973 season presents a clear answer to a muddy national title situation, as in the following year, steps were taken to prevent the Coaches Poll from enduring the embarrassment of picking a champ who would lose a bowl game. But even then, the circumstances of the season leave us to wonder if a clear national title matchup really took place or if the best team in the nation stayed home to watch things unfold.

Notre Dame (11–0) was one of Ara Parseghian's greatest teams, with wins over No. 6 USC and No. 20 Pitt during the regular season. Alabama (11–1) won the SEC, taking down No. 10 Tennessee and No. 7 LSU along the way. The Tide were undefeated and ranked No. 1 going into the Sugar Bowl but lost to No. 3 Notre Dame, 24–23.

Oklahoma (No. 3 AP, 10–0–1) had the highest SRS rating (32.87) and one of the toughest schedules in the country. And Woody Hayes's Ohio State Buckeyes tied No. 4 Michigan to end the regular season before then beating No. 7 USC in the Rose Bowl, 42–21, to finish the season ranked No. 3 in the UPI poll and No. 2 in the AP.

The Coaches Poll published its final ranking before the bowl games, though, and conferred the national title on Alabama. (Had the AP stopped polling before the bowls, as they did through 1968, Alabama would also have been the writers' champ.) UPI changed its practice the next season and started to issue a post-bowl-games poll to determine a champion. The wire service also decided not to rank teams on probation, which took OU (placed on NCAA probation prior to the start of the season) out of the rankings for two years.

Notre Dame Stadium was built and completed in 1930 at the instigation of coach Knute Rockne. At the time, the enclosed bowl seated fifty-four thousand and was one of the largest stadiums in the world. The cost of the initial construction was $750,000 and was paid for in cash. The stadium was expanded with a second deck in the 1990s. AUTHOR-OWNED IMAGE

The AP, FWAA, and NFF all then picked Notre Dame as the top team in the nation for 1973 and did so using the most complete information. This is the second Alabama title claimed where the Tide subsequently lost a bowl game (the other was 1964), and it is one of three questionable titles claimed by the school overall (see the discussion of 1941 in chapter 5).

There was no strong consensus top team after the second week of the season. Preseason No. 1 USC proved weak mettle against No. 8 Oklahoma in September, opening the door to a wide-open vote in both polls. By the end of the regular season, six different teams in the AP poll and five in the Coaches Poll received first-place votes, with the majority going to Alabama, followed by OU. The top four?

FIRST-PLACE VOTES (RANKINGS)

Team	Last Coaches	Last AP	Postseason AP
Alabama	21 (1)	34 (1)	0 (4)
Oklahoma	9 (2)	16 (2)	16 (3)
Ohio State	2 (3)	2 (4)	11 (2)
Notre Dame	1 (4)	2 (3)	33 (1)

The Irish and the Tide settled the issue in the Sugar Bowl, played on New Year's Eve at the old Tulane Stadium in uptown New Orleans (the game moved to the Superdome in 1975). A total of seven lead changes took place. Notre Dame would open with a 6–0 lead, go down 7–6, and then go up 14–7 midway through the second quarter. Alabama then scored ten unanswered points to go ahead 17–14, before Notre Dame scored their final touchdown to take a 21–17 advantage. In the fourth quarter, Alabama crossed the goal line again but a missed the extra point to leave the score 23–21. Irish kicker Bob Thomas then hit a game-winning field goal to secure Parseghian's second national title, 24–23.

The Irish had made it to New Orleans on the legs of a strong ground game with three running backs topping five-hundred rushing yards: Wayne Bullock, Art Best, and Eric Penick. After Oklahoma's defensive battle with USC, the Irish beat the Trojans in South Bend, 23–14, to break USC's twenty-three-game unbeaten streak. The win over Alabama confirmed the Irish as the "more true" champion, winning on the field.

Galen Hall played football at Penn State for Rip Engle (yes, there was a coach in Happy Valley before Joe Paterno). Having entered the coaching ranks with West Virginia in 1964, he moved to Oklahoma two years later to become part of Jim Mackenzie's staff. He then served as Barry Switzer's offensive coordinator, installing the wishbone and coaching Billy "Boomercue" Sims to the 1978 Heisman Trophy. When OU cleaned house in 1983, Hall joined Charley Pell's coaching staff at Florida. Pell was fired over recruiting violations in 1984, and Hall was elevated to interim coach, leading Florida to an 8-0 finish for an overall 9-1-1 record and an SEC championship. The next year, the Gators again went 9-1-1 and earned their first-ever No. 1 ranking in the AP poll on November 5 but lost four days later to Georgia. Hall was eventually forced out of Florida in 1989, coaching in the World League of American Football and then returning to Penn State as an assistant to Joe Paterno. Paterno was ousted amidst scandal in 2011 with Hall and the rest of the coaching staff being let go as well. CREATIVE COMMONS

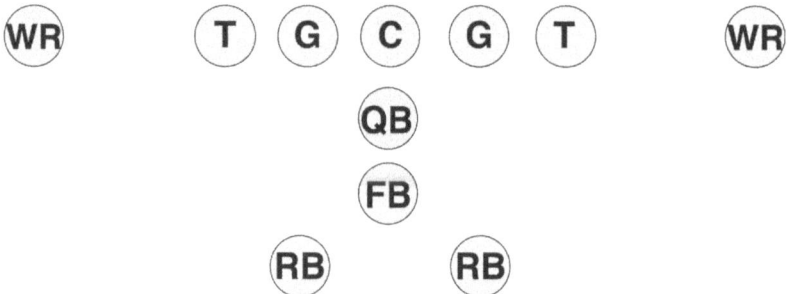

The wishbone. AUTHOR-OWNED IMAGE

But were they really the best team in football that year? The 1973 Sooners are one of the best in both OU and college football history. A season after head coach Chuck Fairbanks departed to take over the New England Patriots, thirty-six-year-old offensive coordinator Barry Switzer took the helm with Galen Hall overseeing the offense. OU opened the season with a road win at Baylor, then tied No. 1 USC, 7–7, in Los Angeles—the first of seven games against top-twenty opponents. The Sooners would go 6–0–1 in those outings and finish undefeated in the Big Eight. Lucious, Lee Roy, and Dewey Selmon fronted the line for a defense ranked fourteenth in the nation, while the sixth-ranked offense averaged over thirty-six points per game with Joe Washington rushing for 1,173 yards.

Just before the season started, OU was placed on probation by the conference and banned from TV and postseason play for two years. They finished No. 2 in the Coaches Poll and No. 3 in the AP poll. The data show Oklahoma, who did not play a bowl, as the strongest team in the nation. The school's power rating is substantially ahead of Notre Dame's, and the Sooners played the fourth-toughest schedule (of the top-ten toughest schedules, seven were teams in the Big Eight). The two things we can definitively say are preseason-pick USC was not the best team in the nation, and Alabama closed poorly, leaving the undefeated, untied Irish with the strongest case on the field.

But the math favors Oklahoma.

TALE OF THE TAPE FOR 1973

Team (AP)	Power	Schedule	Record	Offense	Defense
Notre Dame (1)	25.67 (6)	7.40 (36)	11-0-0	34.7	8.1
Oklahoma (3)	32.87 (1)	13.23 (4)	10-0-1	36.4	12.1
Alabama (4)	26.10 (4)	7.68 (32)	11-1-0	39.8	9.4

1974: OKLAHOMA OR USC?

In 1973, Oklahoma came within spitting distance of a national title, going 10–0–1, finishing the season ranked second in the Coaches Poll, and holding the highest power rating of any team in college football. The next year, the probation-laden Sooners would not be denied. OU's scorching wishbone offense, anchored by quarterback Steve Davis, running back Joe Washington, and fullback Jim Littrell, averaged over forty-three points per game and went undefeated on the way to being voted the top team by the AP writers.

With two of the Selmon brothers (Lee Roy and Dewey) back on the defensive line, the Sooners defense ranked fifth in the nation and gave up just 8.4 points per game. Only one opponent came within two touchdowns of Oklahoma all year (No. 17 Texas).

OU opened the season at No. 1 but slipped to third in the AP poll after an uninspired win over Baylor, which would capture the Southwest Conference title. After two blowout wins, the Sooners went into the Red River Shootout against Texas with confidence but also questions. In the fourth quarter, OU trailed, 13–7, but a forty-yard reverse by Billy Brooks tied the game at 13–13. The defense then hardened, forcing a fumble by the Longhorns that Oklahoma recovered at midfield. In the closing minutes, kicker Tony DiRienzo hit a thirty-seven-yard field goal to give the Sooners a 16–13 victory. Oklahoma then tore through the Big Eight with devastating offensive displays against Colorado, Kansas State, and Missouri.

An upset by Michigan State of then-No. 1 Ohio State, combined by a win over Kansas, put OU back in the No. 1 spot of the AP poll in mid-November. After the Sooners then took down No. 6 Nebraska, a season-closing game against Oklahoma State proved surprisingly close until OU scored five touchdowns in a span of just over seven minutes in the second half for a 44–13 win.

Banned from postseason play by the Big Eight, Oklahoma sat at home as No. 9 Notre Dame beat No. 2 Alabama in the Orange Bowl on New Year's Day. With that, the Sooners held on to the top spot in the final AP poll.

Over in the other reality known as the UPI Coaches Poll, where teams on probation don't get ranked, USC took a less-certain path to the national title. The Trojans opened the season with a road loss in Little Rock to No. 20 Arkansas, but they then bounced back to beat No. 8 Pitt on the road to set off a five-game winning streak. A tie against Cal was followed by a new winning streak that included back-to-back home victories over UCLA and No. 5 Notre Dame. The energized offense led by quarterback Pat Haden and running back Anthony Davis averaged over thirty points

The Los Angeles Memorial Coliseum was commissioned in 1921 and completed in 1923, serving as the home field for USC since opening. The stadium was UCLA's home field from 1928 to 1981 and has also been home to NFL and Major League Baseball teams as well as two Olympics. The original capacity of 75,144 was eventually expanded to 105,000 for football before being reduced more recently to 77,500. Both USC and UCLA won national titles while playing at the Coliseum. AUTHOR-OWNED IMAGE

The Los Angeles Memorial Coliseum while under construction. PUBLIC DOMAIN

per game. USC would win the Rose Bowl, 18–17, over Ohio State to claim the Coaches Poll title since Notre Dame beat Alabama and probation beat Oklahoma.

Barry Switzer played college football at Arkansas and started his coaching career there overseeing running backs before being brought onto Oklahoma's staff as offensive coordinator in 1966 by head coach Jim Mackenzie. Mackenzie had played for Bear Bryant at Kentucky and been an assistant for Frank Broyles before being hired by OU. In the spring after his first 6–4 season, the thirty-seven-year-old Mackenzie died unexpectedly of a heart attack. Chuck Fairbanks, age thirty-three, was promoted to head coach, keeping Switzer on staff. Fairbanks left OU after six seasons, and the thirty-five-year-old Switzer was promoted to the head-coaching job. The Bootlegger's Boy, whose mother had committed suicide when he was twenty-two years old, would win three national titles, including two in his first three years at the helm. He compiled a 157-29-4 record in sixteen seasons with the Sooners while also developing an intense rivalry with Tom Osborne of Nebraska. A series of scandals, both involving the program and his own finances, led to his eventual resignation in 1989. Five years later, he came back to football as head coach of the Dallas Cowboys and won a Super Bowl. Living in Norman, I used to run into Coach Switzer a lot. He remains active in his eighties, engages in the community, and is highly social, always there to make a friend, tell a story, or play a quick joke. At a party once, he introduced himself to my wife, Kim, as Steve Owens, a former Sooner running back and winner of the 1969 Heisman Trophy. WESTERN HISTORY COLLECTION, THE UNIVERSITY OF OKLAHOMA

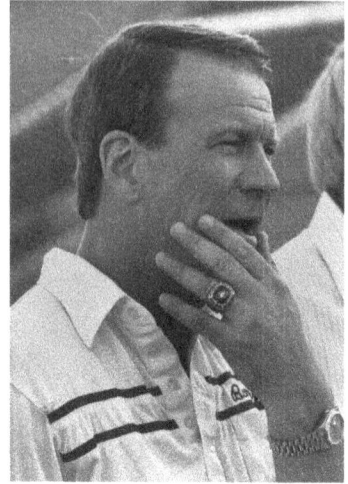

The data are convincing for OU as champion, which was undefeated with far and away the highest power rating of any team in college football that year. Alabama (11–1), despite a loss to Notre Dame, had the second-highest SRS (22.55) and a strength of schedule (7.55) higher than both wire-service champions. USC, while an outstanding team, trailed both the Big Eight and SEC champions in the metrics.

TALE OF THE TAPE FOR 1974

Team (AP)	Power	Schedule	Record	Offense	Defense
Oklahoma (1)	27.80 (1)	7.43 (26)	11-0-0	43.0	8.4
USC (2)	20.90 (4)	6.32 (40)	10-1-1	30.3	11.8

1978: ALABAMA OR USC?

The Alabama Crimson Tide had come up just short in 1977, finishing behind head coach Dan Devine's 11–1 Notre Dame Fighting Irish. Before the season started, Bear Bryant had downplayed his team's quality, observing that the Tide had "a questionable offense, an average kicking game, and a good defense." Alabama's defense ranked nineteenth in average points allowed, while the offense was thirteenth at 28.8 points per game. The Tide also faced the fifth-toughest schedule in the nation.

Alabama began 1978 as the season-opening No. 1 team after a 20–3 victory over head coach Tom Osborne's Nebraska Cornhuskers. They then fell out of the top spot after a disappointing home loss to John Robinson's USC Trojans.

The Oklahoma Sooners, in their sixth season under coach Barry Switzer, moved into the top spot and appeared to be in the driver's seat for the title. But the Bootlegger's Boy and his team came up short in a road game against the No. 4 Cornhuskers in early November, opening the door for Penn State to move into the top spot, followed by Nebraska and Alabama.

The Cornhuskers had lost to Alabama to start their season but then had run off nine straight wins, only to pick up a second loss when they were upset at home by unranked Missouri, 35–31. This left Penn State and Alabama as the top two teams in the writer's poll.

As SEC champion, the Tide awaited a pairing in the Sugar Bowl against the Nittany Lions, but Penn State head coach Joe Paterno preferred going to the Orange Bowl to take on Switzer's Sooners. However, Bryant evidently lobbied Joe Pa into accepting a rematch of the 1975 Sugar Bowl, setting up a showdown between the nation's two top teams.

This Sugar Bowl matchup, which was held for the fourth time at the new Superdome, was one of the greatest defensive struggles in the history of the intersectional rivalry (Alabama leads the series 10–5 all-time). Alabama initially jumped out to a 7–0 lead at the very end of the second quarter. With less than ninety seconds left in the half, Alabama drove eighty yards and scored on a Jeff Rutledge pass to Bruce Bolton from the seven. Penn State got on the board after the half, when Scott Fitzkee pulled in a touchdown pass from Chuck Fusina following an Alabama turnover. Then the Tide went up for good, 14–7, on an option play that resulted in a Major Ogilvie touchdown.

The Nittany Lions had possession of the ball in the fourth quarter when Fusina took aim at the end zone with a pass that was instead intercepted by Alabama. The game refused to be put to bed, though, when three plays later, Penn State recovered an Alabama fumble on the Tide's nineteen-yard line. The Nittany Lions penetrated to the Alabama eight for a first-and-goal with the possibility of scoring the game-tying (or winning) touchdown. But on second down, Penn State was knocked out of bounds just a yard short of the goal line on a passing play, which was then followed by the Tide defense standing tall and surging at the line of scrimmage to keep the Nittany Lions out of the end zone on both third and fourth downs. That goal-line stand basically secured the win and a No. 1 ranking from the AP poll, FWAA, and NFF.

Out west, USC had followed up their road upset of Alabama with a win over Michigan State before being upset by Arizona State at Sun Devil Stadium in Tempe. The Trojans climbed back near the top of the wire-service polls with wins over ranked Washington, UCLA, and Notre Dame before then going to the Rose Bowl as the PAC-10 representative. There, USC bested No. 5 Michigan, 17–10, to take the top position in the Coaches Poll after Penn State was defeated by Alabama.

If you summarize the top ten turmoil that was Bama, USC, Oklahoma, and Penn State, it looks like this: Alabama (11–1) played four ranked opponents during the regular season, defeating No. 10 Nebraska, No. 11 Missouri, and No. 10 LSU while losing early in the season to then No. 7 USC. The Tide won the SEC and wrapped things up by knocking off No. 1 Penn State in the Sugar Bowl. USC (12–1) beat then No. 1 Alabama in the third week of the season and later No. 19 Washington, No. 14 UCLA, and No. 8 Notre Dame while losing to unranked ASU during the regular season. The Trojans defeated No. 5 Michigan in the Rose Bowl. OU (11–1) and Penn State (11–1) were also ranked No. 1 during the regular season and had comparable SRS ratings, although they played weaker schedules. But the Sooners lost to No. 4 Nebraska at a critical juncture, and the Cornhuskers had already fallen to Alabama. Penn State was undefeated and ranked No. 1 at the end of the regular season but lost to Alabama in the Sugar Bowl.

So how do you call it? Alabama has the power rating and beat the last undefeated No. 1 team head-to-head. USC took down Alabama earlier in the season, but when playing its most successful football late in the year, had no path to directly take on the last undefeated major team left standing. So who is the champion?

TALE OF THE TAPE FOR 1978

Team (AP)	Power	Schedule	Record	Offense	Defense
Alabama (1)	25.99 (1)	11.83 (5)	11-1-0	28.8	14.0
USC (2)	25.51 (2)	13.20 (2)	12-1-0	24.5	11.8

1990: COLORADO OR GEORGIA TECH?

Want a mess? Here's a mess. Enjoy the mess, dear reader.

The 1990 season opened with a typical look for the era. The preseason AP top ten was Miami, Notre Dame, Auburn, Florida State, Colorado, Michigan, Nebraska, Tennessee, USC, and Clemson. Then things went sideways as Miami and USC lost almost immediately, bumping Notre Dame to No. 1 with FSU No. 2 by mid-September. Then both of those schools were defeated on the first weekend of October, which moved Michigan to No. 1 and Virginia to No. 2. Michigan promptly lost to Michigan State, so Virginia went to No. 1, followed by Miami. All the while, Georgia Tech had been creeping up the rankings, going from being completely unranked to No. 23 to No 18. And they'd keep climbing.

Colorado's Folsom Field opened in 1924, seating twenty-six thousand and expanding to forty-five thousand in the 1950s and then to fifty-two thousand in the late 1970s. The Buffaloes played in six conferences here, mainly in the Big Eight/Big 12 with a thirteen-year disruption as members of the PAC-12. AUTHOR-OWNED IMAGE

Virginia began the season ranked fifteenth and then reeled off seven straight victories, including a 20–7 win over No. 9 Clemson, to move into the top spot in the polls. Unfortunately, head coach George Welsh's best team then went into a tailspin. Bobby Ross and his No. 16 Yellow Jackets of Georgia Tech came into town on November 3 owning a seven-game unbeaten streak with wins over ranked opponents Clemson and South Carolina (back then an independent in football). Virginia, who had never held the top ranking in the polls, had just blown out Wake Forest the week before.

Virginia opened up a 13–0 lead and was ahead by two touchdowns at the half, 28–14. A fumble recovery to open the second half set up a quick Georgia Tech score, followed by another touchdown later in the third quarter to tie it. The teams then traded touchdowns to tie the score at thirty-five all at the end of the third quarter and then swapped fields goals inside the last eight minutes to even things at thirty-eight apiece.

Tech, starting from deep in its own territory with just over two minutes on the clock, drove to within field goal range, winning the game on a thirty-seven-yard field goal by Scott Sisson with seven seconds left, 41–38.[10]

The Yellow Jackets finished out the season with a win over Georgia and then beat No. 19 Nebraska, 45–21, in the Citrus Bowl. As Atlantic Coast Conference champions, Georgia Tech received an automatic bid to the game, a situation that had consequences in shaping the postseason landscape and contributed to producing a split-poll result as Tech was voted No. 1 in the Coaches Poll.

This marked the first undefeated season for Georgia Tech since 1952, their eighth unbeaten season overall, and also the school's first claimed national title since 1952 (INS, later part of UPI). Ross swept all the Coach of the Year accolades.

Poor Virginia rebounded the next week to beat North Carolina but then fell apart, losing to Maryland, Virginia Tech, and Tennessee to drop out of the rankings entirely.

The other wire-service champion was Colorado, although its rise to No. 1 was helped by a controversial circumstance caused by the incompetence of a Big Eight officiating crew. The Buffaloes had opened the

The 1990 Georgia Tech national title plaque. Georgia Tech coach Bobby Ross had come to Atlanta from Maryland in 1987 after starting his head coaching career at The Citadel. Overall, including these schools and his time later coaching Army, he was 103-101-2, possibly the worst career record ever of any coach with a Consensus Major Selector national title.

CREATIVE COMMONS

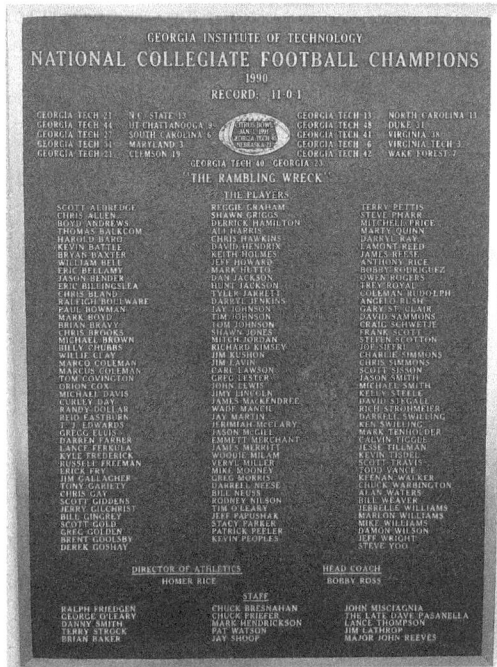

season with a tie against No. 8 Tennessee, a win over Stanford, and a loss to No. 21 Illinois, which tumbled Colorado to No. 20 in the rankings at 1–1–1. But head coach Bill McCartney's team rallied with back-to-back wins over ranked opponents (No. 22 Texas and No. 12 Washington) before sweeping a conference schedule that included victories over No. 22 Oklahoma and No. 3 Nebraska. With the Big Eight title in hand, the Buffaloes would face Notre Dame in the Orange Bowl.[11]

The controversy surrounding Colorado started in October on the road in Columbia, Missouri. It then found legs again in the Orange Bowl. First, October.

In what has become known in college football lore as "The Fifth Down Game," Colorado was down, 31–27, in a seesaw battle with the 2–2–0 Missouri Tigers. Starting from inside their own ten-yard line, the Buffaloes and their predominantly run-based offense drove into Missouri territory before a completed pass left Colorado just short of the goal line with forty seconds left. Quarterback Charles Johnson spiked the ball, bringing second down. Then, after a failed rushing attempt, the Buffaloes called their final timeout, during which the chain crew failed to flip the down marker to third down. Communication problems, rule changes, and even a heart attack in the stands have been blamed for the failed correction of the down marker.

As a result, Colorado ran two second-down plays, a third-down play where Johnson spiked the ball with two seconds left (really fourth down and what should have been a change of possession on downs), and a fourth-down play (really fifth down) with which the Buffaloes scored the winning touchdown on a quarterback keeper. Officials then conferred for twenty minutes while a national TV audience watched.[12] The TD was allowed to stand.

The clock was at 00:00, but with the score being within two points, Colorado was obliged to attempt a conversion after the touchdown. Johnson took a knee, time officially expired, and the Buffaloes salvaged what no one knew at the time would be a championship season. Again, it is worth hearing from Bleacher Report's Michael Pinto: "Had the game been called properly, Colorado would never have been in a position to claim the national championship."[13]

As Big Eight champions, the Buffaloes earned an automatic bid to the Orange Bowl. Head coach Lou Holtz's Notre Dame Fighting Irish, ranked No. 1 earlier in the season, was now No. 5 with two losses. In what was a messy defensive battle, Colorado led 10–9 late in the game due to a successful block of a Notre Dame point-after attempt in the second quarter. Then with forty-three seconds left in the game, the Irish's Rocket Raghib Ismail ran a punt return ninety-two yards for a touchdown. But the potential game-winner was invalidated by a clipping penalty on the punt-return team, leaving the score 10–9 and giving Colorado a controversial national title when the AP writers voted the Buffaloes No. 1, although twenty of the fifty-nine ballots ranked Georgia Tech first. The FWAA and NFF also gave their top rankings to Colorado.

In the Coaches Poll, where the Buffaloes were ranked No. 1 by thirty-eight of forty-seven voters in the last regular-season poll, the final tally showed the Yellow Jackets with thirty first-place ballots to twenty-seven for Colorado and two for two-loss Miami, giving Georgia Tech a narrow championship win in the poll.

It was a season for weak and flawed champions. Though undefeated, Tech ranked fourth in the power rankings, just behind Colorado but well behind Miami and Washington, another two-loss team. Tech also played the weakest schedule of any late-season championship contender.

Colorado, despite a loss and tie, had played one of the toughest schedules in the country but was likely punished by some voters for the controversial wins in Columbia and at the Orange Bowl. Miami and Washington, while stronger on paper and owning major bowl victories, were nonetheless voted down for each having two losses during the regular season.

TALE OF THE TAPE FOR 1990

Team (AP)	Power	Schedule	Record	Offense	Defense
Colorado (1)	19.45 (3)	9.06 (2)	11-1-1	30.7	17.6
Georgia Tech(2)	19.28 (4)	4.28 (28)	11-0-1	31.6	15.5
Miami (3)	23.90 (1)	7.90 (6)	10-2-0	37.3	15.3
Washington (5)	21.62 (2)	6.87 (12)	10-2-0	36.7	15.3

1991: MIAMI OR WASHINGTON?

The Associated Press's No. 1 ranking never left the state of Florida in 1991. Bobby Bowden, head coach of the Florida State Seminoles, appeared poised to overcome several years of frustration, typically at the hands of the Miami Hurricanes. FSU opened the season No. 1 in both polls and was 10–0 coming into the third weekend of November. An upset loss at home, 17–16, to No. 2 Miami—the result of a missed field goal with twenty-nine seconds left (one of the vaunted "wide right" games in Seminole history)—was followed by a season ending loss at No. 5 Florida. After its big victory at FSU, Miami moved into the top spot in both polls, followed by Washington of the PAC-10.

Head coach Dennis Erickson's Hurricanes had the top defense in the country and their usual high-scoring offense, which averaged more than thirty-two points per game. Miami owned solid wins over No. 10 Houston and No. 9 Penn State before going into Tallahassee to upset the Seminoles with a stifling defensive effort. But despite finishing the regular-season schedule with wins over Boston College and San Diego State, the Hurricanes slid from holding the No. 1 slot in both polls to just leading among the writers, confronting a more notable vote melt in the Coaches Poll.

The Miami Orange Bowl's main entrance facade. CREATIVE COMMONS

The Miami Orange Bowl. Burdine Stadium (later called The Miami Orange Bowl) was opened in 1937 and was closed and demolished after the 2007 season. Home field to the Miami Hurricanes and the Miami Dolphins, the venue also hosted the annual Orange Bowl game, numerous national-title matchups in football, and five of the first thirteen Super Bowls. The original capacity of 23,300 was eventually expanded to more than 80,000. The Hurricanes have not contended for a national title since leaving the stadium in 2007 after winning five championships over nineteen seasons from 1983 to 2001. AUTHOR-OWNED IMAGE

Still, the Hurricanes were well positioned as they headed into a post-season Orange Bowl appearance, which would be played on their home turf. Nebraska (9–1–1 and ranked eleventh) would appear as the automatic-qualifying team from the Big Eight Conference, but Miami's defense completely shut down the Huskers' blistering third-ranked offense in a dominating 22–0 victory.

But there was that other contender out west. PAC-10 champion Washington had the No. 2 offense in the country, averaging more than forty-one points per game, as well as the No. 2 defense behind the Hurricanes. The Huskies were undefeated and had regular-season wins over then No. 9 Nebraska and No. 7 Cal, both on the road. The win over the Cornhuskers was not as dominating as Miami's bowl victory but was nonetheless a decisive win in Lincoln. Washington went undefeated and earned a berth in the Rose Bowl, where they devastated No. 4 Michigan, 34–14.

Orange Bowl Playing Surface. Dennis Erikson went 179-96-1 in twenty-three seasons at seven institutions. He was 63-9 in six years at Miami with two national titles and six major bowl appearances, exceeding the performance of each of his two previous predecessors, Jimmy Johnson and Howard Schnellenberger. Under Erikson, the Hurricanes finished no lower than sixth in the final rankings in five of those seasons and only lost more than two games once. He should thank the special-teams gods for cursing Florida State's kicking game, or else that 1991 title doesn't happen. CREATIVE COMMONS

The 1991 Miami Hurricanes were undefeated and champions in the AP poll. Three of Miami's five national titles from 1983 to 2001, including this one, were secured on their home field at the Orange Bowl. Dwayne "The Rock" Johnson (shown here) was a role player on the 1991 squad before later meeting Hulk Hogan and achieving true fame. CREATIVE COMMONS

The polls were close. *Very* close. The writers picked Miami based on a margin of just four first-place votes, while the coaches went the other way by a 33½ to 25½ split. The FWAA and UPI/NFF rankings tabbed Washington as well.

So why did Miami get voted down? Was it ducking Florida in the Sugar Bowl to play at home? Was it the weak finish against Boston College and San Diego State? Was it "Miami Fatigue" since the Hurricanes had already won titles in 1983, 1987, and 1989? Or was it that they got lucky against FSU when the kicking gods again smote Bobby Bowden?

The tale of the tape favors Washington. The Huskies played a far-tougher schedule than Miami and had a similarly impressive win over a common foe, Nebraska. The power ranking places Washington well-above the Hurricanes. Washington had an objectively stronger offense and ranked just behind Miami on defense.

TALE OF THE TAPE FOR 1991

Team (AP)	Power	Schedule	Record	Offense	Defense
Miami (1)	23.76 (2)	4.17 (26)	12-0-0	32.2	8.3
Washington (2)	26.22 (1)	5.97 (8)	12-0-0	41.3	9.6
Penn State (3)	19.90 (3)	5.13 (17)	11-2-0	36.5	14.2
Florida State (4)	19.82 (4)	4.59 (22)	11-2-0	34.5	14.5

1997: MICHIGAN OR NEBRASKA?

The 1997 season opened with no fewer than nine teams getting first-place votes in the polls. As late as October 6, five different teams were still getting first-place votes in the AP poll, and four received first-place ballots in the Coaches Poll as late as the first week of November. Penn State and Florida swapped the top spot back and forth until the Gators lost to LSU on October 11. Nebraska moved into the AP's top spot on October 20 and stayed there until it slipped behind Michigan after avoiding an upset on the road at Missouri on November 8. FSU, always lurking around, took over the second spot in the AP and the top spot in the Coaches Poll for two weeks until losing to No. 10 Florida in Gainesville. Michigan then eased into the top spot of coaches' rankings as well.

This is a powerful season with legendary coaches of the late twentieth century (Tom Osborne, Bobby Bowden, Steve Spurrier, Joe Paterno, Phil Fulmer) all in their primes and all chasing a championship. The Huskers, led by quarterback Scott Frost (later Nebraska's head coach), had the top offense in the nation and averaged 46.7 points per game. The twelfth-ranked defense had two shutouts and would only really be challenged by Colorado and Missouri. Nebraska opened the season at No. 6 in the AP Poll and beat No. 2 Washington and No. 17 Kansas State during the regular season.

Absent the near upset at Missouri, the Huskers likely would have consolidated their position as the consensus top team in both polls. Their victory over No. 14 Texas A&M in the Big 12 Championship Game was a rout. Nebraska hung fifty-four points on the Aggies while holding them to a single field goal until the fourth quarter. The final was 54–15. Ranked No. 2 in the AP going into the bowls, the Huskers beat Fulmer's No. 3-ranked Tennessee squad, the SEC champions, in the Orange Bowl, 42–17, largely containing quarterback Peyton Manning with him and backup Tee Martin each held to a single touchdown throw. Finishing 13–0, Nebraska would claim Tom Osborne's third national title in four seasons and the last of his career, as he retired and entered politics.[14]

Up in Ann Arbor, Michigan, was no one's No. 1 coming into the season. Third-year head coach Lloyd Carr's Wolverines were ranked a respectable fourteenth by the writers and thirteenth in the Coaches Poll.[15] An upset win over No. 8 Colorado to open the season was followed by victories over Notre Dame and ranked Big Ten rivals Iowa and Michigan State. In November, wins over No. 2 Penn State, No. 23 Wisconsin, and No. 4 Ohio

State vaulted Michigan to the top spot, the Big Ten title, and a date with No. 8 Washington State (WSU) in the Rose Bowl.

Michigan finished the season at 12–0 when quarterback Brian Griese led the Wolverines to a 21–16 win.[16] Failing to run out the clock, Michigan punted from the Washington State thirty-three-yard line and pinned the Cougars down on their own seven with sixteen seconds to play. WSU quarterback Ryan Leaf got off two plays (and also took an illegal formation penalty) to get to the Michigan twenty-six yard line with two seconds left. Controversy then arrived, as she often did, when Leaf, out of timeouts, attempted to spike the ball after the chains were moved. However, the SEC crew deemed there was inadequate time after the spike, called the game over, and Leaf's protest went unheeded.

Michigan would finish the season as the AP poll champion, dominating the first-place votes, and would come out on top in the FWAA and NFF rankings. The Coaches Poll was very close and just broke to the advantage of Nebraska, who only claimed the top spot on thirty-two of sixty-two ballots.

A look at common opponents would seem to favor Michigan, albeit slightly. Both teams beat Colorado, though the Wolverines' 27–3 win is more impressive than the Cornhuskers' late-season 27–24 victory over the Buffaloes. The tale of the tape rates Nebraska higher with a stronger power ranking despite playing a relatively weak schedule outside of its dominating victory over Tennessee.

There were a lot of "strong losers" in 1997. The power rankings place both Florida State and Florida as two of the strongest teams in the country that season. Florida State (11–1) has the highest power ranking (23.38), beating No. 23 USC, No. 16 Clemson, No. 21 Georgia Tech, and No. 5 North Carolina, before taking down No. 9 Ohio State in the Sugar Bowl. The Seminoles' only loss came at No. 10 Florida (10–2), who had the No. 3 power ranking (21.07) with wins over No. 4 Tennessee and No. 6 Auburn as well. The Gators finished out their season with a victory against No. 11 Penn State (an early-season No. 1) in the Citrus Bowl, 21–6.

Florida lost to No. 14 LSU on the road and to No. 14 Georgia in Jacksonville. Tennessee, who owned the No. 4 power ranking (20.87), fell to then No. 1 Florida early in the season but beat No. 15 Georgia, No. 25

Southern Miss, and the SEC West division winner, No. 11 Auburn, for the conference crown before losing to Nebraska.

The next season, Tennessee took home the title, beating Bowden and the Seminoles.

TALE OF THE TAPE FOR 1997

Team (AP)	Power	Schedule	Record	Offense	Defense
Michigan (1)	20.14 (5)	4.47 (32)	12-0-0	26.8	9.5
Nebraska (2)	22.30 (2)	2.53 (41)	13-0-0	46.7	16.5

2003: USC OR LSU?

The BCS was supposed to guarantee there'd never be a divided title again. It did not. At the start of this book, we talked about these teams and this situation. Here's a little more detail to add to that discussion—no need to rehash everything.

Now one of the biggest stadiums in the world (102,321), LSU's Tiger Stadium opened in 1924 with a capacity of twelve thousand. Another ten thousand seats were added in 1931, and the legendary 1936 expansion added another twenty-four thousand in a horseshoe configuration. Monies appropriated for dormitories were used to create the stands—built atop student dorms—at the suggestion of athletic director T. P. "Skipper" Heard. The idea is usually attributed to the outlandish governor of Louisiana, Huey P. Long, who was a noted booster of LSU and its football and band programs. He wrote many of LSU's fight songs with composer and LSU band leader Castro Carazo. AUTHOR-OWNED IMAGE

LSU opened the season at No. 14 in the AP poll and defeated No. 7 Georgia, No. 17 Auburn, and No. 15 Ole Miss but lost to unranked Florida. The Tigers then beat No. 5 Georgia in the SEC Championship and ranked in the top two of the BCS standings, which set up a showdown with undefeated Oklahoma (No. 3 in the AP) in the Sugar Bowl. LSU beat the Sooners, 21–14.

USC, ranked No. 1 in the AP and Coaches polls, fell to third in the BCS rankings when the data-driven ratings (the cursed computers) placed them third and out of the title game. The Trojans' one loss was to unranked Cal, but they beat then No. 6 Auburn and later No. 6 Washington State during the regular season before handling No. 4 Michigan in the Rose Bowl, 28–14. The Coaches Poll was committed by the BCS agreement to name the championship game winner No. 1 (even though some of the coaches still voted for USC), but the AP writers, not bound by this obligation, chose USC first on forty-eight of sixty-five ballots in their final poll.

The data in the tale of the tape agree with the writers. The Trojans' power rating is much stronger than LSU's, and they played comparably difficult schedules. The Tigers had a better defense, USC a better offense. LSU did beat Oklahoma, a higher-ranked team, in the Sugar Bowl, but USC's win over similarly powerful Michigan in the Rose Bowl cannot be discounted.

TALE OF THE TAPE FOR 2003

Team (AP)	Power	Schedule	Record	Offense	Defense
USC (1)	23.14 (1)	3.60 (36)	12-1-0	41.1	18.4
LSU (2)	20.85 (2)	3.28 (41)	13-1-0	33.9	11.0

FOUR NOTABLE DISSENTS BY THE FOOTBALL WRITERS ASSOCIATION OF AMERICA

There are two bases of disagreement that can be observed in the Consensus Major Selector titles, which are based on human aggregator polls (and in the case of the National Football Foundation, a committee). One is genuine difference in judgment between the selectors when they act on the same information at the same time. For example, writers and coaches have sincerely different perspectives and make decisions based on different biases, which we talked about earlier.

The other difference is that when the selectors don't act at the same time, one selector has access to more information than the other. This timing problem was what led to the slow-moving reform of how champs were chosen.

When the AP and UP/UPI both picked before the bowl games and "missed" because champions lost their bowls, there was one major selector available to make the correction: the Football Writers Association of America. The FWAA has disagreed with both the AP and UP/UPI on four occasions since its beginning in 1954. In two instances (1960, 1964), the reason was because they selected after the other Consensus Major wire-services champion had lost a bowl game. In two other instances (1958, 1961), the answer is found elsewhere. Since 1964 and through the end of the FWAA's independence in 2014, their choice for champion did not disagree with the wire services but instead either agreed with both or sided with one wire service or the other in a disputed title.[1]

Season	AP Writers	UPI Coaches	FWAA	NFF
1958	LSU	LSU	Iowa	
1960	Minnesota*	Minnesota*	Ole Miss	Minnesota*
1961	Alabama	Alabama	Ohio State	Alabama
1964	Alabama*	Alabama*	Arkansas	Notre Dame

*Lost bowl game after being selected.

1958: LSU OR IOWA?

The LSU Tigers were lightly regarded heading into the 1958 season. Coming off a 5–5 campaign, head coach Paul Dietzel's team was unranked to start the season but moved into the top twenty after opening its schedule with a 26–6 win over Rice. By October 13, the Tigers were ranked ninth with two first-place votes in the AP poll (thirteen teams received first-place votes) and then took over the No. 1 spot in the October 27 poll after top-ranked Army was tied by Pitt. A win over No. 6 Ole Miss the next week was followed by a blowout of Duke, a close win over previously ranked Mississippi State, and a 62–0 annihilation of conference opponent Tulane in the Battle for the Rag at Tulane Stadium in New Orleans. Now 10–0 and

Before coming to Iowa in 1952, Forest "Evy" Evashevski had been the head coach at Hamilton College before joining the military and at Washington State in 1950 and 1951. At Iowa, he was 52-27-4 with two Rose Bowl trips (both wins). He left coaching at age forty-two and then served as athletic director until he was dismissed a decade later amidst a controversy regarding athletic department finances and the treatment of head football coach Ray Nagel. PUBLIC DOMAIN

the SEC champions, LSU returned to Tulane Stadium for the Sugar Bowl and beat Clemson, 7–0. Both wire services named the Tigers national champs.

This was LSU's first national title, and the success resided with both talent and the three-platoon system used by Dietzel. The talent was head-lined by the rushing backfield of quarterback Warren Rabb and halfbacks Billy Cannon and Johnny Robinson. Cannon won the Heisman Trophy in 1959 and later enjoyed an impressive professional career while playing primarily in the American Football League (AFL).

The three-platoon system was Dietzel's solution to the limited sub-stitution model used from 1953 until 1964.[2] Under the rules at the time, a player who came out of the game couldn't come back in until the next quarter—everyone was playing iron-man football. To keep his Tigers rested, Dietzel had a starting unit (the White team) that played on both sides of the ball, a mainly backup offensive unit (the Go team), and a third-string backup defensive unit made up of novice players and scrubs, nicknamed the "Chinese Bandits." Then, while being mindful of the clock, he'd use eleven-man substitutions so that the White team came in fresh with the start of the next quarter. The product was one of the toughest defenses in the country as four of their wins were shutouts. The Bandits were not scored on until LSU played Duke on November 8, and only the Blue Devils scored more than seven points on the Tigers.[3]

Head Coach Forest Evashevski's Iowa Hawkeyes went 8–1–1 and fin-ished the season second in the AP and Coaches polls. But they also trav-eled a tougher road than LSU. The Hawkeyes beat five ranked opponents, including No. 6 TCU, No. 4 Wisconsin, No. 8 Northwestern, and No. 15 Notre Dame. In the Rose Bowl, they faced No. 16 Cal. They likely would have been the top pick of the polls, except a late season loss to No. 16 Ohio State and a tie with Air Force marred their record.

Iowa had the top-rated offense in the country, averaging 405.9 yards per game. The previous two seasons, the Hawkeyes had gone a combined 16–2–1, winning the Big Ten title and making their first trip to the Rose Bowl in 1956, a 35–19 win over Oregon State.

Likewise, this 1959 Rose Bowl was not expected to be much of a con-test. Cal, while ranked sixteenth, was an 18½-point underdog. Iowa shut out the Bears and took an insurmountable lead by the half when quarterback Randy Duncan delivered both running and passing touchdowns (to wide receiver Jeff Langston). In the game overall, running back Willie Fleming rushed for two touchdowns with Bob Jeter and Don Horn also scoring, as the Hawkeyes cruised to a 38–12 win. Cal's productivity was confined to two touchdown rushes by running back Jack Hart.

The case shouldn't seem tough. LSU went undefeated; Iowa did not. LSU went untied; Iowa was not. LSU had a star back who would later win the Heisman. LSU had a novel approach to game management. But when you go to the tale of the tape, the data say Iowa had a stronger power ranking, indeed the best in the nation, while LSU's rating is third behind Wisconsin. Iowa had a better offense. The Hawkeyes played the second-toughest schedule of the season; LSU's was twenty-eighth.

Perhaps the FWAA saw something that wasn't readily evident to the coaches and writers who voted in their respective polls?

TALE OF THE TAPE FOR 1958

Team (AP)	Power	Schedule	Record	Offense	Defense
LSU (1)	21.50 (3)	5.59 (28)	11-0-0	25.6	4.8
Iowa (2)	24.78 (1)	12.28 (2)	8-1-1	27.2	14.6

1960: OLE MISS OR IOWA OR WASHINGTON OR MINNESOTA (OR MISSOURI)?

Ole Miss claims three national titles, although its 1960 title claim has the greatest legitimacy. Ranked second in the polls behind Syracuse to start the season, head coach Johnny Vaught's Rebels moved to No. 1 after a road win over Houston and would cycle in and out of the top spot, swapping it with Syracuse and also Iowa. Ole Miss won five straight games, including a 10–7 victory over No. 14 Arkansas, but a 6–6 tie with LSU on October 29 dropped the Rebels to sixth. They did manage to finish the regular season with three more wins for a No. 2 ranking in the final AP poll. Ole Miss then beat Rice 14–6 in the Sugar Bowl and was named champion by the FWAA, which voted after the bowls.

The wire services had selected Minnesota as national champs. The voting was close. The first-place votes in the final AP poll were 17½ for

Johnny Vaught played football at TCU under razzle-dazzle trick-play innovator Francis Schmidt. Vaught is also the only football coach in Ole Miss history to win the SEC or a national title. After his years playing for the Horned Frogs, he coached the line at North Carolina for former TCU assistant coach Raymond "Bear" Wolf. After service in World War II, he spent a year as an assistant to Harold Drew at Ole Miss, but when Drew left to take over as head coach at Alabama, Vaught was elevated. He had a 190-61-12 record at for the Rebels with only two coaches posting winning records against him in his twenty-five seasons at Ole Miss: Bear Bryant (7-6-1 at Kentucky and Alabama) and General Bob Neyland (3-2 at Tennessee). PUBLIC DOMAIN

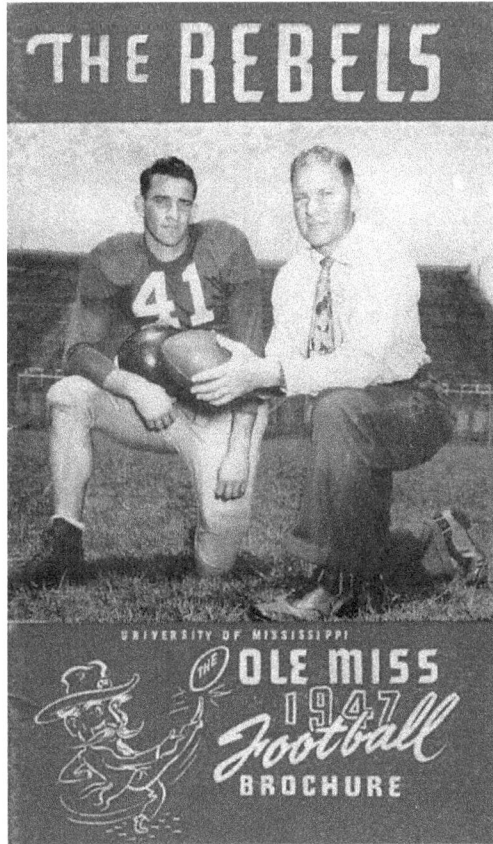

THE REBELS

UNIVERSITY OF MISSISSIPPI

OLE MISS 1947 Football BROCHURE

Minnesota, 16 for Ole Miss, 12½ for Iowa, and 2 for Washington. The coaches voted 21 first-place votes to Minnesota, 9 to Ole Miss, and 5 to Iowa. Ole Miss students burned AP and UPI dummies in effigy while chanting, "We're No. 1! To hell with AP and UPI!"

Perhaps they had a point hidden beneath a protest bearing an unfortunate semblance to a lynching. Head coach Murray Warmath's Golden Gophers were rejuvenating the greatness of Minnesota football in the 1930s. The Gophers opened the 1960 season with a win over No. 12 Nebraska and then ran off six more victories, culminating in a home win over then No. 1 Iowa. The next week the Gophers lost to Purdue, 23–14, but rebounded with a decisive 26–7 road win over No. 4 Wisconsin to earn a share of the Big Ten title and a trip to the Rose Bowl.

Already crowned national champions by the AP, UPI, and NFF, Minnesota would meet one-loss Washington in Pasadena, but the Gophers' sixteenth-ranked offense was held to a single score as the Huskies prevailed in a largely defensive struggle, 17–7.[4] The wire services were left with a national champion who had two losses, including one while wearing the crown. As was noted in Michael Pinto's Bleacher Report article, "Minnesota's 1960 national championship was the last in school history, but it's also one the Golden Gophers wouldn't have received if it had been just five years later."[5]

How do you sort this one out? Iowa has the top power ranking in the nation, played a tougher schedule, and while defeated by then No. 3 Minnesota, also has a better record. The Hawkeyes went 8–1 with wins over seven ranked opponents: No. 10 Oregon State, No. 6 Northwestern, No. 13 Michigan State, No. 12 Wisconsin, No. 10 Purdue, No. 19 Kansas, and No. 3 Ohio State. Iowa was ranked No. 1 at the time of their loss to the Golden Gophers but shared the Big Ten title with Minnesota. The Hawkeyes closed their season with a 28–0 win over Notre Dame to finish second in the Coaches Poll and third in the AP. However, voted No. 1 by the Litkenhous ratings, Iowa claims a title for this season.

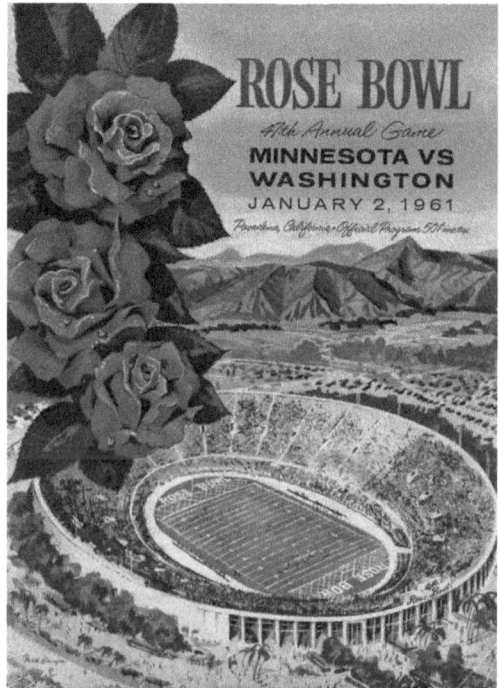

The 1961 Rose Bowl game program. Murray Warmath started his head coaching career at Mississippi State before heading to Minnesota in 1954. Earning a 97-84-10 record in twenty years as a head coach, Warmath's peak season came in 1960 with a conference championship and a national title claim before falling to Washington in the Rose Bowl. He took another Big Ten title in 1967. Among his notable players was Sandy Stephens, who was the first Black man named an All-American at quarterback. PUBLIC DOMAIN

Missouri and Ole Miss also rank ahead of Minnesota in the power rankings and have better records while Ohio State had the second-highest power ranking (22.96) but lost two games, including one to Iowa.

Then there's Washington. The Huskies lost early in the season to No. 17 Navy, then bested No. 15 UCLA and No. 18 Oregon State en route to the Athletic Association of Western Universities title, a precursor to the PAC-10. In the Rose Bowl, then ranked No. 4, Washington beat AP and UPI national champ Minnesota.

Then it gets even weirder. Missouri was designated the national champion by Poling but did not claim the title. The Tigers went 9–1 in the regular season with victories over ranked Penn State (No. 20) and Colorado (No. 18) and were briefly rated No. 1 before losing to Kansas. But the Big Eight later stripped the Jayhawks of both their victory over Missouri and their conference title for using an ineligible player. In turn, the win and the Orange Bowl berth were given to Missouri, who then beat No. 4 Navy, 21–14. The Tigers' regular-season record was changed by the Big Eight to 10–0, although the NCAA still recognizes the one loss.

The University of Mississippi's stadium opened in 1915 and was named for law professor and Ole Miss athletics faculty committee chairman Judge William Hemingway. The original capacity (twenty-four thousand) expanded by a few thousand seats every few years, reaching forty-two thousand in 1988 before major expansions in 1998, 2002, 2015, and 2016 upped the capacity to 64,038. Until expansion in 1998, many rivalry games were played in Memphis and Jackson. PUBLIC DOMAIN

M-59 Memorial Stadium, University of Minnesota, Minneapolis, Minn.

Memorial Stadium, known as the Brick House, was the second on-campus home of the Minnesota Golden Gophers and seated 56,652. From 1924 to 1981, it was the team's home field and the venue where Minnesota claimed all of its national titles. The Gophers moved to the Hubert H. Humphrey Metrodome for the 1982 season and then returned to campus at Huntington Bank Stadium in 2009.

The facade of the original stadium entrance still stands inside the University of Minnesota McNamara Alumni Center. PUBLIC DOMAIN

"The Arch" from the University of Minnesota's original stadium, now located in the McNamara Alumni Center. CREATIVE COMMONS

At the time, one major selector made the logical choice, it would seem. The NCAA places the Football Writers Association of America on par with the two wire-service polls. And the FWAA result is consistent with what the wire-service voters most likely would have done had they known that Minnesota would lose—again—and Ole Miss would handily defeat a Rice team that, despite three regular-season losses, had the tenth-best power ranking in the country.

TALE OF THE TAPE FOR 1960

Team (AP)	Power	Schedule	Record	Offense	Defense
Minnesota (1)	21.49 (5)	10.99	8-2-0	22.8	8.8
Ole Miss (2)	21.64 (4)	6.10	10-0-1	25.5	6.4
Iowa (3)	26.51 (1)	14.95	8-1-0	26.0	12.0
Missouri (5)	21.88 (3)	6.15	10-1-0	26.8	8.5
Washington (6)	14.37 (17)	1.46	10-1-0	24.7	9.7

1961: OHIO STATE OR ALABAMA?

The 1961 season would result in Bear Bryant's first national title and the first of six he would win at Alabama. The Tide opened the season against Georgia and their rookie head coach, Johnny Griffith, winning 32–6 in Athens. At the beginning of November, undefeated and ranked fourth behind Michigan State, Ole Miss, and Texas, Alabama would decisively beat Mississippi State, 24–0, while the No. 2 Rebels lost to LSU, 10–7, and No. 1 Michigan State was upset by Minnesota, 13–0. The Tide moved into the second slot in the polls, just behind the Longhorns.

Two weeks later, the top ten got scrambled again. Texas, hosting TCU at home, was upset, 6–0, by an otherwise decidedly subpar team.[6] Alabama went into the top slot of the polls, initially taking thirty-nine of forty-nine first-place votes. The balloting then tightened for the last two weeks of the season, even as Bama handily beat Georgia Tech and Auburn to earn a date with No. 9 Arkansas in the Sugar Bowl.

How good was Alabama, and why were they so good? It was defense. The Crimson Tide won six of eleven games by shutout. They held all other opponents to single digits and gave up just 2.3 points per game as the top-ranked defense in the country. In the Sugar Bowl, they beat Arkansas,

In the mid-twentieth century, a feature of college football was card stunts, which involved coordinated crowd actions where fans in the stands hold cards that create a recognizable image stretching across the stands. At the 1961 Rose Bowl, the clever pranksters of Cal Tech rigged the Washington Huskies card pattern instructions to spell out "CALTECH" during a halftime stunt. CREATIVE COMMONS

10–3, getting all the points they needed on quarterback Pat Trammell's touchdown. Arkansas was held to a single field goal by Mickey Cissell in the third quarter.

The No. 3 Buckeyes opened their schedule at home against TCU, but head coach Abe Martin's Horned Frogs tied Ohio State, 3–3. Needless to say, the Buckeyes' start to the season was ignominious as TCU would only win three games all year. Ohio State bounced back, though, handily winning its next eight games, including a victory over No. 9 Iowa at home.

Upon capturing the Big Ten crown, Ohio State was extended a formal bid to the Rose Bowl. The invitation was initially accepted by the campus athletics council on a 6–4 vote. But by a 28–25 vote with four not in attendance, the faculty council rejected the bid, reaffirming a previous 1959 "no bowl" decision. In response to the decision, Coach Woody Hayes, who was in Cleveland at time, observed, "We must not let anything happen at the university to cause animosity between the students and the faculty. I respect the integrity of these faculty men who voted against the Rose Bowl, even though I question their intelligence on this one issue."[7]

Minnesota would go to the Rose Bowl in place of the Buckeyes, where it defeated UCLA, 21–3. Ohio State stayed home. A bowl performance was of no consequence to their title hopes anyway, as the AP, UPI and NFF had already selected Alabama as national champion. Bama took twenty-six of forty-seven first-place votes in the AP, and eighteen of thirty-five in the UPI, with the coaches also giving fifteen tallies to Ohio State and one each to Ole Miss and Colorado.[8] Whatever the argument was within the FWAA for making Ohio State champions, the decision was not affected by either an Alabama loss or a strong bowl performance by the Buckeyes. But it did give the legendary coach his third national title.

The tale of the tape might lend some credence to Darrell Royal's Longhorns. Texas had the highest power ranking (25.33) and finished the regular season ranked No. 3 in the AP and No. 4 in the UPI. But that Longhorn loss to TCU in November loomed large over a 33–7 win at No. 10 Arkansas (a common foe to Alabama) and a 12–7 victory against No. 5 Ole Miss in the Cotton Bowl. But when we judge between Alabama and

Abe Martin was head coach at TCU from 1953 to 1966, compiling a 74-64-7 record. He had played for the Horned Frogs under Francis Schmidt. Born Otto Herschel Martin, he got the nickname Abe from a comic strip that Schmidt spotted in the *Fort Worth Star-Telegram*, "Abe Martin Says." He came back to TCU in 1945 as an assistant to Dutch Meyer and became head coach upon Meyer's retirement.
PERMISSION OF TEXAS CHRISTIAN UNIVERSITY

Ohio State, the power ranking and undefeated, untied season speak to Alabama's case.

TALE OF THE TAPE FOR 1961

Team (AP)	Power	Schedule	Record	Offense	Defense
Alabama (1)	24.03 (2)	5.30 (36)	11-0-0	27.0	2.3
Ohio State (2)	19.20 (6)	6.76 (27)	8-0-1	24.6	9.2

1964: ARKANSAS OR ALABAMA?

This is the season that forced the AP to recognize that bowl games matter.

The 1964 campaign opened with Ole Miss, the defending SEC champion, ranked first. But following a win over Memphis State, the Rebels were then upset in Jackson by the Kentucky Wildcats, 27–21, and fell out of the rankings. Remember, during this time the AP poll only consisted of ten teams.

Although Texas moved into first, the Longhorns dropped to sixth after being upset by No. 8 Arkansas at home, 14–13, on October 17. Ohio State and Notre Dame then started swapping No. 1 honors until the Buckeyes were also upset on their home field, 27–0, by Penn State. Given the opening, Alabama jumped to No. 2 and then captured the AP and UPI top spots at the end of the season when Notre Dame was defeated in Los Angeles by USC, 20–17, in the battle for the Jeweled Shillelagh trophy.

The Tide, led by quarterback Joe Namath, were the overwhelming choice of the writers and coaches, followed by Arkansas, the Southwest Conference champion. Both teams were undefeated.

Alabama's defense shut out two opponents and held six others to a single-digit score. Namath[9] led the thirteenth-best scoring offense (22.7 points per game), completing 64 percent of his passing attempts with five touchdown tosses. He finished eleventh in the Heisman Trophy voting.

The most notable wins for Alabama were over No. 9 Florida (quarterbacked by Steve Spurrier), No. 8 LSU, and No. 10 Georgia Tech. Upon finishing the undefeated season with a one-touchdown victory over Auburn in their annual Iron Bowl rivalry game at Legion Field in Birmingham, the Tide then accepted a bid to the Orange Bowl to play No. 5 Texas.

Joe Namath played at Alabama, wore pantyhose on television, and is lately seen selling the Medicare Coverage Helpline on those cable stations that show old TV reruns. Namath never won the Heisman, but he earned a national title with Bama in 1964 and "called his shot" with the New York Jets, winning Super Bowl III in January 1969 over the Baltimore Colts. Bear Bryant said Namath was "the greatest athlete" he'd ever coached. Tampa Bay Buccaneers head coach John McKay noted of the legendary quarterback late in Joe Willie's career, "Namath is still Namath, but I must say that our guys were nice to him. I noticed when they knocked him down, they helped him to his feet. That was gentlemanly. I thought one stood around long enough to get his autograph." IMAGE CREATED BY AUTHOR USING CHATGPT

An assistant on Alabama's staff, Howard Schnellenberger played a critical role in the development of Joe Namath. He would later coach at the University of Miami, earning a 41-16 record and winning the national title in 1983. Schnellenberger also had coaching stops at Louisville (54-56-2), Oklahoma (5-5-1), and Florida Atlantic (58-74). The Colonel cracked the code on the South Florida recruiting market—check out ESPN's *30 for 30* documentaries *The U*, *The U: Part 2*, and *Catholics vs. Convicts*—but never again experienced the level of success he enjoyed in Miami. PUBLIC DOMAIN

Arkansas went to the Cotton Bowl as conference champion. The legendary Frank Broyles, by now in his seventh season at Fayetteville, had coached the Razorbacks to a 10–0 regular-season record, which included

five straight shutout victories to finish out their schedule. With wins over all the traditional SWC powers—TCU, Texas, and Texas A&M—Arkansas faced No. 6 Nebraska in the Cotton Bowl, winning 10–7.

Meanwhile, down in Miami, Alabama went into a deep hole against the Longhorns, 21–7. A touchdown pass to Ray Perkins and a David Ray field goal for the Tide resulted in a final 21–17 Texas victory.

The AP writers and UPI coaches had both voted after the end of the regular season, selecting Alabama by clear margins. With the Tide's loss, the FWAA chose Arkansas after the bowls had been played. The Razorbacks were the only undefeated, untied team in the nation among the large schools. And they had a win over a common opponent with Alabama (Texas).

Notre Dame was selected by the NFF for the MacArthur Bowl, but the university does not claim the title. And the truth is, with one exception, no one claims the NFF as their sole title. Its champion is always in the company of the FWAA, the AP poll, or the Coaches Poll. The exception? Ohio State in 1970, which we explore in just a bit.

The most interesting part of this story is that the Irish do not claim the National Football Foundation's honor. The NFF is the fourth Consensus Major Selector, deemed by the NCAA to be on par with the FWAA, the

Frank Broyles played at Georgia Tech (as a quarterback he held the Orange Bowl game passing record of 304 yards for fifty-five years) and was an assistant to Baylor and Florida head coach Bob Woodruff (son of George). Broyles then returned to Georgia Tech to serve on the staff of his old coach, Bobby Dodd, before being named head man at Missouri in 1957 (as pictured here). He left after one year to take over Arkansas, where he coached Jimmy Johnson (national champion with Miami in 1987 and two Super Bowl wins with the Dallas Cowboys), Barry Switzer (national titles in 1974, 1975, and 1985 with Oklahoma, and one Super Bowl win with the Cowboys), and Jerry Jones (owner of the Cowboys and three Super Bowl titles). All three men either played or coached on Broyles's 1964 national championship Razorbacks team. Broyles was 144-58-5 at Arkansas and won the Southwest Conference seven times in nineteen seasons. THE UNIVERSITY OF MISSOURI, NOW IN THE PUBLIC DOMAIN

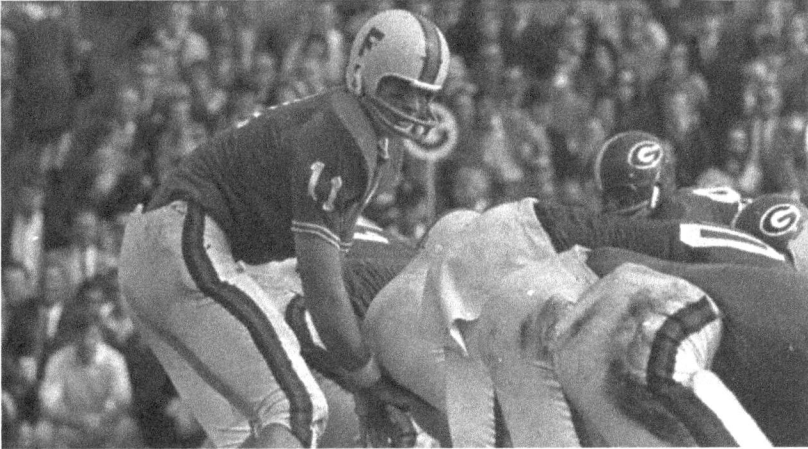

First coaching Duke, then Florida, and then later South Carolina, Steve Spurrier picked up a national championship along the way, winning the title with the Gators in 1996. PUBLIC DOMAIN

AP poll, and the Coaches Poll. But Notre Dame's refusal to claim this title informs an understanding of Consensus Major Selectors that comes from going through all these contests.

The wire services are the most legitimate titles conferred, with the AP writers being the Cadillac standard by virtue of longevity. Econometric

Ray Perkins and the 1964 Alabama Crimson Tide. Ray Perkins played for Bear Bryant at Alabama and was a favorite receiving target for both Joe Namath and Kenny Stabler. He succeeded Bryant as head coach at Bama in 1983, going 32-15-1 over four seasons before being followed by Bill Curry (who had gone 31-43-4 at Georgia Tech) and then Gene Stallings, who had played for Bryant at Texas A&M as one of the Junction Boys. Stallings won a national title in 1992. IMAGE CREATED BY AUTHOR USING CHATGPT

analysis shows there is greater bias of voters observed in the Coaches Poll. The FWAA becomes more impactful when it corrects a demonstrated failure of the wire services to pick the right champion or when it breaks the tie. The NFF is prestigious because of its origins and especially the long shadow of General Douglas MacArthur's association with it. But the NFF is not normally the sole basis for claiming a title. Notre Dame is very much a Cadillac-standard program, so taking a pass on claiming this title is unsurprising.

The tale of the tape favors Notre Dame for power ranking (No. 1), and the strength of schedule is solid. Alabama and Arkansas were third and fourth in the power ranking, respectively, but the Razorbacks hold the trump card—they won their bowl game and defeated a common opponent.

TALE OF THE TAPE FOR 1964

Team (AP)	Power	Schedule	Record	Offense	Defense
Alabama (1)	22.06 (3)	8.15 (20)	10-1-0	22.7	8.0
Arkansas (2)	20.05 (4)	5.51 (44)	11-0-0	21.0	5.8
Notre Dame (3)	27.33 (1)	8.83 (16)	9-1-0	28.7	7.7
Michigan (4)	24.24 (2)	11.04 (9)	9-1-0	23.5	8.3
Texas (5)	18.84 (5)	6.66 (33)	10-1-0	20.0	7.4

CONSEQUENCES FOR THE POLLS

Abraham Lincoln observed, "I am slow to learn and slow to forget that which I have learned. My mind is like a piece of steel, very hard to scratch anything on it and almost impossible after you get it there to rub it out."[10] The same can be said of the wire services. After multiple experiences of declaring a champion, only to see them ignobly lose a postseason bowl game, they decided that perhaps, just perhaps, it would make sense to take a last poll after all the evidence was in. The Associated Press and UP/UPI had several instances of their champion losing a bowl prior to 1964, but it took until 1965 for the sportswriters to move to a postseason poll and until the 1970s for the coaches to do the same.

That, dear reader, is a lot of learning.

The Football Writers Association of America was the one organization that always got it right. Waiting until after the bowl games made sense and proved valuable. When the FWAA came along in 1957, there were seven postseason bowl games being played. In that time until the AP surrendered in 1965 and moved to a postseason poll, the FWAA provided critical correction of national title claims twice, in 1960 and 1964. Being there to correct the polls proved valuable, both in terms of having title claims make sense, and in giving a good rationale for a title claim by the strongest team standing on January 2.

So were FWAA titles persuasive in fixing a bad wire-service choice before the bowls? Or were they just a conflicting decision? First, as a group of sportswriters, they represent a second sample of objective observers—much like the AP writers poll—with no stake in the game of rankings itself. The coaches cannot make this claim. Second, there is the power of the wisdom of crowds. The more eyes you put on a problem, the better solution you get.

And finally, for good or for ill, as we'll see when we look at the BCS/CFP championship puzzle, as much as people think technology and science can provide solutions, at the end of the day there's a distrust of math by people who don't understand the math. This is evident when math is applied to emotional issues like "Who is the champion?" in an intense, fan-driven sport.

Passionate believers don't want a dispassionate science to tell them they are wrong. Clearly the math must be wrong, they might tell you, because it has no soul.

CHAPTER 5

THE DISSENTING TITLE CLAIMS

Adissenting title is not the same as a split title. Split titles occur when the four recognized Consensus Major Selectors disagree on who is the champion. We've looked at those cases already.

Dissenting claims are based on some authority other than the Consensus Major Selectors, who are deemed by the NCAA, experience, and popular consent to be the most credible. The bases of dissenting claims can range from historic selectors who had high credibility at the time of the championship (the contemporary algorithms of the 1930s and 1940s), to simply declaring yourself champions. Some dissenting claims also involve time travel of sorts, as research or math is the basis for a retrospective title claim.

The following teams officially claim at least one national title since the beginning of the wire-service era that is based on a dissenting authority: Pitt, 1936; Cal, 1937; Tennessee, 1938, 1940, 1950, 1967; Cornell, 1939; USC, 1939; Stanford, 1940; Alabama, 1941; Georgia 1942; Oklahoma State, 1945; Army, 1946; Michigan, 1947; Kentucky, 1950; Princeton, 1950; Illinois, 1951; Michigan State, 1951, 1955, 1957; Georgia Tech, 1952; Iowa, 1956, 1960; Ole Miss, 1959, 1962; Washington, 1960; SMU, 1981, 1982; and UCF, 2017.[1]

1936: MINNESOTA OR PITT?

This was the third straight recognized selector title claimed by Minnesota and fifth-year head coach Bennie Bierman and was one of five claimed by the Gophers from 1934 to 1941.

Minnesota had a quality win over No. 5 Purdue but also lost to No.

3 Northwestern. The Gophers had a stifling defense, giving up just four points per game and compiling a scoring margin of 203–32 for the season. And all of this was accomplished against the country's fifth-toughest schedule in 1936.

Pitt, like Minnesota, played one of the toughest schedules in the country as well (ranked eighth) and claimed wins against No. 7 Notre Dame, No. 6 Nebraska, and No. 5 Washington. Those victories were balanced against a home loss against Duquesne, who finished the season 8–2 overall and ranked fourteenth, and with a road tie at No. 5 Fordham, 0–0, at the old Polo Grounds in New York City. Pitt went on to the Rose Bowl and defeated the Pacific Coast Conference champ, No. 5 Washington. Six of Pitt's ten games were shutouts.

Pitt and Minnesota had two common opponents in 1936, Nebraska and Washington. The Golden Gophers opened the season on the road in Seattle, beating Washington, 14–7, at Huskey Stadium. Two weeks later, Minnesota opened at home against the Cornhuskers and collected its second win, 7–0. Nebraska then won four straight over Indiana, Oklahoma, Missouri, and Kansas, climbing to No. 6 in the AP poll before suffering its loss to Pitt at home, 19–6.

Meanwhile, out west the Huskies went 7–0–1 in their next eight games (tied by Stanford) to win the PCC. They then faced the Eastern Independent champion Pitt in Pasadena, losing to the Panthers, 21–0.

The 1936 Minnesota Golden Gophers. PUBLIC DOMAIN

Bernie Moore coached football and track at LSU after starting his head-coaching career at Mercer (where one of his players was future Georgia Bulldogs head coach Wally Butts). Winning the SEC in 1935 and 1936, he was 83–39–6 in thirteen seasons leading the Tigers. In 1948, Moore stepped down from LSU to become commissioner of the Southeastern Conference. PERMISSION OF LOUISIANA STATE UNIVERSITY

But what about LSU? Down in Baton Rouge, the Tigers, under head coach Bernie Moore, had premiered in the initial AP poll at No. 13 and then climbed week after week up the charts, beating No. 19 Tulane at home on November 28. LSU was undefeated in the SEC, tied Texas early in the schedule, and finished the regular season at 9–0–1 with five shutouts to earn the No. 2 ranking. The Tigers then went to the Sugar Bowl where they lost to No. 6 Santa Clara, 21–14. The Broncos of California had only given up thirteen points in seven regular-season wins and just twenty-two points for the year before the Sugar Bowl. Retrospectively awarded a championship by the Sagarin Ratings, LSU makes no claim on the title.

Then there's undefeated Alabama. The Tide's 8–0–1 record in head coach Frank Thomas's sixth season included wins over No. 10 Tulane, Clemson, Mississippi State, Kentucky, and Georgia Tech with a scoreless tie against Tennessee at Legion Field in Birmingham. Alabama climbed as high as No. 3 in the AP poll, but despite beating Vanderbilt, 14–6, on Thanksgiving Day again back at Legion Field, the Tide finished fourth in the final rankings. Bama had four shutout wins and also held three other opponents to single digits to tie for seventh in scoring defense.

The 1936 Sugar Bowl. LSU edged out Alabama for the SEC title in 1936, but then lost to Santa Clara, 21-14 in the Sugar Bowl, thereby making its contribution to the Slippery Rock Argument. PUBLIC DOMAIN

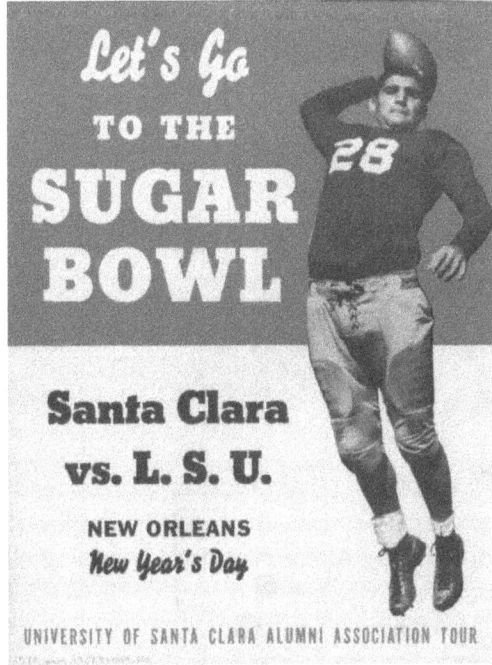

LSU had a nominally better record, though, with one additional win, so the Tigers were crowned SEC champions and received an invitation to the Sugar Bowl. Alabama did not play in the postseason.

THE TALE OF THE TAPE FOR 1936

Team (AP)	Power	Schedule	Record	Offense	Defense
Minnesota (1)	24.61 (1)	8.74 (5)	7-1-0	25.4	4.0
LSU (2)	19.87 (3)	6.51 (15)	9-1-1	26.8	4.9
Pitt (3)	23.10 (2)	8.40 (8)	8-1-1	22.4	3.4
Alabama (4)	16.43 (7)	3.66 (37)	8-0-1	18.7	3.9

1937: PITT OR CAL?

In 1923, Jock Sutherland was head coach at Lafayette College in Easton, Pennsylvania. The next season he succeeded the legendary Pop Warner as head coach at Pitt. The 1937 edition of the Panthers was possibly his finest team. Pitt went 9–0–1 and was named champion in the East by the New York football writers, winning the Lambert Trophy, while also being tabbed national champions by the Associated Press writers in their final season poll. The Panthers were invited to play Cal, the PCC's champion, in the Rose Bowl, but team members voted to decline any bowl invitations.

Pitt Stadium opened in 1925 as the home field for the University of Pittsburgh Panthers. The team's success under Pop Warner while playing at Forbes Field led to the creation of a football venue. Seating nearly seventy thousand when it opened, the stadium was the home field to Pitt football from 1925 to 1999. The NFL's Steelers also played half of their home games at Pitt Stadium starting in 1958 until they moved into Three Rivers Stadium in 1970. AUTHOR-OWNED IMAGE

Pitt's schedule, ranked the tenth toughest in the nation that year, included wins over ranked opponents Wisconsin (No. 16), Notre Dame (No. 12), Nebraska (No. 11), and Duke (No. 18) in its season finale, all of whom were bested by a Panther lineup of ten All-Americans. Lesser lights Ohio Wesleyan, Carnegie Tech (now Carnegie

Born in Scotland, Jock Sutherland coached at Lafayette (33-8-2) and Pitt (111-20-12). He was also a professor of dentistry. After Sutherland succeeded Pop Warner as head coach at Pitt in 1924, the Panthers regularly claimed the Eastern championship and made four trips to the Rose Bowl.
CREATIVE COMMONS

Mellon), West Virginia, and Penn State also joined the list of vanquished. The only real challenge to Pitt was Fordham, who was unranked at the time but headed to a No. 3 spot in the final AP poll, thanks in part to a scoreless tie with the Panthers at the Polo Grounds in New York City. Five of Pitt's nine victories were by shutout, as a defense ranked tenth in the country for points allowed accompanied a top-fifteen offense that featured fullback Frank Patrick and halfbacks Dick Cassiano and Marshall Goldberg.

In the first AP poll, released on October 18, Cal was ranked No. 1 with twenty-four of fifty-two first-place votes, followed by Alabama and Pitt. The only blemish on the Golden Bears' record was a scoreless tie against Washington on November 6 that dropped them from the No. 1 slot they'd held to No. 2. With wins against No. 11 USC and No. 13 Stanford, Cal finished 10–0–1. The Bears ranked second in the last AP poll before hanging a loss on No. 4 Alabama in the Rose Bowl, the Tide's first all season. The Dunkel System named Cal the top team in the nation.

Other than Dunkel, though, the contemporary and retrospective algorithms generally select Pitt as the best team in the nation. The Panthers' overall power ranking is higher, and they played a far tougher schedule. That the team decided to forego postseason play is unfortunate—either a Sugar Bowl matchup with Alabama or a Rose Bowl showdown with Cal would have made for an intriguing end to the season.

Among the other undefeated schools in the final AP rankings, No. 7 Dartmouth has the second-highest

Jock Sutherland. Pitt claims five national titles during his tenure (1924–38) and nine overall. Sutherland's last championship (1937) came from the AP writers poll.
PUBLIC DOMAIN

Paid for with seat subscriptions and designed to resemble the Coliseum in Rome, California Memorial Stadium opened in 1923 and was built at a cost of $1.4 million. Seating seventy-five thousand at the time of construction, the capacity initially expanded to about eighty-one thousand before being reduced to the current sixty-three thousand. The original stands were designed and built to be able to move independently during earthquakes. AUTHOR-OWNED IMAGE

power ranking while No. 3 Fordham, No. 6 Villanova, No. 9 Santa Clara, and No. 14 Holy Cross have both lower power rankings and weaker schedules.

THE TALE OF THE TAPE FOR 1937

Team (AP)	Power	Schedule	Record	Offense	Defense
Pitt (1)	20.05 (1)	6.45 (10)	9-0-1	20.3	3.4
Cal (2)	18.02 (3)	2.02 (53)	10-0-1	19.5	3.0
Fordham (3)	16.63 (7)	3.26 (40)	7-0-1	22.8	2.0
Villanova (6)	16.08 (9)	-0.58 (74)	8-0-1	20.6	0.8
Dartmouth (7)	18.91 (2)	0.91 (62)	7-0-2	27.6	3.7
Santa Clara (9)	12.70 (19)	-2.42 (88)	9-0-0	18.1	1.0
Holy Cross (14)	7.22 (37)	-2.48 (89)	8-0-2	10.7	1.9

1938: TCU OR TENNESSEE?

Texas Christian was ranked No. 1 or No. 2 throughout November and ran the table on the Southwest Conference. Heisman Trophy winner Davey O'Brien led the Horned Frogs through the most successful season in program history, posting a 11–0 mark. TCU's defense held seven of eleven opponents to a single score and had three shutouts. After the Irish lost on December 3 at USC, the Horned Frogs moved into the AP No. 1 slot as national champions and then defeated No. 6 Carnegie Tech in the Sugar Bowl at Tulane Stadium, 15–7. At that point, fifth-year head coach Dutch Meyer was 44–11–4 at TCU; fans of the Horned Frogs did not know that this would be the high-water mark for TCU football for more than seventy years.

Over in Knoxville, another claimant emerged. Tennessee was designated national champions by most of the major designators other than the AP writers (Boand, Dunkel, Houlgate, Litkenhous, and Poling). This

You've heard of the award, given annually since 1981 to the best quarterback in college football. Do you know why it exists? Davey O'Brien was a lanky little guy, just over five feet, seven inches tall, who grew up in Dallas. He came to TCU in 1935 and played for Dutch Meyer, backing up Sammy Baugh. In 1937, he moved into the starting role, and in 1938 led the Horned Frogs to an undefeated season and the national title. He set a Southwest Conference record for passing yards (1,509) that year as well as the collegiate record for running and passing plays by one player. He also won both the Heisman Trophy, the first Texan to do so, and the Maxwell Award, becoming the first player to win both in the same season. (It is worth noting that the Heisman was in its fourth selection year and the Maxwell in its second selection year.) The Davey O'Brien Award, housed at The Fort Worth Club, was initially created in 1977 as the Davey O'Brien Memorial Trophy for the best player in the Southwest. Longhorns running back Earl Campbell was the first winner, followed by Oklahoma's Billy Sims, and then Mike Singletary from Baylor. Since the designation of the award began being given to the nation's best quarterback in 1981, twelve QBs have won the O'Brien, the Heisman, and the Maxwell in the same season: Doug Flutie (Boston College, 1984); Vinny Testaverde (Miami, 1986); Ty Detmer (Brigham Young, 1990); Gino Torretta (Miami, 1992); Charlie Ward (Florida State, 1993); Danny Wuerffel (Florida, 1996); Tim Tebow (Florida, 2007); Cam Newton (Auburn, 2010); Marcus Mariota (Oregon, 2014); Baker Mayfield (Oklahoma, 2017); Joe Burrow (LSU, 2019); Bryce Young (Alabama, 2021). No TCU player had ever won the Davey O'Brien Award until 2022, when Max Duggan claimed the trophy as quarterback for the national championship runner-up Frogs. CREATIVE COMMONS

Dutch Meyer coached the Horned Frogs of TCU from 1934 to 1952, accumulating a 109–79–13 record with three Southwest Conference titles and two national championships (1935 and 1938). Meyer, from Ellinger, Texas, also played at TCU. As a coach, though, he helped elevate the passing game in college football, recruiting the legendary Sammy Baugh off a sandlot and inventing the double-wing formation, initially known as the Meyer Spread. When it came to throwing the ball, he believed in short, sure, and safe. (His thoughts on the game can be found in his 1952 book *Spread Formation Football*.) If you don't remember Dutch Meyer for anything else, remember him for his motivational speech: "Fight 'em until hell freezes over. Then fight 'em on the ice!" PERMISSION OF TEXAS CHRISTIAN UNIVERSITY

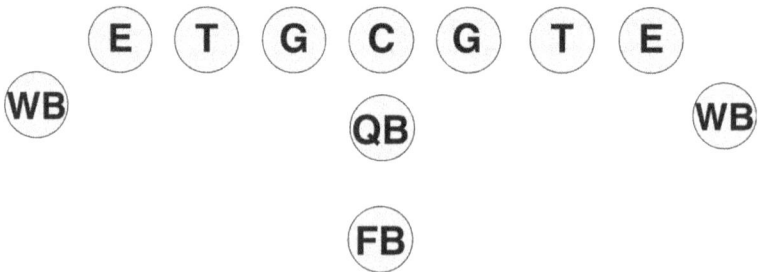

The double-wing formation, foundation to the Meyer Spread offense. IMAGE FROM AUTHOR

was the first of three straight undefeated regular seasons for head coach Robert Neyland's Volunteers. Tennessee started its legendary seventeen-game regular-season shutout streak (seventy-one straight quarters—still an NCAA record) on November 5 against Chattanooga. Only

Amon G. Carter Stadium. In 1923, a major endowment gift to TCU was tied to building a new library, which was to be built on Clark Field, where the Horned Frogs played. A gift from Fort Worth publisher Amon G. Carter financed the construction of a new stadium bearing his name, which opened in 1930 with seating for twenty-two thousand. TCU claimed national championships in 1935 and 1938 playing there. The architect for the stadium, Andrew Poyar, also designed what became Neyland Stadium at the University of Tennessee. CREATIVE COMMONS

three opponents would score on the Volunteers all season as they gave up 1½ points a game and finished second in scoring defense behind Duke. Undefeated in the regular season, Tennessee ranked No. 2 in the final AP poll and beat No. 4 Oklahoma, 17–0, in the Orange Bowl (Oklahoma had previously won fourteen straight). Evidently, the game was rough as the teams combined for 221 yards in penalties. Tennessee claims this as their first national title.

But what about Notre Dame? The Irish do not assert a title claim despite being picked by Dickinson. However, the claim would be intriguing, as Notre Dame would have matched up well against TCU, Tennessee, or Oklahoma. The Irish went 8–1 against a national schedule ranked the second toughest in the nation, beating No. 13 Carnegie Tech (who also lost to TCU), No. 12 Minnesota, No. 16 Northwestern, and both service academies. The Irish finished the season losing to No. 8 USC on the road, which knocked them down from a No. 1 ranking prior to the game to fifth in the final AP poll.

Rocky Top. Tennessee's Shields–Watkins Field (now Neyland Stadium) was built in 1921 and designed by Andrew Poyar. Subsequent design expansion phases were laid down by General Robert Neyland, working with Poyar, while he was still head coach for the Volunteers. These plans have guided the venue's expansion from its original capacity of thirty-two hundred to the current capacity of 102,455. Shown here is the stadium in 1968, when the new east deck increased seating to more than sixty-four thousand. AUTHOR-OWNED IMAGE

TALE OF THE TAPE FOR 1938

Team (AP)	Power	Schedule	Record	Offense	Defense
TCU (1)	20.65 (1)	2.74 (45)	11–0–0	24.5	5.5
Tennessee (2)	20.24 (3)	2.88 (44)	11–0–0	26.6	1.5
Notre Dame (5)	19.31 (4)	9.75 (2)	8–1–0	16.6	4.3

1939: TEXAS A&M OR CORNELL OR USC OR TENNESSEE?

The first poll of the season, released by the AP came on October 16, featured Pitt, Notre Dame, Oklahoma, Tulane, and Tennessee in the top five. USC was seventh, Texas A&M ranked ninth, and Cornell twelfth. That week Pitt was upset by Duquesne while Oklahoma and Tulane both tied.

Tennessee then jumped into the top spot, followed by Notre Dame, who then started to slip. Texas A&M moved into second on November 6 and would take over the No. 1 ranking on November 20. The Volunteers made another brief showing at No. 1 in the December 4 poll, but when the final rankings came out, the Aggies were first and Tennessee second with

USC and Cornell rounding out the top four. The Sooners tumbled after losing their last two games.

The final AP poll would split the first-place votes with Texas A&M earning fifty-five, Tennessee twenty-six, Cornell sixteen, USC nine, and Duke two, although the Trojans were ranked third overall.

Texas A&M was undefeated and untied in 1939, finishing 11–0 with wins over two ranked opponents, including a 14–13 victory over No. 5 Tulane in the Sugar Bowl. Head coach Homer Norton's Aggies had the third-best defense in the country (six shutouts in ten regular season games) and a solid offense led by fullback John Kimbrough[2] that averaged nineteen points per game. Of the thirty-one points the Aggies surrendered in 1939, thirteen were in the game against Tulane.

Football has been played on Kyle Field since 1904, and a concrete grandstand has been there since 1927. Able to seat thirty-three thousand in 1929, the former horseshoe design has been repeatedly expanded to become a fully enclosed bowl with triple decks and official seating of 102,733. PUBLIC DOMAIN

Kyle Field. CREATIVE COMMONS

Schoellkopf Field at Cornell University opened in 1915 and was named for former Big Red player and coach Henry Schoellkopf. AUTHOR-OWNED IMAGE

The halcyon days were quickly passing for those schools who now make up the Ivy League, which formed in 1954. Cornell in 1939 and Princeton in 1950 are the last of the Ivy programs to contend for, and assert, a claim to the national title. Carl Snavely, a College Football Hall of Famer who would ultimately win 180 games as a head coach, had his finest team, which included All-Americans Nick Drahos at tackle and quarterback Walter Matuszczak. The 8–0 Big Red soundly beat No. 4 Ohio State in Columbus on their way to winning the Lambert Trophy as champions in the East. Cornell declined an invitation to play USC in the Rose Bowl for academic reasons—the players needed to study for finals.

The Trojans were led by head coach Howard Jones, a Hall of Famer himself who was 194–64–21 in a career spent mainly at Iowa and USC with stops at Syracuse, Yale, Ohio State, and Duke. Teams he coached claim six national titles, including four at USC.[3] The claim of the 1939 national title by the Trojans is not one Jones knew of; it was made in 2004, based on the 1940 Dickinson System rankings.[4]

The shame is USC had the AP title in their hands—almost. Coming into the last game of the regular season against UCLA, the Trojans were averaging 20.9 points per game, led by All-American quarterback Grenny Lansdell, and the defense was giving up just over four points per contest with four shutouts. USC shutout UCLA. And UCLA shutout USC. The Trojans subsequently beat the Volunteers and their top-ranked defense, 14–0, in the Rose Bowl.

Then there's Tennessee. Head coach Bob Neyland's 1938 team had gone 11–0, ranked second in the AP, and made a legitimate claim to the national title with eight shutouts and just 16 points given up in total. The 1939 edition was even better, at least on defense. No one scored on

Homer Norton coached the Texas Aggies from 1934 to 1947, compiling an 82–53–9 record. Despite taking the national title in 1939, he was fired in 1947 after finishing 3-6-1 and losing to the Texas Longhorns for the eighth season in a row. Norton came to College Station after coaching Centenary in the SIAA for several years. His last Centenary team (1933) is in a four-way tie with Temple (1937), UCLA (1939), and Central Michigan (1991) for the most tie games in a season with four. They had three ties during the regular season (LSU, Texas, and TCU) and then tied Arkansas in the 1934 Dixie Classic (forerunner to the Cotton Bowl). PUBLIC DOMAIN

Texas A&M Stadium in 1939. The 1939 Texas A&M Aggies were 11–0, and the defense gave up just 1.8 points per game. They capped their end-of-regular-season title with a 14–13 win over Tulane in the Sugar Bowl. AUTHOR-OWNED IMAGE

Tennessee during the regular season—the last major college team to go unscored on in the regular season. The offense was less spectacular, but it didn't seem to matter. At the end of the year, Tennessee was undefeated, SEC champs, and ranked No. 2.

A powerful case for a national title could be made . . . except for the Rose Bowl. Journeying to Pasadena, the Volunteers had two touchdowns hung on them by quarterback Ambrose Schindler—one rushing, one passing. The Tennessee offense was shut down by USC's defense as tailback George Cafego was out with a knee injury suffered against The Citadel.

The tale of the tape is mixed. Texas A&M is undefeated, untied, had the stingiest defense of the three contenders claiming titles, played a longer schedule, and is listed second in the power rankings. The team the Aggies are behind is Cornell, who was also undefeated, untied, and played a more difficult schedule. USC soundly defeated the toughest remaining bowl opponent in unbeaten, untied, unscored-upon

Once upon a time, Tulane was a force in the SEC. The 1939 Green Wave went undefeated in conference play and were 8-0-1 at the end of the regular season with intersectional wins over Columbia and Fordham. Only a 14-14 tie against North Carolina blemished their record. Red Dawson, the young head coach who had been a quarterback at Tulane, was 36-19-4 in six seasons at the helm and would later coach the Buffalo Bills, a professional team in the All-America Football Conference. The Wave's defense shut out five opponents during that 1939 season and held two others to less than seven points, while the offense averaged a respectable 19.4 points per game in an era of low scores. Tulane finished the season ranked fifth in the AP Poll, but any retrospective title aspirations were lost in the Sugar Bowl when the Green Wave fell to No. 1 Texas A&M after the final AP poll was released. This is as close as Tulane has ever come to a national championship argument. PUBLIC DOMAIN

Tennessee, but those two ties loomed in the minds of voters in the AP poll and are reflected in the Trojans' far-weaker power ranking. Tulane, Ohio State, Duke, and North Carolina all rated higher on the power ranking than USC.

TALE OF THE TAPE FOR 1939

Team (AP)	Power	Schedule	Record	Offense	Defense
Texas A&M (1)	20.96 (2)	4.60 (30)	11-0-0	19.3	2.8
USC (3)	17.00 (7)	3.30 (42)	8-0-2	18.1	3.3
Cornell (4)	23.02 (1)	7.90 (6)	8-0-0	24.6	6.5

1940: STANFORD OR MINNESOTA OR TENNESSEE OR BOSTON COLLEGE?

Cornell came into 1940 off an undefeated season and riding a twelve-game unbeaten streak extending back to 1938. The Big Red would continue to win, holding the top AP spot through the beginning of November while extending the unbeaten streak to eighteen games. Head coach Carl Snavely's eleven fell to Dartmouth in the seventh game of the season, 3–0, and then lost again at Penn, tumbling in the rankings.

Bennie Bierman was a transitional and transformational figure in college football. He got his first head-coaching job at Montana while in his twenties and later became the head man at then Mississippi A&M, posting a combined 17-17-4 record in five seasons at the two schools. Over five years at Tulane, he was 36-10-2, winning the Southern Conference in 1929, 1930, and 1931 (going 28-2), and at one point reeled off fifteen straight games without a loss. He was 93-35-6 at Minnesota with five national titles, and in 1942 he coached the legendary Iowa Pre-Flight Seahawks, one of the greatest amateur football teams ever assembled. Bierman was a conservative coach, but he also adjusted his game to his situation: "Why did I put so much emphasis on blocking, tackling, and the running game? Well, it was the potential ability of Midwestern lads to block so powerfully which first tempted me to stress the running game as a major part of the Minnesota attack shortly after I arrived in Minneapolis from Tulane in 1932. Under another set of circumstances and blessed with a different type of material, I'd probably have favored the forward pass or the lateral." CREATIVE COMMONS

Minnesota moved into the top spot in the writers poll and would hold it through the end of the season. The Golden Gophers, led by head coach Bernie Bierman, were hunting for a fourth national title in seven years, going 8–0 in 1940 with five one-score wins, which included a pair of one-point victories over No. 8 Northwestern and No. 3 Michigan.

The win over Michigan was critical and stung the Wolverines faithful in a manner one would think would be reserved for an Ohio State game. The student yearbook *Michiganensian* observed the national title situation and Michigan's (sole) loss to the Gophers in rainy, muddy playing conditions: "Minnesota went on to win the National Championship, while Michigan finished third, but here in Ann Arbor, we'll always believe it was rain and not the Gophers which pushed Michigan out of what would have been its first national championship since 1932."

The second, third, fourth, and fifth slots were held at the end of the season by Stanford, Michigan, Tennessee, and Boston College, respectively. All were undefeated except Michigan. Texas A&M had held the second spot going into Thanksgiving but lost to Texas, 7–0, in Austin, slipping to sixth in the AP poll.

The Stanford Indians (they became the Cardinal in 1981) were led by former University of Chicago head coach Clark Shaughnessy. Stanford had gone 1–7–1 the year before while Chicago, which hadn't been winning a lot of games lately either, decided to drop football for academic reasons. Shaughnessy, who was also a physical education professor at Chicago, quit the faculty in order to continue as a coach, a "professor of football" perhaps, at Stanford. One innovation he brought was a resurrection of the nineteenth-century T formation, which is basically the same modern T used today. Shaughnessy hadn't been winning much with the scheme at Chicago, but that would change in California.[5]

Stanford opened with shutout wins over San Francisco and Oregon and then battled Santa Clara, 7–6, before running off five straight victories, including four over ranked opponents, with improved offensive production. The Stanford team and the T formation were a good marriage. A 13–7 road win over rival Cal in the Big Game found Stanford undefeated, ranked second, and headed to the Rose Bowl, where they would beat Big Six champion Nebraska, who had one loss—to Minnesota. The contemporary

Poling System algorithm and the Williamson system declared Stanford's "Wow Boys" the 1940 champion.[6]

Neyland and his Volunteers were back in contention as the dominant defensive force in the South, giving up just twenty-six points in the regular season and shutting out eight opponents. Neyland, who would soon return to the Army and serve in the China-Burma-India Theater in World War II, collected another perfect regular season as Tennessee went 10–0 and returned to the Sugar Bowl at Tulane Stadium. The team was recognized as national champions by the contemporary Dunkel System while the SRS power ranking placed Tennessee seventh, the Vols having faced a very weak schedule that included Mercer, Chattanooga, and Southwestern (now Rhodes College in Memphis).

Tennessee would meet another national title claimant, fifth-ranked Boston College, in the Sugar Bowl. Both teams were undefeated but out of AP title contention. The Eagles were coached by Frank Leahy, in the second year of his first head coaching job.[7] BC opened the season with wins at home against Centre and on the road at Tulane in Tulane Stadium.[8] The balance of the schedule was subpar, with a strength of schedule on the weak side of average. Temple, No. 9 Georgetown, and Auburn stand out as the most notable opponents. Nonetheless, BC won all ten of its games and went to New Orleans for New Year's.

Shields-Watkins Field, circa 1940. The 1940 Tennessee Volunteers, coached by Robert Neyland, went 10–0 in the regular season with eight shutouts before losing to Boston College in the Sugar Bowl. PUBLIC DOMAIN

Boston College Alumni Field opened in 1915 and hosted Eagles games until being replaced by Alumni Stadium in 1957. The original grandstand was eventually expanded to twenty-five thousand seats, but the capacity was inferior to Fenway Park, where most BC games were played. PUBLIC DOMAIN

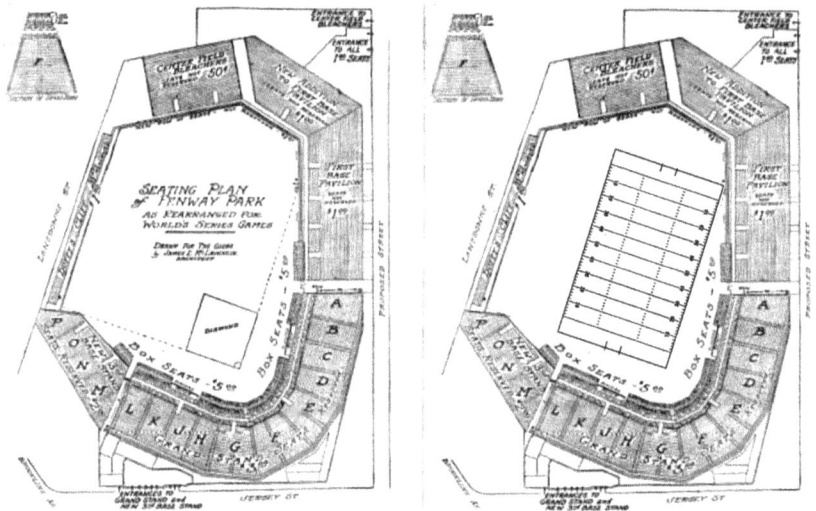

Fenway Park. The self-proclaimed 1940 national champion Boston College Eagles played nine of their eleven games in Boston, including six at Fenway Park. The only road games the Eagles played were in New Orleans, which included a regular-season matchup against Tulane and a Sugar Bowl win over Tennessee (both at Tulane Stadium). PUBLIC DOMAIN

General Neyland's team seemed to be in form during the first half, shutting down Leahy's offense, which averaged more than thirty points per game that season. The score was 7–0 Tennessee at the half on a Van Thompson touchdown run. The teams then alternated touchdowns with the score tied, 13–13, heading into the fourth quarter. Tennessee kicker Bob Foxx missed a field goal, and BC then took over and drove eighty yards to score the winning touchdown, 19–13. Boston College subsequently declared themselves national champs based on beating Tennessee and going undefeated. With that, Leahy departed to take over at his alma mater, Notre Dame, where he led the Irish to four AP championships and a record of 87–11–9.[9]

When we hash everything out, any claim Tennessee makes would appear to be obliterated by the Sugar Bowl loss. For Boston College, they beat a top team, a perennial champion. Stanford has a case, but its best win (Nebraska) was also bested by Minnesota, who was ranked ahead by the reporters. The results of both Nebraska losses are quite similar.

The tale of the tape is all about Minnesota. The Gophers were undefeated, and among the undefeated they have far and away the highest

The 1941 Minnesota Golden Gophers were undefeated, winners of the Big Ten, and AP national champs (here, defeating Nebraska, 9–0). MINNESOTA HISTORIC SOCIETY

Stanford Stadium opened in 1921 as a sixty-thousand-seat horseshoe, but by 1927 the stadium had expanded to over eighty-five thousand seats. It is one of two non-NFL venues to host a Super Bowl (Super Bowl XIX in 1985). Following the Cardinal's 2005 season, the original stadium was demolished and a new 50,424-seat enclosed bowl was erected around the original historic field. PUBLIC DOMAIN

power ranking. The only team with a stronger power ranking is one-loss Michigan, whom Minnesota beat on the field. Boston College, Tennessee, and Stanford had fine campaigns, but the first two faced much weaker competition on the way to being unbeaten in the regular season.

TALE OF THE TAPE FOR 1940

Team (AP)	Power	Schedule	Record	Offense	Defense
Minnesota (1)	27.66 (2)	16.16 (1)	8-0-0	19.3	8.9
Stanford (2)	20.14 (4)	8.54 (13)	10-0-0	19.6	8.5
Michigan (3)	28.21 (1)	13.59 (3)	7-1-0	24.5	4.3
Tennessee (4)	19.06 (7)	0.97 (54)	10-1-0	30.2	4.1
Boston College (5)	16.65 (12)	-1.08 (70)	11-0-0	30.8	5.9

1941: MINNESOTA OR ALABAMA?

Alabama offers one of the more incredible (or uncredible) claims to a national title. In 1941, the Crimson Tide went 9–2 with losses to Mississippi State and No. 7 Vanderbilt and a win over No. 14 Tulane before then beating No. 9 Texas A&M in the Cotton Bowl. We won't spend too much time on this controversy because the circumstance is absurd. This case, along with the two Alabama wire-service champions who lost bowl games (1964 Orange Bowl, 1973 Sugar Bowl) and the school's four claimed pre-wire-service titles (before 1936), only fuel criticism about the Tide's monster title count. Alabama ranked twentieth in the final 1941 AP poll, which was released a month before the Cotton Bowl.

So how does a two-loss, twentieth-ranked team in the eyes of the sportswriters that finished third in the SEC claim a title? The answer is Deke Houlgate and the Houlgate System (described in chapter 2). The Associated Press poll, as well as nearly every other selector at the time, picked Minnesota. As Michael Pinto observed over at the Bleacher Report, "While there are a ton of claims from around the country that can be understood, this one is really just baffling."[10]

The case for Minnesota is clear. Voted national champions by the writers and ranking at the top of every algorithmic selector except two, the Golden Gophers, led by Heisman Trophy winner Bruce Smith, went 8–0 and defeated No. 3 Michigan and No. 9 Northwestern. They did not participate in a postseason bowl game. The power ranking for Minnesota is second in the nation, and they played a far tougher schedule than other contenders.

The most notable alternative to Minnesota would be Texas. The Longhorns were 8–1–1 with a tie against Baylor and a loss to TCU. They had victories over No. 20 SMU and then No. 2 Texas A&M, finishing the season ranked No. 4 in the AP poll. Texas has the highest power ranking of any team in 1941, and the Williamson System also designated the Longhorns as champions. Texas does not claim the title, but it would have a far stronger case than Alabama.

TALE OF THE TAPE FOR 1941

Team (AP)	Power	Schedule	Record	Offense	Defense
Minnesota (1)	25.57 (2)	10.07 (12)	8-0-0	23.3	4.8
Texas (4)	26.32 (1)	7.92 (20)	8-1-1	33.8	5.5
Texas A&M (9)	15.02 (17)	4.39 (41)	9-2-0	25.5	6.8
Alabama (20)	14.87 (18)	3.97 (44)	9-2-0	23.9	7.7

1942: OHIO STATE OR GEORGIA?

The 1942 college football season presents one of the great early arguments for settling things on the field. Ohio State and Georgia finished
1–2 in the Associated Press poll and also ranked at the top of all the
major selector algorithms of the day, with most of the power formulas
breaking toward the Bulldogs. Both teams played sectional schedules
consistent with the challenges of wartime and enjoyed no common
opponents.

UGA, coached by Wally Butts, was led on the field by Heisman winner Frank Sinkwich and future Maxwell Award winner Charlie Trippi.
Playing only three games at home that season, the Dawgs opened their

View of Stanford Stadium from atop the stands at the 1925 Stanford-Cal Big Game. PUBLIC DOMAIN

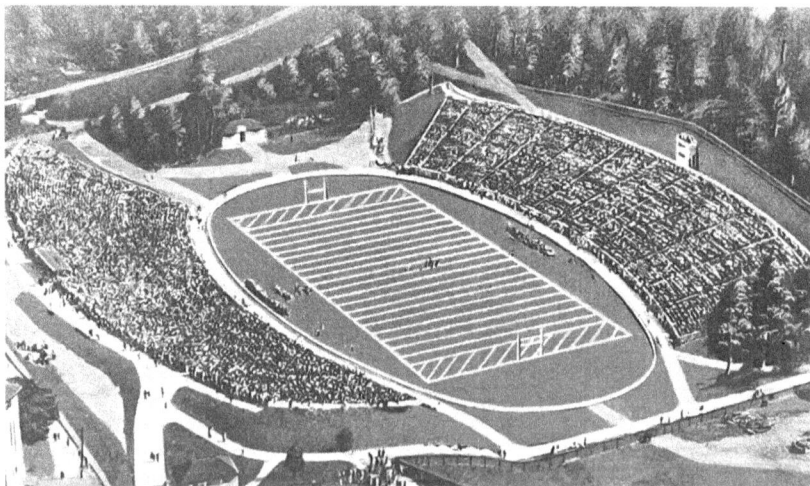

Sanford Stadium was completed in 1929 and named for Georgia professor (later president) Steadman
Sanford, who was also chair of the athletics committee. Seating thirty thousand, the concrete stadium
was constructed with convict labor and was a response to the advantages afforded to Georgia Tech by
Grant Field in Atlanta. Sanford Stadium has been repeatedly expanded to include an enclosed lower
bowl and triple decks with a current capacity of 93,033. One expansion, the 1980s closing of the east
end zone to create a horseshoe, is termed "The seats that Herschel built" in tribute to the popularity of
Heisman-winning running back Herschel Walker. IMAGE OWNED BY AUTHOR

Wally Butts had played college ball at Mercer, where he was coached by Bernie Moore, the future LSU head coach and longtime SEC commissioner. After coaching at Madison A&M (a college prep school in Georgia), Georgia Military College, and Louisville's Male High (where he won the Kentucky state title in 1937), Butts came to Georgia in 1938 as an assistant to new head coach Joel Hunt. When Hunt then left after one season to take the head-coaching job at Wyoming, where he promptly went 0-7-1, Butts was promoted. In fact, Hunt's greatest lasting impact on college football was bringing Butts to UGA. Among his assistants was Shug Jordan, who would later become head coach at Auburn and mentor a quarterback named Vince Dooley. Butts, nicknamed "the little round man," went 140-86-9 at Georgia with four SEC titles and a claimed national championship in 1942. TULANE UNIVERSITY, IMAGE IN PUBLIC DOMAIN

schedule with a close, 7–6, win over Kentucky in Louisville and later took down No. 3 Alabama, 21–10. On their way to finishing 11–1 (6–1 in the SEC), Georgia ranked No. 1 in the AP before falling to No. 5 after losing to Auburn, 27–13, in the third week of November. With a 34–0 win over No. 2 Georgia Tech, though, the Bulldogs rebounded to supplant the Yellow Jackets at No. 2 in the final AP poll. UGA then beat No. 13 UCLA, 9–0, in the Rose Bowl. Four mathematical selectors of the time—Houlgate, Litkenhous, Poling, and Williamson—selected Georgia as national champion, which claimed its first title.

However, Ohio State posts the most powerful case. Halfback Les Horvath and quarterback George Lynn led the Buckeyes; Horvath would later win the Heisman in 1944 while attending dental school. The Buckeyes went 9–1–0 and opened the season as the AP No. 1. Their lone loss, a 17–7 defeat at the hands of No. 6 Wisconsin, came three weeks earlier than Georgia's. Termed "The Bad Water Game," about half of the Ohio State gridiron squad played with an intestinal infection from drinking bad water on the train to Madison. The Buckeyes recovered their intestinal fortitude and beat No. 13 Illinois and No. 4 Michigan. They were ranked No. 1 in the final AP poll and did not play in a postseason bowl game, claiming their first national title.

Frank Sinkwich and Charley Trippi were nicknamed the Touchdown Twins as teammates at the University of Georgia. Head coach Wally Butts ran a variant on the single-wing split-back formation, variously snapping to either Trippi or Sinkwich and allowing both of his backs to accumulate significant offensive yardage in a precursor to modern option offenses. In UGA's 1942 championship season, Sinkwich, who won the Heisman, was voted the top athlete for 1942 by the Associated Press. The second-place finisher? Ted Williams of the Boston Red Sox, who won the American League Triple Crown. Sinkwich enlisted in the Marines in 1943 but was discharged for having flat feet. Playing two seasons for the Detroit Lions, he was named MVP in 1944 before then joining the Army air corps. An injury playing military football debilitated his subsequent professional career. Trippi left UGA in 1944 to also join the Army air corps, largely playing military football. Drafted by the Chicago Cardinals in 1945, he returned to UGA for the 1945 and 1946 seasons and won the Maxwell Award in his final year as Georgia went 11–0. It has been jokingly alleged but never seriously proven that the Bulldogs paid better than the NFL for Trippi to come back for one more season.

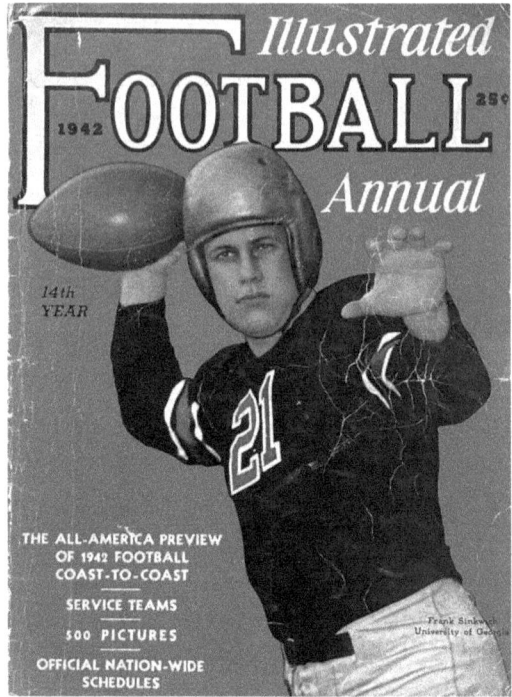

PUBLIC DOMAIN

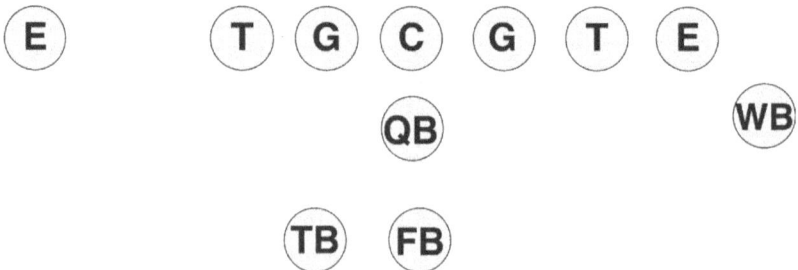

The single-wing split-T formation. AUTHOR IMAGE

The data record is a close one. Based on the power rating, the teams rank 1–2 with an edge toward the Buckeyes. Neither school had a schedule rated in the top twenty, as OSU's slate ranked twenty-first over UGA's thirty-fifth. The offenses finished second and third, respectively, just behind 10–1 Tulsa of the Missouri Valley Conference. The Golden Hurricane finished No. 4 in the AP poll and ranked ninth in the season's power rankings.[11] Where Georgia stood out was on scoring defense, giving up just 6.3 points per game (eleventh) compared to 11.4 points for the Buckeyes (fifty-eighth).

TALE OF THE TAPE FOR 1942

Team (AP)	Power	Schedule	Record	Offense	Defense
Ohio State (1)	21.2 (1)	4.72 (21)	9-1-0	33.7	11.4
Georgia (2)	19.4 (2)	3.34 (35)	11-1-0	31.3	6.3

1945: ARMY OR OKLAHOMA A&M?

The post hoc Oklahoma State claim of a national title is arguably the most absurd assertion of a national title in college football. Bill Connelly, in

Doc Blanchard started his football career at the University of North Carolina (his physician father had played at Tulane and Wake Forest). Having been approached in high school about attending West Point, he enlisted in the army in 1943 and then started at West Point in 1944. During his years playing for head coach Red Blaik, the Cadets went 27-0-1 with the tie coming in 1946 against one of the greatest Notre Dame teams ever. Blanchard won the 1945 Heisman and shared the backfield with Glenn Davis, who would win the Heisman the next season. Blanchard noted years later that his Heisman ceremony consisted of receiving a telegram that read, "You've been selected to win the Heisman Trophy. Please wire collect."

PUBLIC DOMAIN

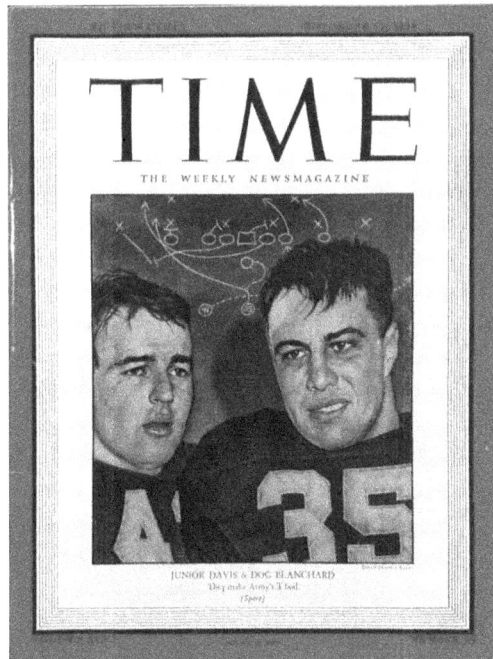

TIME

THE WEEKLY NEWSMAGAZINE

JUNIOR DAVIS & DOC BLANCHARD
(Sport)

his 2016 statistical analysis of the top fifty college football teams since World War II, the 1945 Army squad rated the best.[12] The squad featured ten All-Americans, including fullback Doc Blanchard and halfback Glenn Davis, the 1945 and 1946 Heisman Trophy winners, respectively.

The Cadets were the No. 1 team in the AP poll from start to finish, despite their schedule being the fifth toughest in the nation. Army destroyed four teams in the top 10 during the regular season: a 48–0 win over then No. 2 Notre Dame, a 61–0 destruction of No. 6 Penn, a five-touchdown margin of victory over No. 19 Duke (yes, Duke), and a 32–13 triumph over No. 2 Navy. Producing five shutouts, the Cadets had the top offense (45.8 points per game) and defense (giving up 5.1 points per game), and their overall power ranking (33.35) is far and away the strongest in the nation. Every major selector of the time and the Associated Press named Army national champions.

Still, there is another claimant, one that emerged long after the season was played—the Oklahoma A&M Aggies (now Oklahoma State University), coached by Jim Lookabaugh.[13] This is one of two post hoc

Michie Stadium at West Point is named for Army's first football coach, cadet Dennis Michie, who organized the team at the Academy in 1890. Originally built with seating for sixteen thousand, several expansions throughout the years have led to the current capacity of thirty thousand. The playing field was named for Red Blaik in 1999, in honor of his coaching consecutive national championships at Army from 1944 to 1946. AUTHOR-OWNED IMAGE

Football has been played at Lewis Field since 1901 with an eight thousand-seat grandstand erected in the current east-west field orientation in 1920. Initial plans for a horseshoe stadium did not come to fruition, but in 1924 the first concrete stands were built on the south side with permanent seating then constructed on the north side in 1930 to raise the capacity to thirteen thousand once completed. After the 1946 season, the stadium was expanded to thirty thousand. Numerous expansions and renovations over the next five decades led to a substantially larger, enclosed venue and seating for over fifty-two thousand. The stadium is now named for the late Oklahoma State athletics benefactor T. Boone Pickens.
OKLAHOMA STATE UNIVERSITY; IN PUBLIC DOMAIN

selector titles ever claimed by major college programs and one of three retrospective title claims from the middle of the twentieth century made by programs during the twenty-first century.

This was a fine team, and possibly the best one in the history of Stillwater. The Aggies, who used the nickname Cowboys back then, went 9–0 with a regular-season win over No. 19 Tulsa and a Sugar Bowl victory over No. 7 Saint Mary's. While A&M's ranked No. 5 in the final AP poll, their overall power rating (18.66) ranks eighth in the nation and is nearly half that of Army's. Their schedule was the thirty-ninth toughest in the nation (1.22). The Aggies offense (31.7 points per game, fourth) and defense (8.4 points per game, seventeenth) were quite good but pale when compared to a far higher-performing Army team that played a much tougher schedule.

The other thing that troubles me about Oklahoma A&M is, irrespective of the overwhelming evidence of Army's dominance on the field, the Aggies don't even have the best claim to be ranked immediately behind Army among the undefeated. That status belongs to Alabama. The Crimson Tide went 10–0 in 1945 and finished third in the AP poll behind Army and Navy. The power ranking for Alabama (23.51) is also third behind those same two teams and substantially higher than that of Oklahoma A&M. And while that record was achieved against the thirty-second-ranked schedule, it nonetheless was a tougher slate than what Oklahoma A&M faced. None of mathematical algorithm selectors of the time picked the Aggies; only one obscure selector crafting post hoc championships designated them as champion. This result is not validated by any other algorithm, but the honor is recognized by the American Football Coaches Association.

TALE OF THE TAPE FOR 1945

Team (AP)	Power	Schedule	Record	Offense	Defense
Army (1)	33.35 (1)	10.24 (5)	9-0-0	45.8	5.1
Oklahoma A&M (5)	18.66 (8)	1.22 (39)	9-0-0	31.7	8.4

1946: NOTRE DAME OR ARMY (OR GEORGIA)?

In 1946, traditional powers reigned and new powers from the South and West rose. But in the end, the national title debate came down to two of the grand programs of the early twentieth century—Army and Notre Dame.

The AP's initial poll of the season, published on October 7, had Texas ranked on top, followed by defending champion Army and then Notre Dame. Georgia was ranked eighth. The Longhorns slipped to third on October 14 as Army took over the top spot with Notre Dame now second. A loss to sixteenth-ranked Rice[14] two weeks later caused the Longhorns to tumble. At the beginning of November, Georgia entered the No. 3 spot and stayed there.

Frank Leahy's 8-0-1 Notre Dame squad shut out five opponents and held the other four to six points per game each to lead the nation in total defense and average points allowed. The Irish also featured the top-ranked offense in the country. They had wins over No. 17 Iowa and No. 16 USC with a 0-0 tie against Army. George Connor won the Outland Trophy as that year's best offensive lineman, and the squad included seven future College Football Hall of Fame players.

Army's defense was less robust, but in addition to the tie with the Irish, they owned wins over four ranked opponents—No. 4 Michigan, No. 11 Columbia, No. 13 Duke, and No. 5 Penn—and also defeated Oklahoma and Navy. Head coach Earl Blaik was closing out a three-title run at Army, although his thirty-two-game unbeaten streak would not be broken until 1947. The Cadets returned Doc Blanchard (who won the Heisman as a junior in 1945) and Glenn Davis (who won the Heisman in 1946) from the 1945 champions, the greatest collegiate team in history.

Army and Notre Dame confronted each other on November 9 and battled to a scoreless tie at Yankee Stadium in what was effectively the national title game. Georgia would have to make their case away from the national media with a capstone game in the Sugar Bowl.

The Bulldogs had the second-best offense in the nation, led by Maxwell Award winner Charley Trippi, who also finished second on the Heisman ballot. Georgia was not pressed all season, winning every game handily, including a 41–0 victory over Auburn. Head coach Wally Butts and his Bulldogs went 10–0 in the regular season with wins over No. 19 Kentucky (coached by Bear Bryant),[15] No. 15 Alabama (coached by Frank Thomas), and No. 7 Georgia Tech (coached by Bobby Dodd) before then downing No. 9 North Carolina (coached by Carl Snavely) in the Sugar Bowl at Tulane Stadium. All four coaches are now in the Hall of Fame.

Aggregator analysis identifies Georgia as a potential national champion, but the Bulldogs don't claim the title. And there's a good reason why. Despite being undefeated and indeed one of the strongest teams ever fielded by UGA, the light at the very top was blinding. In terms of power ranking, strength of schedule, defense, and the historic talent on their rosters, Notre Dame and Army were far better teams.

Coach Carl Snavely

Carl Snavely had a long career coaching at several institutions, including two separate tours at North Carolina. With the Tar Heels, he went 59-35-5 with two Southern Conference titles and had ranked teams from 1946 to 1949. He also produced a 42-16-8 record in seven seasons at Bucknell. Snavely's greatest success, though, was at Cornell, where the Big Red went 46-26-3 and were undefeated in 1939. Among his players at North Carolina was future Oklahoma, Maryland, and UNC head coach Jim Tatum. PUBLIC DOMAIN

The controversy is between the Cadets and Irish. They played. They tied. And the tale of the tape gives the nod to Notre Dame, who played a somewhat tougher schedule and had a better offense and defense. The Irish have a stronger overall power ranking as well. It looks like the AP writers got it right in their vote.

But on the field, the two teams played to a draw and took down all comers.

TALE OF THE TAPE FOR 1946

Team (AP)	Power	Schedule	Record	Offense	Defense
Notre Dame (1)	32.88 (1)	12.44 (7)	8-0-1	30.1	2.7
Army (2)	30.48 (2)	14.28 (3)	9-0-1	26.3	8.0
Georgia (3)	25.17 (3)	5.35 (35)	11-0-0	35.6	10.0

1947: MICHIGAN OR NOTRE DAME?

The 1947 national championship is an unresolvable debate. Two of the greatest college football teams of the twentieth century went undefeated, decisively beating most of their opponents.

The Wolverines, coached by Fritz Crisler, and Notre Dame, led by Frank Leahy, traded the top spot in the AP poll until the Fighting Irish (after blowing out Tulane, 59–6, on November 22) settled in as the No. 1 team. Notre Dame and Michigan were effectively tied on December 2, but when the Irish then captured a 38–7 win over USC[16] just before the final AP poll, that pushed the voting decisively their way. Following the end of the regular season, Notre Dame did not accept a bowl game invitation as a matter of school policy.

Three weeks later, though, Michigan, as Big Nine champions, went to the Rose Bowl and took on the No. 8 Trojans. The Wolverines routed USC, 49–0, tying a Rose Bowl record for points scored and margin of victory while also setting off a debate about whether Michigan should be champs instead of Notre Dame. Sportswriter Pete Rozelle[17] observed that, in the press box, the consensus was "the offensive-minded Ann Arbor squad deserved no less than a co-rating with the Irish as America's Number One Collegiate eleven." Grantland Rice called Michigan the best team he'd seen all year.

Fritz Crisler started his career playing and assisting at the University of Chicago under the tutelage of the legendary Amos Alonzo Stagg. He then served as head coach at Minnesota (going 10-7-1 combined in 1930 and 1931 and coaching Biggie Munn), moved to Princeton (35-9-5 from 1932 to 1937 with two 9-0 teams that both claim national titles), and finally joined Michigan (71-16-3 with two Big Ten titles from 1938 to 1947). With the Wolverines, he coached Heisman winner Tom Harmon and legendary Iowa coach Evi Evashevski. In addition to being the principal promoter of the two-platoon system, Crisler was an innovator in speeding up and refining offensive play, making the game faster and more nuanced to negate opponents' power, especially in the running game. After 1947, he stepped off the sidelines to focus solely on being Michigan's athletic director. PUBLIC DOMAIN

The outcry was such that the AP took an unprecedented post-bowl poll of sports editors. The editor of the *Detroit Free Press*, in arguing to revote, observed that a look at their three common opponents—Pitt, Northwestern, and USC—reveals Michigan played better defense, showed a stronger offense, and beat all three teams more decisively:

	Michigan vs.	Notre Dame vs.
USC	49-0	38-7
Northwestern	49-21	26-19
Pitt	69-0	40-6

He also pointed to the relative weakness of Notre Dame's schedule compared to Michigan's, noting that opponents of the Irish were 30–45–6 while the Wolverines' opponents finished 42–48–5 (closer to .500). The tale of the tape leans toward Michigan as well based on both the power rankings and strength of schedule.

This special post-bowl AP poll went 226 for Michigan to 119 for Notre Dame. However, the final regular-season AP poll remains the official ranking for 1947 and so both schools claim a title. Representatives of the two institutions were magnanimous. Fans never gave up the debate.

TALE OF THE TAPE FOR 1947

Team (AP)	Power	Schedule	Record	Offense	Defense
Notre Dame (1)	28.31 (3)	7.97 (26)	9-0-0	32.3	5.8
Michigan (2)	30.39 (1)	10.09 (16)	10-0-0	39.4	5.3

1950: OKLAHOMA OR KENTUCKY OR TENNESSEE OR PRINCETON?

The premier of the United Press Coaches poll in 1950 set up dueling human polls for the national title. The AP and UP would be joined the next year by the International News Service (Hearst) writers poll.

Oklahoma, named by AP and UP (also Helms, Litkenhous, Williamson), was the first consensus national champion chosen by both major wire-service polls. The Sooners, led by thirty-four-year-old fourth-year head coach Bud Wilkinson went 10-0 in the regular season with wins

The stadium at Owen Field (now called Gaylord Family - Oklahoma Memorial Stadium) was finished in 1925 on a site where football was first played in 1923. Head coach Bennie Owen helped raise the $293,000 used to build the sixteen-thousand-seat facility. Now expanded to over eighty thousand, the stadium has been home to seven national champions. I lived across Lindsey Street for six years as head of house for Headington College, an academic residential college at OU. AUTHOR-OWNED IMAGE

The 1950 Oklahoma Sooners. UNIVERSITY OF OKLAHOMA WESTERN HISTORY COLLECTION

over No. 4 Texas and No. 16 Nebraska. The Sooners moved into the No. 1 spot just before Thanksgiving after No. 1 Ohio State was upset by No. 8 Illinois. Oklahoma would face No. 7 Kentucky, coached by Bear Bryant, in the Sugar Bowl. The Wildcats upset the Sooners 13–7, leading the entire way behind the quarterback play of Babe Parilli.[18] As Michael Pinto observed of the situation after the 1951 Sugar Bowl, "Kentucky shocked the world in one of the biggest upsets of the first half of the 20th century. But it is also one that didn't quite get the result it deserved."[19]

Bryant's Kentucky team was outstanding, arguably the best in the history of a generally mediocre program. The Wildcats decided in 2016 to fully claim their NCAA-recognized national championship, based on the Sagarin retrospective rating generated in 1990, by creating and displaying a trophy for the title. Sagarin, an official selector, is highly regarded among the algorithms and has a long history of sophisticated analysis and publicity in major news outlets.

Back in 1950, the Wildcats had climbed to No. 3 in the AP poll by Thanksgiving, having beat No. 17 Florida two weeks earlier. But in the tradition of UK football, they were shutout, 7–0, by Tennessee in Knoxville on November 25 and finished the season at No. 7 in both wire services.

The vanquisher of Kentucky, Tennessee (DeVold, Dunkel) was 11–1 after defeating No. 3 Texas in the Cotton Bowl. The Volunteers started the season at No. 4 but lost the second game on their schedule to Mississippi State and tumbled out of the top twenty. Tennessee, though, climbed back to No. 4 by the final AP poll of the season with wins over No. 14 Duke and

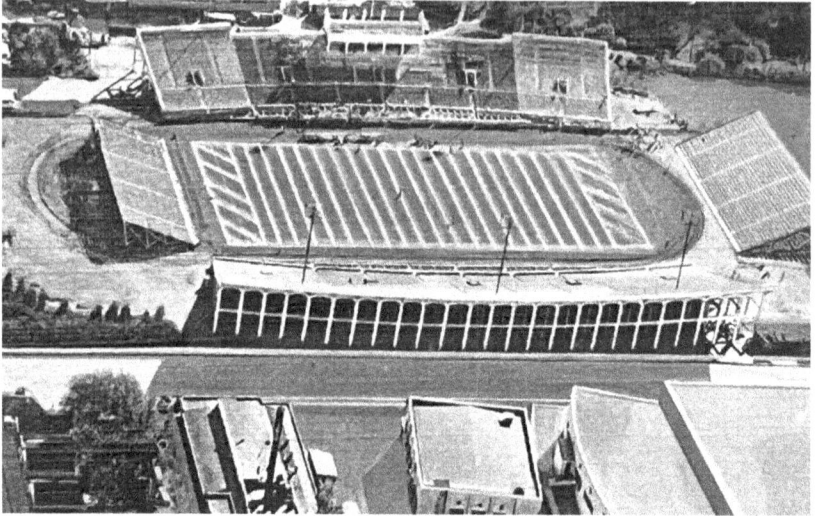

Kentucky Stoll Field/McLean Stadium. Football on this site was first played in 1880 in a cow pasture that became Stoll Field. The concrete stands were erected in 1916 with the name being changed to McLean Stadium in 1924. Used until 1972, the facility had a seating capacity of thirty-seven thousand and hosted Kentucky's first SEC football champions in 1950, coached by Bear Bryant. AUTHOR-OWNED IMAGE

The University of Kentucky would eventually claim the 1950 season and cite the Wildcats' 1951 Sugar Bowl win over Oklahoma as justification for a national title, one that is recognized by the NCAA. Bear Bryant was the coach of that team. If we could call him and ask if he would claim the title, I do not know for certain what he would say. I do suspect he'd ask me if I'd called my momma today because I'm sure he wishes he could call his. (Pictured here at Maryland, 1945.) CREATIVE COMMONS IMAGE

No. 3 Kentucky along the way.

Applying superficial transitivity to common opponents isn't much help. Kentucky and Tennessee both beat Ole Miss quite soundly, while Mississippi State defeated the Volunteers by one score but got blown out by twenty-seven against the Wildcats. Oklahoma bested Texas by one point, but Tennessee beat them by six. And Kentucky defeated the Sooners in the Sugar Bowl by six, but the Vols took down the Wildcats by seven.

Palmer Stadium was home to Princeton football from 1914 to 1996. The horseshoe was modeled on the Greek Olympic Stadium and seated forty-two thousand at its peak. Princeton claims twenty-eight national titles from 1869 to 1950, including seven since the legalization of the forward pass. AUTHOR-OWNED IMAGE

Then there's Princeton, which Board and Poling placed at the top of the pack. The Tigers went 9–0 with a 27–0 trouncing of No. 10 Cornell to finish the season ranked No. 6 in the AP and No. 8 in the UP Coaches Poll. They were one of two undefeated Eastern independents with nine wins, along with Franklin & Marshall.

The power rating data say the strongest team in the country at the end of the season was 6–3 Ohio State, who played a far tougher schedule than any of the contenders above, followed by 8–1 Army. Then come Oklahoma (third), Texas (fourth), Illinois (fifth), and Kentucky (sixth). Tennessee and Princeton finished tenth and fourteenth, respectively. While the power ratings, overall records, and polling-service ratings usually closely align, in 1950 there's a good bit of divergence, and I doubt anyone would take a three-loss "champion" seriously.

TALE OF THE TAPE FOR 1950

Team (AP)	Power	Schedule	Record	Offense	Defense
Oklahoma (1)	19.21 (3)	4.76 (31)	10-1	32.0	13.5
Tennessee (4)	17.11 (10)	2.28 (49)	11-1	27.9	5.9
Princeton (6)	15.69 (14)	-2.65 (81)	9-0-0	38.8	10.4
Kentucky (7)	17.95 (6)	-0.39 (65)	11-1	32.8	5.8

1951: MICHIGAN STATE OR ILLINOIS OR TENNESSEE?

Head Coach Clarence Munn's Michigan State squad featured four All-Americans and went 9–0 with wins over Ohio State (then ranked seventh) and Notre Dame (ranked eleventh). Briefly atop the polls in the middle of October, a close game against a Marquette team that went 4–6–1 dropped the Spartans to No. 3 behind Cal and Tennessee. The first week of November there were still eight undefeated teams in the nation and a fractured vote among the coaches and writers—thirteen different teams received first-place votes. Michigan State slipped into the top spot again, only to be dropped to second after a close road win against a weak Indiana team. With that, Tennessee made its way into the top spot to stay. Michigan State finished the season ranked No. 2 in the AP and UP Coaches polls. The Spartans, an independent at the time, did not play in a postseason bowl.

Down in Knoxville, the twentieth edition of General Neyland's Vols had assembled an undefeated 10–0 regular season. Tennessee, arguably the best team in the nation in 1950, scored over thirty-five points per game and had the twelfth-best defense in the country. Hank Lauricella, playing running back out of Neyland's single-wing offense, was runner-up for

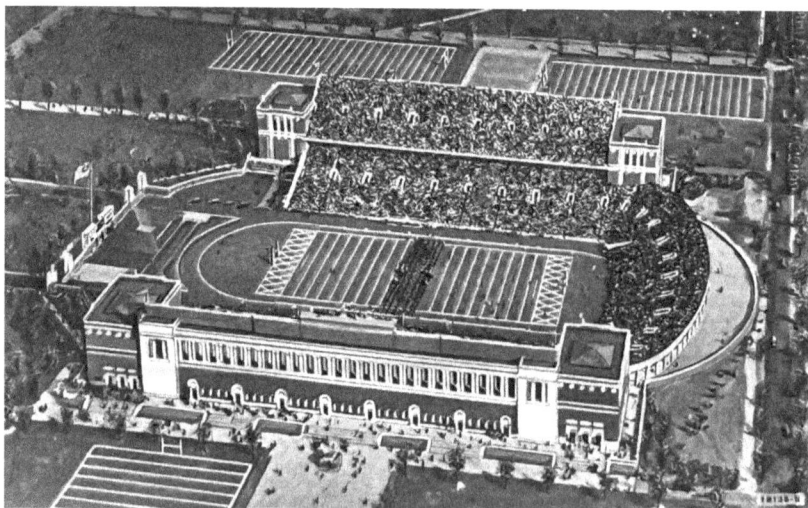

The University of Illinois's Memorial Stadium opened in 1923 with its U-shaped stands emulating Harvard Stadium. Renovations and expansions have increased the seating to 60,670 from about fifty-two thousand at the time of the Fighting Illini's 1951 national title. AUTHOR-OWNED IMAGE

Harvard Stadium. AUTHOR-OWNED IMAGE

the Heisman Trophy (behind Princeton's Dick Kazmaier). Lauricella had touches on most offensive plays, earning the nickname "Mr. Everything." Despite owning wins over No. 16 Duke and No. 9 Kentucky, Tennessee had not played a particularly tough schedule (forty-second) but spent the entire season ranked in the top three and finished as both the AP and UP's No. 1.

The Volunteers took on head coach Jim Tatum's No. 3 Maryland Terrapins in the Sugar Bowl in front of more than eighty-two thousand fans, losing 28–13. Maryland scored quickly and had hung three touchdowns on Tennessee in the first half to claim a 21–6 lead. A pick-six interception in the third quarter by Ed Fullerton gave the Terrapins their fourth score and sealed the fate of the Vols. Maryland, 10–0, was recognized by DeVold and Dunkel but does not claim the title.

Meanwhile, Boand recognized Dodd's Georgia Tech eleven from the SEC, but the Yellow Jackets don't claim the title. Tech had two wins over ranked teams, including an Orange Bowl victory over No. 9 Baylor, but was tied by Duke in the regular season. Bleacher Report's look at bogus national titles notes that "the Volunteers are better recognized as one of the most disappointing teams in history" after losing to Maryland. But in addition to 9–0–1 Michigan State, Michael Pinto points us in a different direction, stating that "there was a third unbeaten team

Jim Tatum played football at Chapel Hill and then went with The Grey Fox, Carl Snavely, to Cornell as an assistant coach. After returning to North Carolina as an assistant to Raymond Wolf in 1939, he was named head coach three years later at the age twenty-nine when Wolf joined the military. Tatum joined the Navy a year later, helping coach the legendary Iowa Pre-Flight school, where he picked up the split-T formation. It was also in the Navy that he started a lasting friendship with Bud Wilkinson and Bear Bryant. After the war, Tatum coached Oklahoma for one season, then coached Maryland from 1947 to 1955 (picking up a national title in 1953 and moving the Terps to the ACC) before then returning to Chapel Hill. Tatum's career was cut tragically short when he died of an infection in the summer of 1959 at age forty-six. PUBLIC DOMAIN

that year that deserves more recognition," and that team was 9–0–1 Illinois.[20]

Illinois, which was also named a champion by Boand, had a tie at Ohio State during the regular season, along with wins over No. 20 Washington and No. 15 Michigan. The Illini defeated No. 7 Stanford in the Rose Bowl, 40–7.

If we go and look at common opponents, the nod goes to MSU. Both teams played Michigan and Ohio State in the regular season. Illinois beat the Wolverines, 7–0, while the Spartans had a more dominating 25–0 win. Michigan State also beat Ohio State, 24–20, while the Buckeyes played the Illini to a scoreless tie. The SRS power rating places Illinois as the best team in the nation, just ahead of MSU. However, one wonders if the Spartans had been given an opportunity to play in a bowl and won, they might have vaulted ahead of Illinois, who are beneficiaries in the algorithm for their Rose Bowl victory.

TALE OF THE TAPE FOR 1951

Team (AP)	Power	Schedule	Record	Offense	Defense
Tennessee (1)	20.39 (5)	3.21 (42)	10-1-0	35.1	10.5
Michigan State (2)	23.06 (2)	8.06 (24)	9-0-0	30.0	12.7
Maryland (3)	22.74 (3)	1.84 (53)	10-0-0	38.1	7.5
Illinois (4)	24.08 (1)	10.88 (6)	9-0-1	22.0	8.3
Georgia Tech (5)	20.10 (6)	4.35 (36)	11-0-1	24.6	7.5

1955: OKLAHOMA OR MICHIGAN STATE?

The AP poll on September 19 was fractured. UCLA, the preseason No. 1, led with thirty-four first-place votes, followed by Georgia Tech, Oklahoma, Michigan, and Maryland. The Bruins fell to Maryland the next week while Michigan State would enter the top twenty two weeks after that. Contenders started to fall away as undefeated Michigan, Maryland, and Oklahoma cycled among the top three through October. On November 7, Oklahoma moved into the top spot to stay with one-loss Michigan State eventually taking over the second spot and undefeated Maryland slipping to third. Nine teams received first-place votes in the final AP poll, which was handily won by Oklahoma. The final Coaches Poll had the same order of finish.

The Oklahoma Sooners were national champions. But there were questions. Maryland, led by former OU head coach Jim Tatum, was also undefeated and ranked No. 3 in the country; the Terrapins counted an early season win over the defending national champion, No. 1 UCLA, (coached by Red Sanders) among their victories.

And lurking about at No. 2 in the polls was one-loss Michigan State. The Spartans had emerged as a power in the 1950s, and in 1955 they recovered from an early-season loss at No. 2 Michigan to storm into the top three.

The 1956 Oklahoma Sooners went 10-0 to repeat as national champions in the wire-service polls. Here, a stub from the 1956 game with Notre Dame. PUBLIC DOMAIN

Oklahoma had gone 10–0 in the regular season, having won the Big Seven for the eighth year in a row and extending their unbeaten streak to thirty-one games, dating back to October 1953 (it would go on for seventeen more games into the 1957 season, when it was broken by Notre Dame on Nov. 16). Oklahoma had five shutout wins and held another three opponents to single digits. Sooners coach Bud Wilkinson and Tatum were old friends. When Tatum took the OU head coaching job after World War II, he brought Wilkinson along as an assistant coach, and the Sooners promoted Wilkinson after Tatum jumped to Maryland.

In the Orange Bowl, the Terrapins shut down Oklahoma in the first half, jumping out to a 6–0 lead. Then OU scored twenty unanswered points in the second half to give Wilkinson another undefeated season and an unblemished championship. Remember, the 1950 Sooners had lost the Sugar Bowl to Kentucky after being crowned national champs in the polls.

Michigan State makes a claim for the title, though, based on the Board System. Much like the later Tennessee claim to a Litkenhous title in 1967, this claim is made by a very strong team. Indeed, the tale of the tape says that the Spartans have both a higher power ranking and a tougher schedule than Oklahoma. But this case also illustrates a factor that is evident over and over in looking at all these titles: an undefeated team is more impressive than a statistically strong one when it comes to choosing a champ.

Sometimes the power rankings elevate multi-loss teams, especially those with narrow defeats in strong schedules. In 1955, UCLA (23.59) and head coach Abe Martin's TCU (22.19) have stronger power ratings than the wire-services champion, and both were conference winners. But each also had a regular-season loss and then lost its bowl game. UCLA fell to No. 5 Maryland early in the season and then dropped the Rose Bowl to Michigan State. TCU lost to No. 19 Texas A&M in the regular season before coming up short in the Cotton Bowl to the No. 10 Ole Miss Rebels.

TALE OF THE TAPE FOR 1955

Team (AP)	Power	Schedule	Record	Offense	Defense
Oklahoma (1)	21.62 (4)	1.89 (50)	11-0-0	35.0	5.5
Michigan State (2)	24.00 (1)	8.50 (14)	9-1-0	25.3	8.3

1956: OKLAHOMA OR IOWA?

The high-water mark of Bud Wilkinson's tenure at the University of Oklahoma came in 1956. The Sooners went undefeated for the third straight season and extended their NCAA-record winning streak to forty games. With four All-Americans, led by Heisman finalist Jerry Tubbs, Oklahoma won its ninth straight Big Seven title. The Sooners' second-best defense in the nation had six shutouts, while the top-ranked offense scored 46.6 points per game and hung half a hundred four times, including fifty-four points on Nebraska and fifty-three on Oklahoma A&M to close the season. OU did not appear in a postseason bowl due to the conference's use of a no-repeat rule for bowls, but all of the Consensus Major Selectors chose the Sooners as national champs.

The 1956 Iowa Hawkeyes won the Big Ten Conference, going 8–1 during the regular season with nonconference wins over Oregon State, Hawaii, and Notre Dame. The Oregon State victory was a comeback as Iowa trailed 13–0 after two OSU field goals and a third-quarter touchdown, but Iowa came back late in the fourth with a pair of touchdown passes. Absent that comeback, there is no discussion of even a hypothetical Iowa national title.

The Hawkeyes suffered a November loss at home to No. 17 Michigan, 17–14, after blowing a 14–3 lead at the half when allowing Wolverine touchdowns in the third quarter and with a minute left in the fourth. The loss dropped Iowa to fifteenth in the polls.

Finishing out its schedule with victories over ranked Minnesota and Ohio State, as well as a blowout 48–8 win over Notre Dame, Iowa climbed back up to No. 3 in the final polls. In the Rose Bowl, head coach Forest Evashevski's Hawkeyes then decisively won a rematch with Oregon State, 35–19. Alex Karras won All-America honors.

The AP poll had Oklahoma ranked either first or second all season. Duffy Daugherty's Michigan State had briefly moved into the top spot before being upset by Illinois. Tennessee moved into first for a week in November but then slipped behind the Sooners before the final AP and UP polls were released. Although the Vols would go 10–0 to win the SEC, they lost to No. 13 Baylor in the Sugar Bowl after the polls. Texas A&M (9–0–1) and Miami (8–0–1) also went undefeated.

The tale-of-the-tape comparison of Oklahoma and Iowa easily favors the Sooners. OU had the better offense, the stronger defense, and was undefeated. The Sooners have a higher overall power ranking. A look at the power rankings for 1956 shows one-loss Georgia Tech, one-loss Tennessee, and two-loss Michigan as stronger teams than Oklahoma. Iowa ranks sixth. Giving some credit where credit is due, Oklahoma and Iowa both beat one of the worst teams in Notre Dame history by forty.

TALE OF THE TAPE FOR 1956

Team (AP)	Power	Schedule	Record	Offense	Defense
Oklahoma (1)	21.08 (4)	-1.12 (65)	10-0-0	46.6	5.1
Iowa (3)	19.50 (6)	7.90 (22)	9-1-0	21.9	8.4

1959: OLE MISS OR SYRACUSE?

The 1959 season opened with LSU and Oklahoma at the top of the polls. The Sooners immediately tumbled out of the top twenty after a loss to No. 10 Northwestern on September 26 up in Evanston, Illinois. Northwestern then moved into the second spot behind LSU, but upsets of both (LSU by No. 13 Tennessee, 14–13; Northwestern by No. 9 Wisconsin,

Archbold Stadium at Syracuse opened in 1907 with seating for thirty thousand. The capacity was expanded and maximized to forty thousand in the 1950s, but then changes in the fire code two decades later reduced that capacity to twenty-six thousand. The inability to expand the venue led to Syracuse football (and basketball) moving to the new Carrier Dome in 1980. IMAGE OWNED BY AUTHOR

Ben Schwartzwalder. Among the players Ben Schwartzwalder coached at Syracuse were legendary running backs Jim Brown, Larry Csonka, Floyd Little, and also the first Black Heisman winner, Ernie Davis. Davis was the top pick in the 1962 NFL draft. Tragically, he never played a down of pro ball, having been diagnosed with leukemia and dying at the age of twenty-three. Schwartzwalder had bounced around high school coaching until he served in World War II, where he commanded a company of the 82nd Airborne on D-Day. He became head coach at Muhlenberg College after the war, then took over at Syracuse in 1949, compiling a 153-91-3 record with eleven ranked teams, including being named the wire-service champions in 1959. CREATIVE COMMONS

24–19) on November 7 scrambled the top of the polls, allowing Syracuse to rise to the top followed by Texas. The Orangemen had bested No. 7 Penn State that same day, 20–18, to move into the top slot in the major polls and then beat No. 17 UCLA on the road. By the end of the regular season, Syracuse, under head coach Ben Schwartzwalder, stood alone at the top of the rankings by a large margin, the only undefeated team in the nation. The Orangemen met No. 4 Texas in the Cotton Bowl and led the entire way to win by a finale of 23–14. It was the first-ever bowl win for Syracuse.

Syracuse had the top offense in the nation, scoring 413 points behind the play of running back Ernie Davis, who would win the Heisman in 1961, and a sixth-ranked defense that posted five shutout wins. All of the major selectors named Syracuse national champs.

Down in Oxford, longtime Ole Miss head coach Johnny Vaught fielded one of the best teams in the history of the institution and would contend for the national title over the next four seasons as well. The Rebels had the best defense in football, giving up just twenty-one points all season while posting eight shutout wins. In its only loss of the season, to then top-ranked LSU, Mississippi surrendered a single

Vince Dooley, Maker of Titles. As a head coach and athletic director in the 1980s, Vince Dooley claimed two national titles: one for himself and one for Wally Butts in 1942. According to the NCAA, Georgia can claim eight national titles, although the Dawgs only claim four: 1942, 1980, 2021, and 2022. After winning it all as a head coach in 1980, Dooley was reading through an NCAA record book and discovered that Georgia had a title in 1942, based on designations by the contemporary algorithms Houlgate, Litkenhous, Poling, and Williamson. As a Georgia alum, I've always been self-conscious about the 1942 title. It wasn't awarded by a Consensus Major Selector. I excuse myself by observing that in the early days of the AP poll, other selector titles got greater consideration because they were given greater validity at the time. It helps that the data behind claims like this one, or some of the Tennessee claims of the era, are more sound than, say, the 1941 Alabama claim that doesn't pass the face-validity test. When you look at Alabama that season, they don't look like a champion. The titles Georgia doesn't claim include 1920 (Berryman), 8-0-1, 20.42 power ranking; 1927 (Berryman, Board, Poling), 9-1, 20.41 power ranking; 1946 (Williamson), 11-0, 25.17 power ranking; and 1968 (Litkenhous), 8-1-2, 21.44 power ranking. PUBLIC DOMAIN BASED ON DUE DILIGENCE SEARCH

touchdown in losing 7–3 to the Tigers and Heisman-winner Billy Cannon. The Rebels finished second in the wire-service polls but at the time were also named champions by the Dunkel System, which Ole Miss claims. In a rematch with LSU in the Sugar Bowl, Mississippi then won 21–0, shutting down Cannon and holding the Tigers to 74 yards of total offense.

The power ranking rates Ole Miss as the stronger team, despite the lone loss to LSU, and the Rebels did play a tougher schedule.

TALE OF THE TAPE FOR 1959

Team (AP)	Power	Schedule	Record	Offense	Defense
Syracuse (1)	23.36 (2)	3.18 (50)	11-0-0	37.5	6.6
Ole Miss (2)	24.12 (1)	4.67 (38)	10-1-0	31.8	1.9

1962: OLE MISS OR USC?

John McKay took over as head coach at USC in 1960.[21] McKay's first two seasons were subpar—his teams went 4–6 and 4–5–1, due in part to playing while on probation and suffering a recruiting disadvantage after the dissolution of the Pacific Coast Conference amid scandal.[22] Alumni pressure was growing going into the 1962 season, but the administration resisted pulling the trigger. The result was McKay won the first of four national titles over the next thirteen seasons.

The 1962 Trojans were quarterbacked by Pete Beathard, backed up by the equally effective Bill Nelsen, and featured running back Willie Brown and College Football Hall of Famer and All-American receiver Hal Bedsole. The Trojans had the fifteenth-ranked offense (24.7 points per game) and the thirteenth-ranked defense, which surrendered 8.4 points per game with three shutouts and five other opponents held to single digits. USC went 10–0 in the regular season, finished the year ranked No. 1 by the wire services, and then beat No. 2 Wisconsin in the Rose Bowl, 42–37.

Ole Miss went undefeated in the regular season and was ranked as high as No. 2 in the polls before finishing the year third behind one-loss Wisconsin. The Rebels' third-ranked defense had three shutouts with six other opponents managing a single score. The offense, led by All-American quarterback Glynn Griffing, scored almost twenty-five points per game, placing just ahead of Oklahoma and USC. Mississippi's schedule was not particularly strong, forty-eighth in the nation, with LSU being its only ranked opponent. But having defeated No. 6 Arkansas in the Sugar Bowl, the Rebels finished with the seventh-highest power ranking. The 1962 Ole Miss squad remains the only undefeated and untied team in the history of the school.[23] Vaught was named SEC Coach of the Year. The Ole Miss title claim is based on the Litkenhous rankings, which is also the basis of the 1967 Tennessee title claim.

John McKay was known for having a brilliant, biting wit, which shone through most when his teams were at their least. The man who former UCLA and Philadelphia Eagles head coach Dick Vermeil called "Dial-a-Quote" had a line for every question or occasion. My favorite two are, "We didn't tackle well today, but we made up for it by not blocking," and in response to a question about how he felt about his team's execution, McKay said, "I'm in favor of it." IMAGE BY ART ROGERS, *LOS ANGELES TIMES*, OBTAINED UNDER CREATIVE COMMONS ATTRIBUTION 4.0 INTERNATIONAL LICENSE

The tale of the tape favors the Trojans, who have the second-highest power ranking in the country behind only Wisconsin, whom USC defeated in the Rose Bowl. There's the suspicion in southern circles that the Bama and Ole Miss teams of this era were "voted down" over the extreme segregation of the Deep South and the resistance of the schools to integrate. But the body of work that McKay's Trojans put together, including wins over three top-ten opponents, is just too impressive.

TALE OF THE TAPE FOR 1962

Team (AP)	Power	Schedule	Record	Offense	Defense
USC (1)	23.29 (2)	8.66 (17)	11-0-0	23.7	8.4
Ole Miss (3)	18.68 (7)	3.08 (48)	10-0-0	24.7	5.3

1967: TENNESSEE OR USC?

The 1967 USC Trojans were the greatest in a series of great John McKay teams. Offensive tackle Ron Yary won the Outland Trophy. O. J. Simpson, a junior playing in his first season of major college ball after a two-year stint in the junior college ranks, led the nation in rushing with 1,543 yards. He would win the Walter Camp Award in 1967 and 1968, adding the Heisman Trophy and Maxwell Award in his senior season. Quarterback Steve Sogge and Simpson led an offense that ranked twenty-seventh overall, although the Trojans' stifling second-ranked defense gave up

Doug Dickey was a highly successful coach with great tenures at Tennessee and Florida. He will forever be remembered in Georgia football lore for one play call in the 1976 "World's Largest Outdoor Cocktail Party," the name given to the annual rivalry game between the Bulldogs and Gators. By then, Dickey had left Tennessee and was coaching at Florida, and his team was in the driver's seat for its first-ever SEC title. With the Gators leading, 27-20, late in the third quarter, Dickey went for it on fourth and short from his own twenty-nine yard line, only to have Georgia's Junkyard Dawgs defense stop Florida short. Quarterback Ray Goff, running the veer offense, then led UGA on a three-score rally to win the game, 41-27, and the SEC title. The play is immortalized as "Fourth and Dumb." PUBLIC DOMAIN

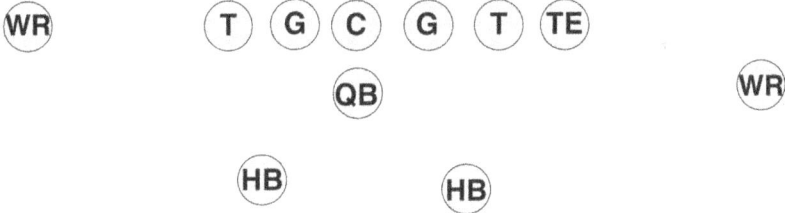

The veer. IMAGE FROM AUTHOR

less than eight points a game, held five teams to single digits, and also had two shutouts. USC beat Texas and Notre Dame, both ranked No. 5 at the time they met, Michigan State, and No. 1 UCLA during the regular season. The Trojans then defeated No. 4 Indiana in the Rose Bowl, 14–3, confirming the titles conferred on them in December and also earning the FWAA postseason title.

The only blemish on USC's 9–1 record was a 3–0 upset on November 11 by Oregon State, who finished the season ranked seventh in the AP

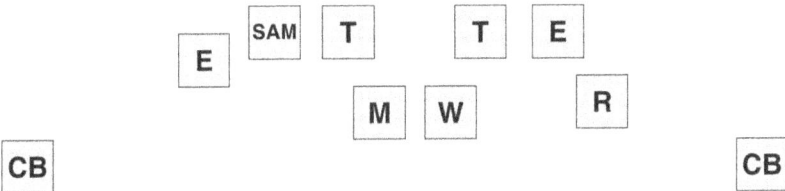

The 60 Junkyard Dawg defense. IMAGE FROM AUTHOR

poll with a 7–2–1 mark. Ronald Reagan, then governor of California, attended the game and bet a box of oranges on the outcome, which he promised to personally pick. The game was played on a rain-soaked field, which made for poor conditions for the Trojans' run-based offense. The only score of the game, with five minutes left in the first half, was a Mike Haggard field goal for the Beavers from the USC fourteen yard line. Simpson ran for 188 yards in the game but could not get into the end zone. The game was marred with turnovers, and USC never had favorable starting position.

The next week, USC beat UCLA, 21–20, on a sixty-four-yard Simpson rush in the fourth quarter. The wire services selected the Trojans as national champion before the bowl games. USC had made the statement case in beating UCLA.

The University of Tennessee, though, also claims the 1967 national title, conferred by Litkenhous, an NCAA-recognized selector. This was a fine Volunteers team, led by fourth-year head coach Doug Dickey, that went undefeated in the SEC.

A remarkable number of dissenting titles involve the University of Tennessee in some form or fashion. Often, the Volunteers have a great case to make. As with the Alabama's 1941 dissent, we won't spend too much time on this one, not because Tennessee wasn't a great team and a contender, but because championships are made on the breaks. And the breaks didn't go for Tennessee in 1967.

The Volunteers lost their season opener to No. 8 UCLA before winning nine straight games, including a 24–13 win over No. 6 Alabama. Tennessee was ranked second at the end of the season in both the AP poll and the Coaches Poll. The Vols then faced No. 3 Oklahoma in the Orange Bowl and lost, 26–24. Had a postseason poll been around, Tennessee likely falls to fifth in the rankings, and Oklahoma goes to second or even first in the wire-service polls.

But what about Oklahoma? The Sooners (10–1) have the fifth-highest power ranking in the nation and were designated champion by Poling, which is as credible as Litkenhous. The Sooners don't claim the championship, as the program historically only claims major selector wire-service titles.[24]

Of course, if we are going to talk about two-loss teams as contenders, Notre Dame (8–2) has the second-best power ranking for the season (19.56) and was designated champion by Dunkel, though they also don't claim the title.[25]

Ultimately, Tennessee's claim suffers from a case of the bad breaks, a series of close, connected outcomes that can be displayed by looking at common opponents. USC beat Texas, 17–13, and Texas beat Oklahoma, 9–7, and Oklahoma beat Tennessee, 26–24. USC beat UCLA, 21–20, and UCLA opened the season by beating Tennessee, 20–16.

It is a series of close outcomes. If UCLA head coach Tommy Prothro doesn't get one more great play out of Gary Beban and the Bruin offense on fourth and two in a game where UCLA had trailed the whole way, then Tennessee's Dewey "Swamp Rat" Warren wins a season-opening duel of great quarterbacks, the Volunteers run the table in the SEC, and they go into the Orange Bowl as the consensus champion. Sadly for Dickey, the dominoes fell the other way.

TALE OF THE TAPE FOR 1967

Team (AP)	Power	Schedule	Record	Offense	Defense
USC (1)	20.33 (1)	6.88 (17)	10-1-0	23.5	7.9
Tennessee (2)	18.14 (4)	7.14 (14)	9-2-0	25.7	12.8

1981: CLEMSON OR SMU?

Clemson was the choice of all of the Consensus Major Selectors (AP, UPI, FWAA, NFF) and also all of the algorithms, aside from Dunkel. Head coach Danny Ford's Tigers went 11–0 in the regular season, opening with warm-up wins over Wofford and Tulane and then beating the defending national champion and fourth-ranked Georgia Bulldogs, 13–3, shutting down Heisman runner-up Herschel Walker. Rising from No. 18 to No. 2 over the coming weeks, which included a victory over No. 9 North Carolina, 10–8, in Chapel Hill, Clemson finished the regular season two weeks later as the undefeated ACC champions.

Top ranked with No. 2 Georgia (10–1) and No. 3 Alabama (9–1–1) immediately behind them, the Tigers had already beat the SEC champion, who was locked into the Sugar Bowl. The No. 4 team, 9–2 Nebraska, was headed to the Orange Bowl, so Clemson accepted the invitation to play in Miami. The Tide had tied UGA for the SEC title, but the Sugar Bowl picked Georgia, thereby violating the unwritten rule that "Bear Bryant always goes to the Sugar Bowl." The Bulldogs lost to Jackie Sherrill's Pitt Panthers and quarterback Dan Marino while Alabama would instead head to the Cotton Bowl to face No. 6 Texas; the Longhorns won, 14–12.

The Orange Bowl was the last bowl played on New Year's Day. Alabama had lost to Texas, and Georgia had lost to Jackie Sherrill's Pitt and Dan Marino in the Sugar Bowl. After initially trading scores in the old Orange Bowl stadium, Clemson opened up a 22–7 lead in the third quarter. Running back Roger Craig scored for the Huskers in the fourth, and a two-point conversion made the final score 22–15.

The other claimant, Southern Methodist, had come a long way in a short period of time. For the better part of three decades, the Mustangs had struggled in the Southwest Conference, long removed from their days as national title contenders in the 1940s, when Matty Bell had coached and Doak Walker had won the Heisman. Long-term head coach Hayden Fry (later a legend at Iowa) had occasional success in the 1960s and early 1970s, but later that decade, change had come. From 1976 until 1979, Ron Meyer (previously a Division II winner at UNLV) had compiled a 16–27–1

Clemson's Memorial Stadium, popularly referred to as Death Valley, opened in 1942 with seating for 20,500. By 1960, the capacity was expanded to nearly forty-five thousand. The upper decks were added in 1978 and 1983, respectively. AUTHOR-OWNED IMAGE

From the 1930s until 1978, and then again for a period of time in the 1990s, SMU played its home games at the Cotton Bowl, which is located on the grounds of the Texas State Fair. The current bowl replaced a wooden grandstand in 1930 and seated 45,507. Periodic expansions have increased the seating to its current capacity of 92,100. AUTHOR-OWNED IMAGE

record.[26] With demands for success loud among the oil-rich alumni, Meyer's 1980 team went 8–4 but lost in the Holiday Bowl. The program was subsequently placed on probation for the 1981 season and deemed ineligible for postseason play. SMU went 10–1 overall and 7–1 in conference play, winning the SWC title, but was prohibited from going to the Cotton Bowl.

The Mustangs' last game of the season, against Arkansas, became their bowl game. Head coach Lou Holtz's Razorbacks were ranked No. 16 in the nation with previous losses to TCU and Houston. SMU came into Fayetteville ranked No. 6 with one loss, 9–7, to No. 10 Texas. Dubbed the "Polyester Bowl," the Mustangs won, 32–18, to improve their record to 10–1. They would finish at No. 5 in the final AP poll (the Coaches Poll did not rank probation teams).

The basis of SMU's national title claim is being one of five teams declared champions by the National Championship Foundation, which had recently made several retrospective selections and was assessing a current champion(s) for just the second time.

As it turned out, SMU's pattern of behavior ran deep. The 1970s was a period of aggressive violation of recruiting rules and norms, mainly in

Jackie Sherrill played college football at Alabama for Bear Bryant and was a member of two national title teams. After working for Johnny Majors at Pitt, he went to Washington State in 1976 to be a head coach at age thirty-three. He returned to the Panthers one year later when Majors, fresh off winning the national title, left to take over his alma mater, Tennessee. Sherill was 50–9–1 in five seasons at Pitt with future Miami coach Jimmy Johnson on his staff. In 1982, he headed to Texas A&M, going 52–28–1 in seven seasons with three straight Southwest Conference titles from 1985 to 1987. Sherill introduced both tradition and controversy. As coach for the Aggies, he created the 12th Man Kickoff Team using walk-on players for special teams kickoff coverage, a tradition that continues today with now just one walk-on player wearing the number twelve. But he was viewed by clean-program avatar Joe Paterno as part of the ugly problems of college sports. When asked about possibly retiring, Joe Pat observed that he couldn't leave college football to "the Jackie Sherrills and the Barry Switzers." (Joe Pa subsequently apologized to Switzer but pointedly said he "didn't give a damn about what Sherrill felt.") When Texas A&M joined most of the rest of the Southwest Conference on probation in 1988, Sherrill resigned but then resurfaced two seasons later at Mississippi State. While there, he once motivated his team by having a bull castrated and went 75–75–2 in thirteen seasons. After he retired in 2003, the Bulldogs were placed on probation for four years. UNIVERSITY OF PITTSBURGH

pursuit of Texas high school players. It paid off, as from 1980 to 1984 SMU went 49–5–1.

But what about Penn State? Or Pitt? When we look at the analytics for the season, the two-loss Nittany Lions have the highest SRS in the nation (25.02), with regular-season losses to Miami and No. 6 Alabama, and finished No. 3 in the wire-service polls. The No. 2 SRS belongs to the Panthers, who lost to No. 11 Penn State late in the regular season, beat

No. 2 Georgia in the Sugar Bowl, and finished No. 4 in the AP poll and second overall in the Coaches Poll. The straight math of the SRS, which differs in this season with the algorithms, places both Clemson and SMU behind Penn State, Pitt, Nebraska, and Georgia. However, the Tigers beat two of these teams on the field.

TALE OF THE TAPE FOR 1981

Team (AP)	Power	Schedule	Record	Offense	Defense
Clemson (1)	21.34 (5)	5.84 (37)	12-0-0	28.2	8.8
SMU (5)	19.45 (6)	2.36 (67)	10-1-0	33.2	12.5

1982: PENN STATE OR SMU?

As SMU emerged as a national contender, the aggressive nature of Meyer's Texas-based recruiting strategy became evident. The Lone Star State is historically the strongest recruiting territory in the nation, and to dominate that talent is to be a dominant force in college football. As it turned out, SMU was paying recruits directly through recruiting staff. The practice became institutionalized. The spending escalated. The benefits came on the field. And the risk to the program grew.

Penn State's Beaver Stadium. The original Beaver Field hosted Penn State football in 1893. Then New Beaver Field opened in 1909. In 1960, the thirty-thousand-seat stadium was dismantled and reassembled at its current location and expanded to 46,284 seats. Renovations and expansions through 2011 have grown the venue to 106,572 seats. CREATIVE COMMONS

Some will humorously note that no one is sure exactly when Joe Paterno was born or if they even used helmets (or leather helmets) back when he played. He was Penn State's head coach for nearly five decades, winning national titles in 1982 and 1986, and taking home a litany of awards while coaching the Nittany Lions. ("Nittany" is supposedly derived from the Algonquian Native American word "Nit-A-Nee," meaning "single mountain.") CREATIVE COMMONS

As noted in discussing 1981, the strategy started to pay off in 1980. Behind the play of running backs Craig James and Eric Dickerson, SMU finished with an 8–4 season and a losing trip to the Holiday Bowl. Probation came soon after, resulting in a one-year bowl-ban.

The 1982 season, though, was SMU's high-water mark. The Mustangs went unbeaten, 11–0–1, winning the Southwest Conference and going to the Cotton Bowl, where they defeated No. 6 Pitt. The Mustangs were ranked No. 2 in the final AP poll, while the Helms Foundation, from their bakery in Southern California, declared SMU national champions.

Doak Walker won the Heisman at SMU in 1948. An electrifying multidimensional player, he excited interest in SMU football, which led to the expansion of the Cotton Bowl. The Mustangs now play on campus, but Walker's statue stands outside SMU's Gerald Ford stadium (not that Gerald Ford). Walker played for the legendary Matty Bell, who had played football for Centre College's 1919 national champs before going 153-88-7 as a coach at TCU, Texas A&M, and SMU, where he won a mythical title in 1935. CREATIVE COMMONS

The Mustangs beat No. 19 Texas in Austin and were tied at home by No. 9 Arkansas at the end of the regular season.[27] Ranked No. 2 going into the Arkansas game, SMU dropped to No. 4. Had Southern Methodist defeated the Razorbacks, it would have presented a championship-scheduling dilemma, as SEC champion and No. 1 Georgia was locked into the Sugar Bowl, and SMU was similarly committed to the Cotton Bowl. Instead, when the Mustangs tied Arkansas, Penn State and Nebraska, both one-loss teams, vaulted to No. 2 and No. 3 in the polls, respectively. The Nittany Lions met Georgia in a one-two matchup while the Cornhuskers played No. 13 LSU in the Orange Bowl.

Up in Happy Valley, head coach Joe Paterno's Penn State squad went 10–1 in the regular season with only a road loss at No. 4 Alabama marring its record. The Nittany Lions beat No. 2 Nebraska, No. 13 West Virginia, No. 13 Notre Dame, and No. 5 Pitt before then taking down No. 1 Georgia in the Sugar Bowl. Their schedule was the third toughest in the country. The win over the Bulldogs, who were playing in their third-straight title game, clearly stated Penn State's case. The Lions finished with the highest power rating in college football that year.

By comparison, nineteen teams between Penn State and SMU have better power-rating scores than the Mustangs. Their persistent performance in not losing to a mediocre schedule kept them unbeaten and secured a No. 2 ranking in both the AP and Coaches polls.

TALE OF THE TAPE FOR 1982

Team (AP)	Power	Schedule	Record	Offense	Defense
Penn State (1)	23.10 (1)	10.27 (3)	11-1-0	32.9	16.3
SMU (2)	13.36 (21)	-0.39 (73)	11-0-1	29.5	13.3

CODA:

This is the beginning of the end of competitive SMU football for a quarter century. The Mustangs program was subsequently hit in 1985 with another probation and in 1987 became the first (and to date only) major college football program to trigger the NCAA's death penalty. After the 1986 season, recruiting violations (again) came to light, indicating a pattern of multiple and repeated infractions. The NCAA canceled the Mustangs' season for 1987 and allowed an "away only" schedule for

1988, although SMU voluntarily canceled the 1988 season. Probation with scholarship limits followed. From 1980 to 1986, the year before the probation shutdown, SMU football went 61–19–1 with an average power ranking of 10.9 against an average schedule, in terms of difficulty. After being shut down for two years, SMU came back to play, and from 1989 through 1995 (the last season of the Southwest Conference before the Big Eight/SWC merger), SMU went 13–61–3 with an average power ranking of minus-10.42 and an even easier schedule. For the first twenty years after the death penalty, SMU had one winning season. And it was thirty years before the Mustangs again appeared in a wire-service top twenty-five.[28]

2017: ALABAMA OR UCF?

Alabama won the College Football Playoff, defeating defending national champion Clemson in the semifinals and SEC champion Georgia in the title game. The Tide was also declared champion by all of the Consensus Major Selectors and nearly all of the algorithms. Having gone 11–1 in the regular season, Alabama's only loss came against No. 6 Auburn with wins over No. 3 Florida State, No. 19 LSU, and No. 16 Mississippi State. Head coach Nick Saban's Tide qualified as the fourth-seeded team in the CFP when No. 3 UGA beat Auburn for the SEC title.

The outcome was nearly very different. In the CFP championship game, Alabama got down 13–0 as Georgia contained starting quarterback Jalen Hurts. Pulled in the second half in favor of true freshman backup Tua Tagovailoa, the Tide scored twenty points over the final two quarters while Bama's defense contained Georgia quarterback Jake Fromm. Near the end of regulation, with the score tied at twenty, kicker Andy Pappanastos could have won it for Alabama, but his kick was wide-left on a thirty-six-yard field goal attempt. In overtime, the Bulldogs added three points on a fifty-one-yard field goal by Rodrigo Blankenship, which was answered by a forty-one-yard touchdown reception by DeVonta Smith from Tagovailoa, giving the Tide a 26–23 win.

Alabama won on the field and against top competition. However, this was not the strongest of Tide teams. Four schools—Wisconsin, Georgia, Ohio State, and Penn State—have higher power ratings than Alabama. This metric must be balanced against the fact that none of the three Big Ten schools played in the CFP. All four finalists finished with wins over highly ranked opponents, while three of the four CFP participants necessarily finished with losses. And the winner of the CFP played the second-weakest schedule (though twenty-second) of all the playoff participants.

Then there was University of Central Florida, champion of the American Athletic Conference. The Knights started the season unranked, then went 13–0 against a below-average schedule (seventy-fifth of 130 FBS programs) that included legacy powers Maryland, Navy, and SMU. UCF notched wins over No. 22 South Florida and No. 20 Memphis before outlasting No. 7 Auburn in the Peach Bowl to go undefeated. The Knights' top-rated offense scored an average of just over forty-eight points per game, but their fifty-second-ranked defense gave up more than twenty-five. Three wins—SMU, Memphis, and Auburn—were by a one-score margin.

UCF remains the only program to ever claim a Colley Matrix national title. The Florida legislature also proclaimed the Knights national champions, presenting one of the more peculiar uses of states' rights versus federalism in American politics. It was a great team, the greatest in UCF history. Was it the best in the country or even better than Alabama? The power rankings place the Knights tenth among FBS programs for 2017, and the nine teams ahead of them, including all four CFP participants, also had more quality wins and far stronger schedules. However, there is one indisputable fact: UCF beat a team that beat Alabama—Auburn.

TALE OF THE TAPE FOR 2017

Team (AP)	Power	Schedule	Record	Offense	Defense
Alabama (1)	21.25 (5)	5.46 (22)	13-1	37.1	11.9
Georgia (2)	22.47 (2)	7.01 (8)	13-2	35.4	16.4
Oklahoma (3)	19.05 (8)	5.26 (25)	12-2	45.1	27.1
Clemson (4)	20.62 (6)	6.84 (10)	12-2	33.3	13.6
Ohio State (5)	21.82 (3)	7.89 (5)	12-2	41.1	19
UCF (6)	16.9 (10)	-0.8 (75)	13-0	48.2	25.3
Wisconsin (7)	22.61 (1)	6.18 (15)	13-1	33.8	13.9
Penn State (8)	21.62 (4)	6.31 (12)	11-2	41.1	16.5
Auburn (10)	17.95 (9)	6.38 (11)	10-4	33.9	18.5
Notre Dame (11)	19.41 (7)	8.94 (2)	10-3	34.2	21.5

BCS:
A FIX AS GOOD AS
THE PROBLEM

Before the Bowl Championship Series and the College Football Play-off, the declaration of a champion depended on opinions. Opinions varied, and the result was controversy over who was champion. The BCS and its expansive successor, the CFP, were supposed to fix this, taking away controversy and declaring a champion on the field.

Why the BCS? Three times in the eight years before 1998, the AP writers and UPI/*USA Today* Coaches polls split their championship selections. In 1990, the coaches picked unbeaten, once-tied Georgia Tech instead of once-beaten, once-tied Big Eight–champ Colorado, who was the choice of both the AP writers and the FWAA. In 1991, the AP selected undefeated Miami while the FWAA and Coaches Poll, which was now sponsored by *USA Today,* went with undefeated Washington. Then in 1997, they split again with the writers picking Michigan and the coaches taking Big 12 champ Nebraska. Controversy ensued.

What's funny is, amidst all this media-ginned controversy over a controversy the sportswriters helped contrive, the loose market system worked hard, and somewhat successfully, to put the No. 1 versus No. 2 teams on the field at the end of the season to settle the issue. They did so with some interesting constraints, most notably the bowl-conference lock-ins. Until the twenty-first century, champions for all the major conferences had rigid bowl tie-ins from the 1960s forward. The SEC (Sugar), Big Eight (Orange), Southwest (Cotton), Big Ten (Rose), and PAC-12 (Rose) all had commitments that made it difficult for conference champs who were ranked first and second overall to go head-to-head, except in the Rose Bowl where the PAC-12 and Big Ten were locked in.

Negotiated pairings of the top two teams was moderately successful from the mid-1980s until the mid-1990s due to the dominance of strong independents. Miami, Notre Dame, Penn State, and Florida State made No. 1 versus No. 2 scheduling easier because the independents avoided bowl lock-ins while playing at the very highest levels. From the year after the last title won by a mid-major program (BYU, 1984) until 1994, the year before the Bowl Alliance came into being, there were four No. 1 versus No. 2 matchups in ten opportunities (1986, 1987, 1992, 1993). Three were won by the second-ranked team. In the six games played by an AP No. 1 against other ranked opponents, the top school lost just twice, in 1985 when No. 3 Oklahoma defeated No. 1 Penn State, and in 1989 when No. 1 Colorado fell to No. 4 Notre Dame.

The No. 1 versus No. 2 matchup made for the most exciting game and heightened the prospect of revealing a weak or unworthy No. 1. It also made for good television. Eyeballs are attracted to a definitive showdown.

In an effort to help facilitate these one versus two matchups, the College Football Bowl Coalition (CFBC) entered the picture after the 1990 and 1991 seasons resulted in split national titles by the wire services. The CFBC consisted of the Southeastern Conference, Big Eight, Southwest Conference (now defunct), Atlantic Coast Conference, Big East (which transformed into the American Athletic Conference[1] but at the time was home to some of the top former eastern independents, such as Miami, Pitt, and West Virginia), and Notre Dame (also known as the Conference of One).

Members of the CFBC committed to a No. 1 versus No. 2 matchup involving an alliance of seven bowls and the five conference champions, as well as the top five at-large teams available. The Big Ten and then PAC-10 did not participate in the No. 1 versus No. 2 deal due to their Rose Bowl tie-ins.

In 1992 and 1993, the CFBC produced expected matchups (Miami vs. Alabama and FSU vs. Nebraska) and then in 1994 produced the best available matchup of No. 1 Nebraska versus No. 3 Miami (Nebraska would win, 24–17). In this last year, No. 2 Penn State, which was by now in the Big Ten, was locked into the Rose Bowl. The Nittany Lions finished the season undefeated after a 38–20 defeat of Oregon in the Rose Bowl, earning several first-place votes in both polls.[2] Starting in 1995, the CFBC evolved into the Bowl Alliance, driven largely by the Sugar, Orange, and Fiesta Bowls but involving the same conferences—everyone except the Big Ten and PAC-10.

Under the Bowl Alliance agreement in use for 1995, 1996, and 1997, the participating major conferences and Notre Dame committed to have the No. 1 and No. 2 teams meet in one of the three bowls. Contenders were picked by adding the AP and Coaches polls together. This alignment produced a No. 1 versus No. 2 matchup in 1995, as top-ranked Nebraska bested Florida. In 1996, a No. 1 versus No. 3 "rematch" occurred as No. 1 Florida State took on No. 3 Florida (FSU beat UF in the regular season).[3] The No. 2 team, Arizona State (11–0), was unavailable as the PAC-10 champion and so faced one-loss No. 4 Ohio State in the Rose Bowl. The Sun Devils lost while Florida defeated FSU to take the national title.

Then in 1997, everything fell apart as Michigan (No. 1 in both polls) beat No. 8 Washington State in the Rose Bowl while Nebraska (No. 2 in both) defeated No. 3 Tennessee in the Orange Bowl. The Wolverines were named champions by the AP but the Coaches Poll leapfrogged the Cornhuskers to the top spot.

The introduction of the Bowl Championship Series in 1998 was designed to fix this problem. As the third iteration of the CFBC solution first articulated in 1992, the BCS resolved the obvious Rose Bowl problem, which was the structural flaw. The previous two split titles were a product of the Big Ten and PAC-10 tie-ins with the Rose Bowl. The new plan would also avoid the possibility of a repeat of the 1990 split, where Colorado played Notre Dame in the Orange Bowl while Georgia Tech met Nebraska in the Citrus Bowl. Surely all would be well.

It was not.

Six years later, in 2003, the BCS resulted in another split title, bringing just as much controversy. The debate arose largely due to the logic of its creation—that biased judgment within human polls was inadequate to pick a champ, and math and other indicators of objective quality should prevail. And when attempting to fix this problem, the BCS did so by layering additional levels of arithmetic complexity onto the process that did not engage the fundamental flaw. In fact, the issue was only enhanced: the human equation.

That the BCS method worked too well can also be argued. When the choice of participants disagreed with the judgments of sportswriters and coaches, the response was tweaking and changing the formula, and repeatedly doing so until the math was aligned to affirm the prejudices of the human voters.

The original 1998 BCS formula combined human polling data (the AP writers and *USA Today* Coaches Poll), three computer rankings (Jeff Sagarin/*USA Today,* Anderson & Hester/*Seattle Times,* and the *New York Times*), strength of schedule, margin of victory, and team losses. The Billingsley, Dunkel, Massey, Matthews/Scripps Howard, and Rothman computer systems were added to the formula in 1999. The Wolfe and Colley/*Atlanta Journal-Constitution* computers replaced the *New York Times* and Dunkel in 2001, and a "quality win" measure was added. Through 2003, systems were modified or purged from the BCS recipe to get rid of margin-of-victory influences.

After the disagreement between the AP writers and the computers over the 2003 rankings, which left eventual AP champion USC out of the national title game (LSU versus Oklahoma), the BCS recipe was rewritten again to make use of the two human polls—the AP and Coaches with the Harris Interactive poll replacing the AP after 2004—and six computer rankings (Sagarin, Anderson & Hester, Billingsley, Colley Matrix, Massey, and Wolfe). The two human polls accounted for two-thirds of the BCS formula weight with the six computer rankings comprising the remaining one-third.

Herein resides one lesson that cannot be dismissed: given a system where writers and math disagree, there are no advocates for math to prevail. Clearly, when the use of objective mathematics disagrees with human writers, the math gets it wrong. And this is kind of funny because, as the website The Power Rank states, "Preseason AP and Coaches polls have remarkable predictive power, even during Bowl season. Human polls from later in the season do not." Sports-Reference's Simple Rating System (used here) and Power Rank do a better job of predicting bowl outcomes than either the preseason or pre-bowl coaches and writers surveys, with pre-bowl surveys being the worst.[4]

So still there was controversy, which eventually led us to the College Football Playoff, which would only bring different controversy.

How so? Read on.

1998: TENNESSEE VS. FLORIDA STATE

TENNESSEE (1)	23
FLORIDA STATE (2)	16

In the beginning, coming off three split titles in eight years, the Bowl Championship Series produced a No. 1 versus No. 2 matchup featuring two historic southern powers. The 1998 Tennessee Volunteers, coached by Phil Fulmer and offensive coordinator David Cutcliffe, are one of the greatest college football teams of all time. The pro-style offense run so successfully by the recently departed Peyton Manning had cut through the SEC undefeated behind the successful leadership of new quarterback Tee Martin. Tennessee had moved into the top spot in the polls in early November after Ohio State was upset by Michigan State at home.[5] Tennessee went on to win one of the toughest divisions in college football, the SEC East, defeated Mississippi State in the SEC Championship, and headed into Tempe, Arizona, as the top-ranked team in the nation.

The Volunteers' opponent, the Florida State Seminoles, had decidedly backed into the BCS finale. Top contenders for the national title for a decade, head coach Bobby Bowden's road warriors had opened the

Phillip Fulmer played football at Tennessee for head coaches Doug Dickey and then Bill Battle and spent twenty seasons as an assistant (thirteen with the Volunteers) before being elevated to head coach in 1993, taking over for his longtime boss, Johnny Majors. Fulmer won the SEC East six times in a span of eleven seasons and took the 1998 national title in the first BCS championship game. He subsequently served as Tennessee's athletic director from 2017 to 2021. PHOTO COURTESY OF UNIVERSITY OF TENNESSEE MEDIA RELATIONS

season at No. 2 in the polls before being upset by North Carolina State in week two of the season. They went into the last weekend of regular season play ranked No. 5 but then beat No. 4 Florida at home in Doak Campbell Stadium. The ACC had no title game, so FSU sat at home and watched events in the Big 12, Big Ten, and PAC-10 unfold over the next two weeks.

Going into the end of the regular season, No. 1 Tennessee, No. 2 Kansas State, and No. 3 UCLA were all undefeated. On December 5, freshly minted PAC-10 champion UCLA had to do some makeup work. A September matchup with Miami had been postponed due to the threat of Hurricane Georges. The game was moved to the end of the season, and the Bruins went into Coral Gables looking to clinch their spot in the Fiesta Bowl. Leading 38–28 at the end of three quarters, head coach Bob Toledo's UCLA squad then collapsed in the face of a comeback by Butch Davis's Hurricanes. Miami scored three touchdowns in the

Bobby Bowden was 377–129–4 as a head coach, mainly in thirty-four seasons spent at Florida State, where he won two national championships (and several near misses) and twelve conference titles in eighteen ACC seasons. There's a lot one can write about Bowden, but I'll just note this: Bowden was portrayed by Mike Pniewski in the 2006 feel-good drama We Are Marshall, starring noted University of Texas faculty member Matthew McConaughey as Jack Lengyel. Bowden had actually been offered the Marshall job two years before the crash, and West Virginia did wear green crosses and the initials "MU" on their helmets in honor of the victims who perished on November 14, 1970, in the crash of Southern Airways Flight 932 that took seventy-five lives, including thirty-seven players on the Marshall Thundering Herd. CREATIVE COMMONS

fourth quarter to win, 49–45. Controversy accompanied the win as one of the Hurricanes' scores might never have happened had an instant-replay appeal been available. A fumble by the Bruins occurred after the ball carrier was down. Miami then drove for a score. The Bruins' loss ended their twenty-game winning streak and took them out of title contention.

Later that afternoon, Bill Snyder's Wildcats, winners of the Big 12 North division, went into the conference title game in Saint Louis, Missouri, and were bested by the Big 12 South winners, Texas A&M, coached by R. C. Slocum. K-State was favored by more than two touchdowns but folded. It would not be the last time the Wildcats would come so close to a title shot only to be denied by a champion from the Big 12 South, although at least this defeat occurred on the field rather than in the BCS formula's calculus. No. 4 Kansas State then lost in the Alamo Bowl to unranked Purdue, 37–34.

Florida State was in, however unlikely. Was there a problem in the formula? Probably not. By most every form of math, the Seminoles should

Tommy Bowden, second-oldest son of Bobby, played at West Virginia and had been a college assistant coach for twenty years when he became Tulane's head coach in 1997. After going 7-4 and 12-0, he took over at Clemson, where he posted a 72-45 record from 1999 to 2008, although he never won the ACC in part because he was coaching against his dad's Florida State teams. The "Bowden Bowl" was split, 5-4, with the edge going to Bobby. The younger Bowden resigned midway through the 2008 season, and Clemson elevated Dabo Swinney, who prior to joining Bowden's coaching staff had been a graduate assistant and position coach at Alabama. Swinney had also played wide receiver on the Tide's 1992 national championship team.

have been there with undefeated Tennessee. The pollsters all put FSU at No. 2 behind Tennessee. The computers all averaged out to put FSU at No. 2 behind Tennessee. FSU had the toughest schedule of any one-loss team in the nation. And they were smart not to lose late, as stupid as that sounds. According to the BCS Guru, Samuel Chi, applying the final revised BCS formula that was instituted in 2003 would have still put FSU and Tennessee in the Fiesta Bowl game.[6]

There was one unbeaten left. Tulane had gone 11–0 under head coach Tommy Bowden, son of the legendary FSU coach. The Green Wave was ranked No. 10 in the final regular-season AP and Coaches polls as well as by the BCS. And while Bowden left for Clemson at the end of the regular season, interim coach Chris Scelfo led the team to a 41–27 Liberty Bowl victory over BYU. Tulane would finish the year undefeated and ranked No. 7 in both final postseason polls—a high-water mark for the Green Wave since their near-miss run at a national title in 1939.[7]

TALE OF THE TAPE FOR 1998

Team (BCS)	Power	Schedule	Record	Offense	Defense
Tennessee (1)	19.96 (3)	4.42 (26)	13-0	33.2	14.5
Florida State (2)	20.34 (2)	6.57 (5)	11-2	30.8	12.4

2000: OKLAHOMA VS. FLORIDA STATE

OKLAHOMA (1)	13
FLORIDA STATE (2)	2

The national title chase and accompanying BCS selection elicited a lot of controversy wrapped up in what was very nearly an elite-program love triangle. The University of Oklahoma, led by second-year head coach Bob Stoops,[8] had stormed through the Big 12 with epic wins over No. 11 Texas (63–14), No. 2 Kansas State (41–31), and No. 1 Nebraska (31–14) in three consecutive weeks. The Sooners finished an undefeated season with a repeat win (27–24) over the Wildcats in the Big 12 title game. Senior quarterback Josh Heupel led a power offense which was complimented by a clutch defense that gave up less than fifteen points a game.[9] At the end of the conference championships, the polls had the Sooners at No. 1, as did the BCS rankings.

No. 2 in both polls? The Miami Hurricanes, who had lost to No. 15 Washington early in the season after a warm-up blowout of McNeese State. But Miami had then run the table with nine consecutive wins, including a three-point upset of No. 1 Florida State, the defending BCS champs.

However, the BCS's computer algorithms had the Seminoles ranked *ahead* of Miami (the computers put FSU ahead of Oklahoma too) substantially enough to offset the human polls, so one-loss FSU jumped past the Hurricanes to claim the other spot in the playoff. The Seminoles had a tougher schedule, with Heisman winner Chris Weinke helming the offense.[10]

The Orange Bowl was a surprise in that the game turned into the forte of the Stoops family—a defensive battle. The Seminoles (39.3 points per game) and Sooners (37 points) had come into the championship showdown with two of the top offenses in college football. The Sooners offense was held to just thirteen points, but that proved to be more than enough. Oklahoma shut out the FSU offense; the Noles' lone score was a safety in the fourth quarter. By then the issue had been decided, leaving Bobby Bowden's best chance for a third national title grounded into the turf of South Florida. It was the Sooners third straight Orange Bowl victory over FSU and Bowden.

The BCS formula was then recalibrated to account for quality wins while diluting the impact of computer algorithms, although the rejiggered metrics would still have ranked Florida State ahead of Miami. Chi, the BCS Guru, observed they were "bowing more to an ignorant media than any real pressure from public opinion."[11]

Does Miami have a case? Yes, they have a hell of a case for taking on OU, especially after FSU's flat performance. Head-to-head, the Hurricanes beat Florida State, 27–24, in Coral Gables, and they had similar victories over Florida—FSU won at home by twenty-three while Miami prevailed over the Gators on a neutral field (the Sugar Bowl) by seventeen. But the "involved" math of the BCS lays out why FSU was preferred—a tougher schedule, a higher power rating, and a stronger defense, which contributed to the Seminoles' better average margin of victory compared to Miami. The problem was that nuanced math makes for a poor argument against the writers who have had their judgment reversed by the same said math.

TALE OF THE TAPE FOR 2000

Team (BCS)	Power	Schedule	Record	Offense	Defense
Oklahoma (1)	21.56 (3)	5.32 (14)	13-0	37.0	14.9
Florida State (2)	23.13 (2)	5.59 (11)	11-2	39.3	10.5

2001: MIAMI VS. NEBRASKA

MIAMI (1)	37
NEBRASKA (2)	14

As if the 2000 election hadn't been hard enough on the integrity of voting, the 2001 BCS would rock the world of people who followed football like hardcore pundits. Miami and Nebraska had been ranked one and two, respectively, ever since the Cornhuskers had beaten undefeated defending champ Oklahoma, 20–10, on October 27. But Nebraska lost to No. 14 Colorado in the last game of the regular season and tumbled in the rankings and out of the Big 12 title game.

Then things got weird. Florida had moved into the No. 2 spot but got beat by Tennessee in a December 1 makeup of an SEC game postponed by the 9/11 attacks on New York City and Washington, DC. The Volunteers jumped into second when Colorado beat Texas the same day for the Big 12 title. But then Tennessee lost to No. 21 LSU, 31–20, in the SEC title game (Tennessee had beaten LSU in Knoxville earlier that season but was carrying a loss to Georgia).

Meanwhile, one-loss Oregon sat stuck at No. 5 in the BCS standings due to the math and a 49–42 loss to Stanford (9–3, 12.13 SRS in 2001). The annual Stanford-Oregon matchup might be one of the most important and underappreciated rivalries in major college football. Upsets are frequent, and Oregon has seen their conference and national title ambitions frustrated by the Cardinal on more than one occasion. Jere Longman of the *New York Times* observed that this happened with "maddening regularity" to Oregon, putting together a perfect season and then losing to Stanford.[12]

By the end of the season, the impact of this one loss showed through in the BCS standings, as the formula produced a weird ranking from the perspective of the writers and coaches. If you wanted an example of how humans and the computers could view the football world completely different, look no further than here. The AP writers and the BCS agreed on the top team, Miami, but the AP's No. 2 (Oregon) was the BCS's No. 4, and the BCS's No. 2 (Nebraska) was the AP's No. 4. The No. 6 team in the AP (Maryland) was No. 10 in the BCS, and the No. 6 in the BCS (Tennessee) was the AP's No. 8.

Colorado had two losses, including Fresno State in its season opener, and was 1–1 against Texas but ranked ahead of one-loss Oregon, who had only lost to a Stanford team that was better than Fresno State. The Buffaloes were somehow ranked behind Nebraska, a team they had defeated and who had not even won its conference. And Colorado did win the Big 12 in part because the Buffaloes defeated a team ranked ahead of them.

As a general rule, writers, coaches, and even the algorithms correlate highly and come up with the same rankings. But there are times they'll disagree, and 2001 brought the most extreme case.

So head coach Gary Barnett's Colorado and Mike Bellotti's Oregon both got sidelined from the BCS game. On January 1, Oregon beat Colorado by twenty-two points in the Fiesta Bowl. Meanwhile, Miami devastated Nebraska, 37–14, for their fifth national title. But there's every

FINAL REGULAR-SEASON RANKINGS, DECEMBER 9, 2001

AP Rank	Team (First Votes)	W/L	AP Points	BCS Rank
1	Miami (FL) (72)	11-0	1,800	1
2	Oregon	10-1	1,698	4
3	Colorado	10-2	1,649	3
4	Nebraska	11-1	1,556	2
5	Florida	9-2	1,396	5
6	Maryland	10-1	1,384	10
7	Illinois	10-1	1,381	8
8	Tennessee	10-2	1,309	6

reason to believe that Oregon largely lost out on the pleasure of getting blown out by Miami. Power ratings for 2001 put Florida, Tennessee, and Texas ahead of Oregon. The Ducks' SRS score (16.92) was approximately the same as Nebraska's (16.48), but both teams paled when compared to the Hurricanes (26.17).

The 2001 Miami Hurricanes were one of the best teams of the era. Head coach Larry Coker's squad was in the midst of a thirty-four-game winning streak, which would not be broken until they encountered Ohio State in the Fiesta Bowl after the 2002 season. The year's BCS matched up undefeated Miami and undefeated Ohio State without controversy, although the weak relationship between the writers poll and the computers was again in evidence.[13] Miami has not returned to the national title game again as of 2024.

TALE OF THE TAPE FOR 2001

Team (BCS)	Power	Schedule	Record	Offense	Defense
Miami (1)	26.17 (1)	5.09 (22)	12-0	42.7	9.8
Nebraska (2)	16.48 (6)	4.33 (29)	11-2	35.6	17.4

2003: OKLAHOMA VS. LSU VS. USC VS. THE FORMULA

OKLAHOMA (1)	14
LSU (2)	21

I won't spend too much time revisiting this case, which gets a lot of attention at the front of the book, but this is the biggie. The BCS plainly and completely failed to produce a public consensus on a champion and also laid bare the dispute between the human polls (especially the writers) and the algorithms.

The game board got set in this manner: USC lost to Cal in three overtimes, 34–31, on September 27, but then won out the rest of the season, culminating in a 52–28 win over unranked Oregon State for the PAC-10 title. LSU lost at home to Florida on October 11 and then won seven straight. That run included three victories over ranked opponents, the last a 34–13 drubbing of No. 5 Georgia for the SEC title.

Going into the conference championship weekend, Oklahoma was rock-solid with the computers, almost immune to movement even if they

FINAL REGULAR-SEASON RANKINGS, DECEMBER 7, 2002

AP Rank	Team (First Votes)	W/L	AP Points	BCS Rank
1	USC (42)	11-1	1,595	3
2	LSU (21)	12-1	1,580	2
3	Oklahoma (2)	12-1	1,491	1
4	Michigan	10-2	1,437	4
5	Texas	10-2	1,322	6
6	Tennessee	10-2	1,228	8
7	Ohio State	10-2	1,208	5
8	Kansas State	11-3	1,151	10

were to lose to Kansas State. And they did in the Big 12 title game, getting shellacked by the Wildcats, 35–7.

But strange things occurred in the math, which is inclined to happen when you play with Bayes.[14] The conference title games on December 6 demonstrated this, as the BCS formula produced a football-rankings version of the Butterfly Effect. At the start of the day, Syracuse beat Notre Dame, 38–12, the Irish having previously lost to USC, 45–14. At the end of the day, Boise State beat Hawaii, 45–28, in Honolulu with the Trojans having also beaten the Rainbow Warriors, 61–32, back in September.

The ripple effect worked its way through the BCS formula via the strength-of-schedule component to weaken USC's overall BCS score. The result vaulted LSU and Oklahoma over the Trojans into the national championship game.[15] Again, the BCS picked a team that was not a conference champion to play for the national title.

TALE OF THE TAPE FOR 2003

Team (BCS)	Power	Schedule	Record	Offense	Defense
Oklahoma (1)	20.27 (3)	4.06 (32)	12-2	42.9	15.3
LSU (2)	20.85 (2)	3.28 (41)	13-1	33.9	11.0

2004: USC VS. OKLAHOMA

USC (1)	55
OKLAHOMA (2)	19

All of the ambitions and hopes of the BCS crashed into the ground after the 2003 season. A split title with two champions had resulted because the AP poll disagreed with the BCS about who the best teams in the nation were. But it also gave the writers something that always sells—a controversy with a villain.

The controversy was that the vaunted BCS, designed to fix the college-football-championship issue, was deeply flawed and had resulted in the exact outcome it was supposed to prevent. The villain was technology. The mysterious computers and the arcane algorithms that did exactly what they were supposed to do—illuminate information which might be missed in the human subjectivity of the wisdom of crowds, also known as the polls.[16] And because algorithms didn't have news columns and radio shows, the algorithms had to be changed to conform to the very human imperfections that had created the demand for an on-field solution! So following the nightmare of 2003, the BCS changed its formula. Again. And in 2004, an undefeated team got left out of the championship game. Again. In fact, three did. But this is what the BCS was designed to do—to make the best of five fit into two.

Which it did. Barely.

USC, Oklahoma, Auburn, Utah, and Boise State were all undefeated at the end of the conference title games. The circumstance, though, was one the BCS was designed to deal with, discriminating among numerous high-quality teams to determine who should play for all the marbles. There was a consensus between the polls and BCS standings among the top three with USC first, Oklahoma second, and Auburn third. Utah, coming out of the Mountain West (and making the case for its later invitation into what would become the PAC-12), ranked fifth in the AP and sixth in the BCS, trailing one-loss Cal of the PAC-10 in the AP and one-loss Texas and Cal in the BCS rankings. Boise was tenth in the AP, trailing Louisville, Georgia, and Virginia Tech, in addition to the others already mentioned, but ninth in the BCS.

Bob Stoops's Sooners and Pete Carroll's Trojans got the nod, but the story was Auburn, the undefeated SEC champions. Head coach Tommy Tuberville's Tigers tore up the conference, beating Alabama and Georgia on the road to the Sugar Bowl. Tuberville, in his sixth season at Auburn, had assembled a team that would include four first-round National Football League (NFL) picks. The Tigers featured the top defense in the country, giving up just 11.3 points a game, and were better defending the pass than Oklahoma (OU would get shredded for 332 yards and five touchdowns through the air by USC quarterback Matt Leinert in the title game).

Could Auburn have done better than the Sooners? Unknown. USC had a higher power ranking and played a tougher strength of schedule, but it is unlikely the Tigers could have done worse than losing by thirty-six points. Auburn beat Virginia Tech in the Sugar Bowl, 16–13, finished the year ranked No. 2 in the AP and Coaches polls, and for a time declared themselves champs, complete with rings.[17] However, the university does not formally claim a title for the season despite some selectors awarding Auburn the crown after USC's title was vacated due to a cheating scandal involving a sports agent paying a player.

Calculations by the BCS Guru indicate that Auburn and Utah still miss the 2004 title game, even if the formula is not tweaked. Chi's analysis indicates that the Tigers suffered from a "slow start." They were ranked only seventeenth when the season began and therefore had inadequate

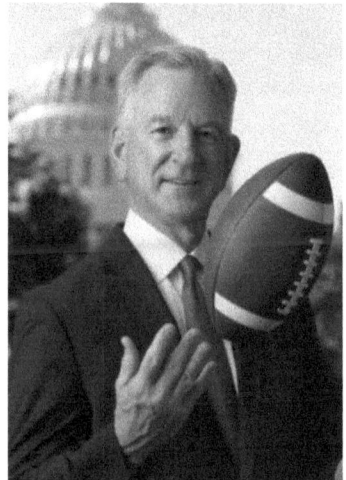

Tommy Tuberville was an assistant coach to Jimmy Johnson (Miami) and R. C. Slocum (Texas A&M) before being named head coach at Ole Miss in 1995. After announcing to the Rebels faithful at the end of the 1998 season that "they'll have to carry me out of here in a pine box," within a week Tuberville (25–20 in Oxford) announced he was taking over at Auburn. With the Tigers, he went 85–40 and won the SEC West in year two. Subsequent coaching tours at Texas Tech and the University of Cincinnati were followed by a stint in the private sector. He then was elected to the US Senate from Alabama in 2020. CREATIVE COMMONS

The 2004 Auburn Tigers went 13-0, won the SEC and the Sugar Bowl, and finished in second place in both AP and Coaches polls. After the Tigers went undefeated, rings were made for the team that said National Champions. Auburn's sports information office said that the rings were "a Coach Tuberville decision." Auburn does not claim the title, but it is a beautiful ring. PUBLIC DOMAIN

momentum to overtake USC and Oklahoma. Perhaps. But three other times since 1990, teams ranked at the top of a wire-service poll at the end of the season had started the year ranked even lower—Georgia Tech (32nd) in 1990, Auburn (23rd) in 2010, and Oklahoma (19th) in 2000. It can be done.

Nonetheless, the often star-crossed Tigers might have a case this time, especially given the Sooners' back-to-back implosions. As Michael Pinto from Bleacher Report observed, "USC's 2004 championship is not only tainted by the Reggie Bush fiasco that forced the Trojans to vacate two wins from the season, including the win over Oklahoma in the Orange Bowl, but also because of yet another mess-up by the BCS."[18]

TALE OF THE TAPE FOR 2004

Team (BCS)	Power	Schedule	Record	Offense	Defense
USC (1)	26.06 (1)	8.22 (5)	13-0	38.2	13.0
Oklahoma (2)	21.23 (4)	6.85 (11)	12-1	34.8	16.8

2006: OHIO STATE VS. FLORIDA

OHIO STATE (1)	14
FLORIDA (2)	41

In 2006, the Big Ten very nearly gave us epic controversy. Head coach Jim Tressel's Ohio State Buckeyes were ranked No. 1 in the AP poll and were set to take on the No. 2 Wolverines at home in The Shoe on November 18. However, the BCS rankings had Michigan ranked higher. Ohio State bested Michigan by three, 42–39, but the rankings didn't move. The Wolverines stayed one behind the Buckeyes in both the polls and BCS rankings after the road loss.

The 2006 Michigan Wolverines started the season with eleven straight wins before a 42–39 loss at top-ranked Ohio State on November 18. Michigan then went on to maintain a Wolverines tradition by losing the Rose Bowl to USC (Michigan is 9–12 all-time in the Rose Bowl with just five wins since 1970). CREATIVE COMMONS ATTRIBUTION-SHARE ALIKE 2.0 GENERIC

Then came the ripple-effect weirdness that was the BCS. USC beat No. 6 Notre Dame and then was upset by UCLA. The Trojans, at one point ranked ninth after an October loss to Oregon State, had clawed ahead of Michigan to second in the BCS standings, only to drop to fifth after falling to the Bruins. That set up a possible rematch between the Wolverines and Ohio State.

But then Florida (coached by Urban Meyer) beat Arkansas (coached by Houston Nutt prior to the arrival, crash, and departure of Bobby Petrino) to win the SEC and secure the other title-game berth—by just .01 points over the Wolverines. The Gators would face Big Ten champ Ohio State.

And without playing a down, Michigan had gone out and in and out of the BCS title game hunt. Why? Because even though the Wolverines' case had been determined after the final game in Columbus, the human voting started to realign. Both the Harris Interactive and the Coaches Polls shifted Florida above Michigan in the rankings after the Gators' victory in the SEC championship. The result was just enough movement to also bump Michigan out of contention in the BCS algorithm.

Why the shift? Was it because Florida had the chance to restate its case while Michigan was idle? Did Meyer have the audacity to campaign for the slot? The impact in the computer algorithm was predictable, explained by performance. The change came in the human element. Was it deliberate to preclude an all-Big Ten rematch for the title?

According to the BCS Guru, that theory is a possibility. In his "BCS Formula Review" postmortem, Chi observed that the only revelation in 2006 was that the Harris Poll proved to be no better or worse than any other human poll. The Harris voters, like the coaches (and the writers in the AP poll), defected from Michigan to push first USC and then Florida into the BCS title game. As the human polls now accounted for two-thirds of the BCS formula, essentially the computer rankings were rendered meaningless in a tight race.[19]

Those computers, with their lack of evolving biases, were no match for the bar conversation going on in the human polls. But the shift toward the human equation still left some strange results once we get past the top four teams in the country. After the conference championships, the order in the BCS standings and the AP poll agreed: Ohio State, Florida, Michigan, and LSU. The No. 5 (Louisville) and No. 6 (Wisconsin) in the AP are the No. 6 and No. 7, respectively, in the BCS. The BCS No. 5 (USC) was No. 8 in the AP.[20]

In terms of a matchup, the writers did everyone a service. Ohio State came into the BCS championship game against Florida as a seven-point favorite. But the Gators and quarterback Chris Leak hung forty-one points on the Buckeyes, who had previously given up just 10.4 points per game. Ohio State's Heisman-winning quarterback, Troy Smith, had an interception, a fumble, and completed just four passes for a total of thirty-five yards. As Ron Johnson over at Bleacher Report observed after the game, "God loves underdogs. And we've got the evidence to back it up."[21]

TALE OF THE TAPE FOR 2006

Team (BCS)	Power	Schedule	Record	Offense	Defense
Ohio State (1)	18.76 (5)	2.07 (34)	12-1	34.6	12.8
Florida (2)	19.66 (3)	6.95 (4)	13-1	29.7	13.5

2007: OHIO STATE VS. LSU
(VS. CAN ANYONE WIN THIS THING?)

OHIO STATE (1)	24
LSU (2)	38

If ever a season demanded the BCS, it was 2007. The was the year of four No. 1s (USC, LSU, Missouri, and Ohio State) and the year that No. 2 always kept losing (Cal, South Florida, Boston College, Oregon, Kansas, and West Virginia would all peak at No. 2 in the AP poll). Of the teams in the final AP top ten, all but one had at least two losses, including Nos. 1 through 6. Only head coach Mark Mangino's Kansas Jayhawks had one loss, to rival Missouri in the last week of the Big 12 regular season.

Heading into the weekend of conference championship games, Missouri, coached by Gary Pinkel, was No. 1 in the AP and Harris polls. But the Tigers lost to No. 9 Oklahoma, 38–7, on December 1, giving the Sooners the Big 12 title while tumbling to No. 7.

The LSU Tigers had occupied the No. 1 spot in the polls twice before suffering regular-season losses in overtime to both No. 17 Kentucky (!) and unranked Arkansas (!!). Now led by former Oklahoma State head coach Les Miles, LSU was at No. 5 before beating No. 14 Tennessee for the SEC title, which vaulted them up to No. 2 in the polls. When then No. 2 West Virginia was upset by unranked Pitt (5–7) on the same day, a huge hole was left for LSU and Ohio State, who was lurking around at No. 3 and idle after the Michigan game. The Buckeyes made their way to No. 1 while the Tigers ("undefeated in regulation") jumped three spots in the human polls and the BCS standings. LSU soundly beat Ohio State in the national championship, 38–24, to become the first two-loss national champ in the BCS era.

At the end of the season, two teams lurked who seemingly had better records. Kansas, with only a single regular-season loss to contender Missouri, got no traction and had played the sixty-ninth-ranked schedule in the county. Hawaii, coached to a WAC title by June Jones, owned a 12–0 record at the end of its regular season but had basically played a puff schedule (109 of 120 in FBS). Ranked No. 10 in the BCS, the Rainbow Warriors were clobbered by head coach Mark Richt's fourth-ranked Georgia Bulldogs, 41–10, in the Sugar Bowl.

TALE OF THE TAPE FOR 2007

Team (BCS)	Power	Schedule	Record	Offense	Defense
Ohio State (1)	14.84 (9)	0.53 (56)	11-2	31.4	12.8
LSU (2)	18.41 (2)	5.77 (14)	12-2	38.6	19.9

2008: OKLAHOMA VS. FLORIDA
(VS. TEXAS SAYS IT WAS SETTLED ON THE FIELD)

OKLAHOMA (1)	14
FLORIDA (2)	24

The 2008 season presented an unlikely comeback. Florida had opened the season at No. 5 in the AP poll and had inched up to No. 4 before losing at home to Ole Miss, 31–30, on September 27. Dropped to No. 12, the Gators then stormed back into the BCS title hunt, going on a nine-game winning streak with victories over five ranked opponents. That included beating No. 23 FSU, 45–15, on the road and then besting undefeated, No. 1 Alabama in the SEC title game, 31–20, which set up a confrontation with perennial Big 12 champ and BCS No. 1-seeded Oklahoma (12–1).

The AP and Harris polls ranked the Gators and Sooners one and two, respectively, while the Coaches Poll had them flipped. The computers had Florida third, but all the selectors pointed to a matchup between the SEC and Big 12 champs.

This was not satisfactory to the Texas Longhorns. Texas had won a national title in 2005 and hoped to do so again for head coach Mack Brown. The Longhorns finished the regular season with an 11–1 record and owned a head-to-head win over Oklahoma, 45–35, in the Red River Shootout. After beating No. 11 Missouri by twenty-five points on October 18, Texas was ranked No. 1 in the BCS standings. But the Longhorns then lost at No. 6 Texas Tech, who in turn jumped to No. 2 before losing two weeks later to OU, 65–21. At the end of the regular season campaign, all three teams were 7–1 in the Big 12 South division. Under league rules, the BCS rankings served to break the three-way tie to determine who would play in the conference title game. Oklahoma (No. 2) was ranked ahead of Texas (No. 3) and Tech (No. 7) in the BCS, so the Sooners were chosen to take on Missouri, winners of the Big 12 North.

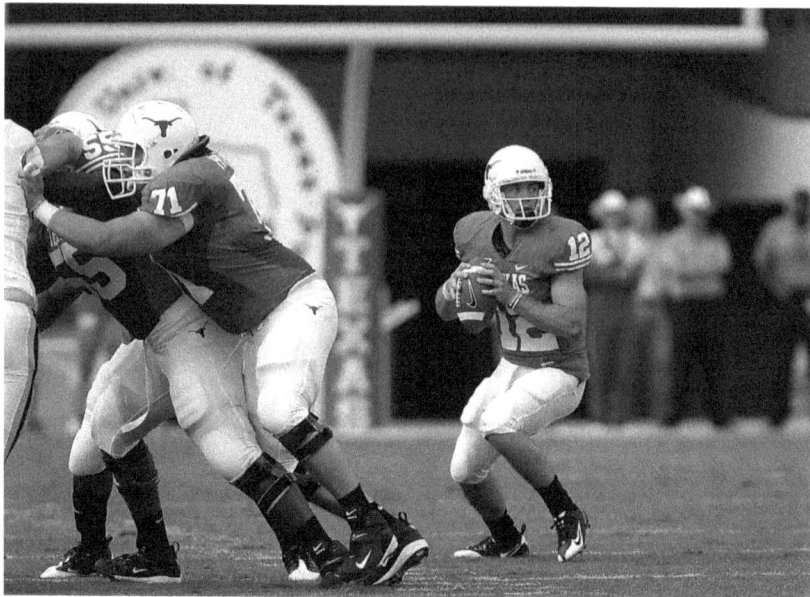

Colt McCoy and the 2008 Texas Longhorns defeated Oklahoma on the field but were leapfrogged in the final BCS rankings by the Sooners and Heisman winner Sam Bradford, who would then lose to Florida and previous Heisman winner Tim Tebow in the Orange Bowl. CREATIVE COMMONS

The Texas faithful were not pleased. Heading into the Texas A&M matchup needing a win, which the Longhorns got, 49–9, over the unranked Aggies, students raised money to print signs for the game that read "45–35" and a plane was hired to fly a banner saying "Texas 45 OU 35—settled on a neutral field" over Oklahoma State's stadium prior to its showdown against Oklahoma. The voters in the Coaches Poll were unpersuaded, splitting with the algorithms and placing Stoops's Sooners ahead of Texas. The writers in the AP and Harris polls put OU just behind Texas headed into the Big 12 title game.

It wouldn't matter. The Sooners pummeled head coach Gary Pinkel's Missouri Tigers, 62–21, on a neutral field and vaulted back over Texas (OU averaged over sixty-two points a game in their last five outings of the regular season and conference championship). Texas finished the season ranked No. 3 in the final Coaches Poll and No. 4 in the AP balloting after beating Ohio State, 24–21, in the Fiesta Bowl. The highly regarded Sagarin rankings had Texas as the top team in the nation.

As to the other potential contenders, both Utah and Boise State were undefeated in the regular season. Head coach Chris Petersen's No. 9 Smurf Turf Broncos lost to Gary Patterson's No. 11 TCU Horned Frogs, 17–16, in the Poinsettia Bowl, while No. 7 Utah beat No. 4 Alabama, 31–17, in the Sugar Bowl to finish themselves at No. 4 in the Coaches Poll and No. 2 in the AP poll. In a bit of protest, Kyle Whittingham, Utah's head coach, was good enough to vote his own team No. 1 in the final Coaches Poll.

In the national title game, it was Florida in a surprisingly low-scoring battle despite featuring two of the best quarterbacks in the nation. Gators quarterback Tim Tebow had won the Heisman trophy in 2007, the first sophomore to ever do so. Oklahoma's redshirt-sophomore quarterback Sam Bradford then won the Heisman for the 2008 season, setting up an unprecedented Heisman-versus-Heisman national title matchup in Miami Gardens. It proved to be a defensive fight, as Florida held OU to two scores while Tebow threw for two touchdown strikes and running back Percy Harvin rushed for another in the Gators' 24–14 win. This would mark Bob Stoops's fourth and final appearance coaching in a national title game.

TALE OF THE TAPE FOR 2008

Team (BCS)	Power	Schedule	Record	Offense	Defense
Oklahoma (1)	24.79 (2)	6.72 (2)	12-2	51.1	24.5
Florida (2)	25.37 (1)	5.59 (5)	13-1	43.6	12.9

2010: AUBURN VS. OREGON

AUBURN (1)	22
OREGON (2)	19

In 2010, three undefeated teams stood at the end of the season. Auburn was there again, but this time they got a shot at the title.

The Plainsmen of East Alabama Male College had started the season barely in the top twenty-five, but behind the play of superstar quarterback Cam Newton, who would win the Heisman that season, the Tigers had run the table in SEC with wins over five ranked teams, including besting No. 19 South Carolina in the SEC title game, 56–17. Of their thirteen wins at the end of the season, five were by three points or less.

Behind them loomed Oregon, the undefeated PAC-10 champion who was ranked No. 2 in the AP and Harris polls but was No. 1 in the Coaches

Poll at the end of the regular season. Then came the undefeated Mountain West champion TCU. The Horned Frogs were third in the human polls and also trailed the other undefeated teams in the computer rankings. TCU's schedule was among the weakest in the nation, ranking eighty-first, although the Frogs averaged more than forty-one points per game.

Auburn had played the ninth-toughest schedule in the country, and Oregon's was among the top twenty-five in terms of difficulty. So the one-two matchup made both popular and arithmetic sense. Head coach Gene Chizik's Tigers won a tight title game, 22–19, while out in the Rose Bowl, TCU beat Big Ten champion Wisconsin, 21–19, to finish No. 2 in all the final polls.

TALE OF THE TAPE FOR 2010

Team (BCS)	Power	Schedule	Record	Offense	Defense
Auburn (1)	20.66 (3)	5.95 (9)	14-0	41.2	24.1
Oregon (2)	21.54 (2)	3.92 (24)	12-1	47.0	18.7

2011: LSU VS. ALABAMA REDUX VS. OKLAHOMA STATE

LSU (1)	0
ALABAMA (2)	21

The 2011 season gave us the first of what would be three all-SEC title matchups for the national title through 2023. The clock-challenged Les Miles LSU Tigers had beaten head coach Nick Saban's Alabama squad, 9–6, in overtime during the regular season, and then defeated Mark Richt's No. 12 UGA Bulldogs in the SEC title game, 42–10. Alabama was otherwise undefeated and had wins over five top-twenty-five teams during the season with only the defensive struggle against the Tigers blemishing their record.

So why did LSU play Alabama again in the championship game? Under the BCS regime, the "best two teams" would meet for the title. A conference championship was not necessary. Prior to the BCS, all national title contenders (AP and Coaches polls) had been conference champs or top-ranked independents such as Miami, Notre Dame, or Penn State. In 2001 (Nebraska) and 2003 (Oklahoma), nonchampions from the Big 12 qualified for the BCS title game.

The team left at the alter in 2011? Oklahoma State. Head coach Mike Gundy's Cowboys ranked just behind the Tide in the polls at No. 3 and were 11–1 with only an overtime road loss to Iowa State on November 18. However, Iowa State is neither Alabama nor LSU. The computers rated Oklahoma State over Bama, so it was the human perception that the Big 12 was weaker than the SEC that penalized the Pokes.

Oklahoma State was well regarded by most of the computers—the Colley Matrix named them the best team in the nation, though as we've noted elsewhere, the CM has a habit of contrarianism in the twenty-first century. But the Cowboys got beat out due to the very human prejudice the BCS was supposed to eliminate. They then beat No. 4 Stanford in the Fiesta Bowl, 41–38, only to watch as Alabama dominated LSU, 21–0, in the New Orleans Superdome. It was suggested by more than one Oklahoma-based commentator that the Cowboys should have had Oklahoma State athletics benefactor Boone Pickens fly them all to New Orleans and sit on the front row of the Superdome, in pads, waiting to take on the winner of the "SEC championship 2.0."

The other controversy is that LSU, by virtue of having beaten Alabama, shouldn't have had to play them again. And the math sort of makes the case. If we look at the twenty-five rematches through 2023 that saw teams from the regular season play again in a postseason bowl, in two instances there were initially ties, so any change in outcome was most likely. But in the remaining twenty-three cases, the winner of the first game prevailed in the rematch just seven times (30 percent), including Georgia's revenge win over Alabama in the 2021 season's CFP final.

If, on the other hand, we look at the universe of conference championship games in the Power 5 since the SEC introduced the concept in 1992, there have been sixty rematches, and the winner of the first game won the rematch thirty-six times (60 percent). So the evidence is, all in all, a wash on the fairness of rematches when it comes to bias or advantage.

TALE OF THE TAPE FOR 2011

Team (BCS)	Power	Schedule	Record	Offense	Defense
LSU (1)	24.27 (2)	6.27 (8)	13-1	35.7	11.3
Alabama (2)	24.44 (1)	4.21 (17)	12-1	34.8	8.2

2012: NOTRE DAME VS. ALABAMA
(VS. WHEN PROBATION ROARS)

NOTRE DAME (1)	14
ALABAMA (2)	42

Notre Dame was ranked No. 1 heading into the 2012 bowl season, but then head coach Brian Kelly's Irish were unmasked in the national title game, 42–14, by Alabama. There is, though, a question to raise about 2012: should it have been Alabama or Ohio State (now coached by Urban Meyer) doing the unmasking? This decision was not in the hands of the voters or the BCS. The Buckeyes were deemed ineligible for the Big Ten championship game or postseason bowl play due to NCAA rules infractions disclosed in 2010.

Alabama's damning November loss to No. 15 Texas A&M on the road at College Station was followed two weeks later by a solid, 49–0, victory over Auburn. A 38–28 win in the SEC title game over No. 3 Georgia then solidified Bama's claim on the second slot in the BCS championship game, if not as the best team in the country.

The 2012 Ohio State Buckeyes were undefeated under first-year head coach Urban Meyer but ineligible for the Big Ten championship game and any bowl invites due to NCAA sanctions. They finished the year ranked third behind Alabama (13-1) and Oregon (12-1) in the final AP poll. Ohio State has subsequently found itself on both sides of the CFP selection controversy. In 2014, the Buckeyes, at 11-1, were arguably the fifth-best team eligible, but the Big Ten champions nonetheless leapfrogged over Big 12 cochampions Baylor (11-1) and TCU (11-1) to make the playoff, which they would go on to win, defeating Oregon in the title game. However, the 2017 team also won the Big Ten, albeit with two losses, and was passed over for the CFP in favor of one-loss Alabama. The Tide had finished second in the SEC West and missed the conference title game entirely but would ultimately play Georgia for the national championship. Kirby Hocutt, chair of the Playoff Selection Committee, observed, "The selection committee just favored Alabama's full body of work over that of Ohio State." CREATIVE COMMONS

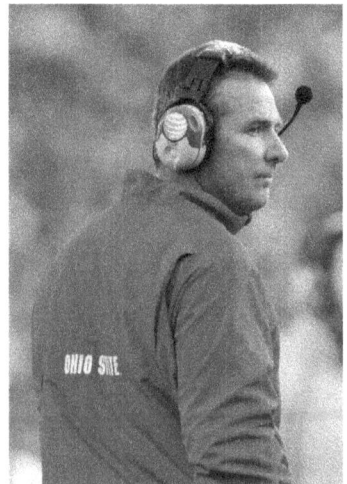

In an instance of rules and standards superseding on-the-field factors, one might ask, Was the best team in college football left out of the title game? Probably not. Although the Buckeyes finished undefeated at 12–0, they played a mediocre schedule that included uninspired nonconference wins over Cal and the University of Alabama at Birmingham. Neither their offense nor defense was in the top twenty. The end-of-season SRS power rankings place Ohio State only thirteenth (13.81), well behind the power ratings of Alabama (first, 24.51) and Notre Dame (sixth, 16.98), and the Irish were doubtlessly higher going into the national championship game. Both of the BCS participants played far tougher schedules as well.

And in the end, Alabama got the job done.

TALE OF THE TAPE FOR 2012

Team (BCS)	Power	Schedule	Record	Offense	Defense
Notre Dame (1)	16.98 (6)	6.14 (8)	12-1	25.8	12.8
Alabama (2)	24.51 (1)	5.51 (14)	13-1	38.7	10.9

THE CFP: FIGHTING OVER PECKING ORDER

T he College Football Playoff has proved to be largely uncontroversial in its selection of teams to compete for the national title, as the schools picked by the CFP for the four-team playoff have been consistent with the top four in the AP writers poll.[1] From 2015 through 2022, the teams chosen by the CFP would have been the same if the AP top four had been chosen. There is only a real dispute in the first year, 2014. Perhaps this will not always be the case, but at least in the context of "writers versus metrics and algorithms," the CFP is proving better than the BCS.

Then came 2023.

The media does try to generate controversy over the fairness of the CFP, but that basis for controversy is thin and weak and usually focuses on (1) the inclusion of a team that didn't win its conference (typically coming from the SEC); (2) the exclusion of a particular conference champion; or (3) the failure to consider or include teams from outside the Power 5 conferences.

With four slots and five power conferences (plus Notre Dame) the odds are certain that a champion gets left out. And with the variable strength and the concentration of quality teams in the SEC and Big Ten, the odds are good that a one-loss conference runner-up, especially from the SEC, has more merit as a playoff team. This also extends to the Group of 5 conferences, which suffer from weak schedules.

2014–2020: DISAGREEMENTS IN THE CFP

The 2014 CFP did feature disagreement in identifying the top four. The Coaches Poll was generally in line with the CFP committee, but the AP poll, which dues not contribute to the CFP, was less so. Each had either a different top four or at least a different ordering.

The Coaches and CFP both put Alabama (SEC), Florida State (ACC), Oregon (PAC), and Ohio State (Big 10) in the top four. However, the Coaches ranked the Seminoles No. 2 and the Ducks No. 3, while the CFP reversed the two teams, who then played each other in the Rose Bowl. Oregon handed Florida State one of the worst defeats in its program history, 59–20.

The more pressing issue was Ohio State versus Baylor as the fourth participant. The Buckeyes had blown out No. 13 Wisconsin, 59–0, in the Big Ten championship game while the Bears, also with just one loss, had defeated No. 10 Kansas State, 38–27, to finish the regular season ranked fourth by the AP writers. The Coaches and the CFP disagreed, slotting Ohio State in at No. 4, and so the co–Big 12 champion didn't get the nod.

So how good was Baylor compared to Ohio State or Oregon? In the eyes of the writers, it was basically a pick'em. The Bears finished just three points ahead of Ohio State and eight points above TCU in the final AP poll before the bowl games. The Coaches Poll was similarly close. Given the choice of either of two Texas Big 12 programs or the Big Ten champion, the CFP went with Ohio State and their statement win over Wisconsin. One wonders if a Texas or Oklahoma would have been similarly edged out?

FINAL REGULAR-SEASON RANKINGS, DECEMBER 7, 2014

AP Rank	Team (First Votes)	W/L	AP Points	CFP Rank
1	Alabama (27)	12-1	1,452	1
2	Florida State (25)	13-0	1,436	3
3	Oregon (8)	12-1	1,426	2
4	Baylor	11-1	1,265	5
5	Ohio State	12-1	1,262	4
6	TCU	11-1	1,257	6
7	Michigan State	10-2	1,105	8
8	Mississippi State	9-3	1,070	7

The 2017 CFP brought another controversy. Clemson (defending champs, coached by Dabo Swinney), Oklahoma (coached by rookie phenom Lincoln Riley), and Georgia (coached by Saban protégé Kirby Smart) were all conference champions and the clear contenders who were left standing after previous No. 3 Wisconsin went down in the Big 10 title game.

Then came the tough choice: Alabama or Ohio State? The gap between the Buckeyes and Crimson Tide was razor thin at the end of the regular season and conference championships. The rhetorical case for Ohio State is compelling: conference champion, season-ending win over a top-ranked opponent, and then a 24–7 Cotton Bowl victory over No. 8 USC, the PAC-12 champion. Those factors spoke to a powerful "what might have been" run in the playoff. The Buckeyes, though, may have knocked head coach Paul Chryst and the Badgers out of contention with a 27–21 win in the Big Ten championship, but previous road losses to Oklahoma and Iowa weighed against them.

Alabama had lost to Auburn to end the regular season and missed the SEC title game but slipped into the playoff and would ultimately win the national championship in overtime over Georgia, 26–23, thanks to a second-half rally in the CFP finale. The Bulldogs had sealed their position by defeating No. 4 Auburn in the SEC championship.

Then there was the Potemkin[2] controversy, that of Central Florida. Ranked No. 10 in the AP poll and undefeated in the AAC, the Knights were never within sniffing distance of a playoff berth. Relegated to the Peach Bowl in Atlanta, they finished out the season with a 34–27 victory over No. 7 Auburn. Four voters in the AP cast ballots for UCF in the last poll, and it is possible they would have made a credible challenge in the CFP. (The UCF national title claim was described in chapter 5.) But the Knights' own "what might have been" was obliterated when head coach Scott Frost left for Nebraska, where he'd been a championship quarterback, although UCF looked no further than Oklahoma's 2000 national-champion quarterback Josh Heupel as a replacement.

Another thin but somewhat interesting controversy came in 2020, the Pandemic Playoff. The choices feature a balancing act of the normal issues—undefeated Group of 5 programs that miss the playoff, a team

FINAL REGULAR-SEASON RANKINGS, DECEMBER 20, 2020

AP Rank	Team (First Votes)	W/L	AP Points	CFP Rank
1	Alabama (62)	11-0	1,550	1
2	Clemson	10-1	1,482	2
3	Ohio State	6-0	1,424	3
4	Notre Dame	10-1	1,338	4
5	Texas A&M	8-1	1,297	5
6	Cincinnati	9-0	1,262	8
7	Indiana	6-1	1,123	11
8	Oklahoma	8-2	1,088	6

which lost its conference title game making the playoff, and the added presence of wildly uneven seasons with Ohio State playing just six games compared to the eleven played by the ACC and SEC champs.

The CFP rankings were divergent after the top five. Cincinnati was ranked sixth by both the AP and coaches polls, while Indiana was listed seventh by the AP and eighth by the coaches. The committee ranked them lower at eighth and eleventh, respectively. Conversely, Oklahoma was rated higher by the CFP (No. 6) than by the polls (No. 8 by the writers and No. 7 by the coaches).

Notre Dame, the fourth team in the playoff, was ranked closer to No. 5 Texas A&M and No. 6 Cincinnati than to No. 3 Ohio State. The Irish had finished the regular season with a three-score loss in the ACC title game to Clemson, who was the AP's No. 4 at the time, and would then lose by seventeen to Alabama in the Rose Bowl game, which was played in Arlington, Texas. Meanwhile, the Aggies had finished the regular season with seven straight wins and only had an early-season loss to Alabama on their record. Texas A&M then soundly defeated No. 13 North Carolina in the Orange Bowl, 41–27.

Could a case have been made for leaping the Aggies into the playoff? Perhaps. Like Notre Dame, they had a loss to a playoff team but also earned a win over then No. 4 Florida. Using power measures is suspect for 2020 because the SEC played a conference-only schedule, which precludes using the algorithms to fold them into the larger matrix of competition that underlies the estimation of strength of schedule and, implicitly, the power rankings too.

CHANGE ARRIVES

The good news for major college football is, after years of deliberation, debate, and negotiation, the Division I Football Bowl Subdivision got a proper playoff. As I was writing this book, the CFP announced an expansion from four teams to twelve and then subsequently announced that the expansion would take place in 2024. Expansion might have arrived sooner, for the 2023 season, if not for the summer of 2022 objections of some Autonomy 5 leaders (the Power 5 conferences plus Notre Dame), including the ACC and Big Ten conferences.

On the one hand, better late than never. Expansion largely addressed the challenges and controversies from a century of picking champions. The field is big enough to accommodate conference champions (the top five) and also at-large teams. A playoff brings all the major bowls into the process, giving them relevance and continuity for another century of football. The plan also provides for on-campus first-round games, followed by two rounds in the bowls, followed by the championship game.

In the context of SEC and Big Ten expansion, which basically created three tiers in the FBS (SEC/Big Ten, the other two in the Power 4 with the demise of the PAC-12, and the Group of 5 or 6), it mattered greatly. As Stewart Mandel wrote for *The Athletic*, "The 11 university presidents who oversee the College Football Playoff went and threw the 99 FBS programs not in or headed to those two conferences a big fat life preserver."[3]

As to the other logistical and season-length issues, they will quickly fade. We know a playoff is workable because larger fields have engaged in a postseason tournament at other levels of college football for decades. We know on-campus playoffs are workable because they're already in use at other levels. Questions remaining include, Do we continue the conference championship games? Are these games really necessary? Doesn't the presence of seven at-large bids just extend the season of the major conference runners-up in most instances?

For sports journalism, which has enjoyed both the drama of controversy and the authority of picking champions for nearly a century, the expanded playoff seemingly spells the end of the myth that Bo Schembechler described with his quote at the beginning of chapter 1. The various polls and algorithms confront the challenge of one team surviving a vetted competition to win the title on the field. Doubtlessly, the polls will inform the selection and seeding, but the power of their authoritative check on the system, which proved valuable in 2003, is deeply diminished.

As a fan, this new world of college football is a shame, kind of like learning the illusionist's trick or finding out about Santa Claus.

The magic and mystery are gone.

Perhaps.

2023: THE LAST RIDE AND THE LAST CONTROVERSY OF THE FINAL FOUR

The 2023 college football season laid to rest the model for nearly a century of modern college football competition. Four years of disruption in the courts, in the conferences, and on the field ended with the last four-team college football playoff in 2023. Beyond the issues of player compensation and the apparent emergence of an unlimited, unregulated transfer portal, this final playoff provided its own controversy, as the committee struggled with fitting five major conference champions, three undefeated teams, and a one-loss two-time defending national champion (six potential contenders) into a four-team bracket.

The season started with the ongoing ripples of conference realignment turning into a tsunami. Oklahoma and Texas had started things in the summer of 2021 by announcing they would be leaving the Big 12 Conference for the SEC. Then in June 2022, UCLA and USC revealed they would be departing the PAC-12 to join the Big Ten. The Big 12, deprived of their two marquee programs, would subsequently reload in two waves, initially inviting BYU, UCF, Cincinnati, and Houston to the Autonomy 5 club starting with the 2023 season, and then taking in Colorado, Utah, Arizona, and Arizona State from the PAC-12 after Oregon and Washington declared in August 2023 their intentions to transfer to the Big Ten. Finally, Stanford and Cal announced at the beginning of September that they, along with SMU in Dallas, were joining the Atlantic Coast Conference.[4]

Two of the five major conference champions (Texas and Washington) were taking the trophy with them as they headed out the door to the SEC and Big Ten. Twelve of the top thirteen teams in the last AP poll following the regular season and conference championships (and fourteen of the top twenty-five) would play in the SEC or Big Ten the next year.

Name-Image-Likeness (NIL) and transfer portal effects continued to tear at the fabric of amateurism, which formally died at the end of the 2023 regular season when the NCAA's president, Charlie Baker, issued a letter proposing a new "power division" for the big-money programs that would incorporate player compensation rules while also complying with Title IX gender equity concerns. The specter of antitrust litigation threatened to bankrupt the NCAA, and conferences and colleges confronted the reality of significant player compensation costs, which would undermine their existing economic model where few athletic programs broke even, let alone made profits. Market estimates set the NIL value of the top one hundred players in Division I football at over $500,000 a season, peaking at nearly $4 million for the most valued commodity, Colorado quarterback Shedeur Sanders.

And talent would not sit still. By the end of the 2023 season, roughly one thousand players out of the eleven thousand scholarship players in Division I had entered the transfer portal. A record number of players sat out the postseason bowl games, which were rendered less and less relevant by the CFP. For Florida State University, the exodus of a quarter of its roster would deplete the team in advance of its Orange Bowl game versus Georgia, the reigning back-to-back national champions. The Bulldogs, who also had key players not participating, demolished the Seminoles, 63–3, in the worst bowl game blowout in history.

The mass FSU migration followed what was a particularly disappointing season's end for the team. The Seminoles had gone undefeated in the ACC and were consistently ranked among the AP's top four for most of the season. But Heisman contender and starting quarterback Jordan Travis then suffered a season-ending injury on November 18 during a game with Northern Alabama, an FCS school. With that, pundits and also the CFP committee questioned the quality of Florida State's team without Travis, even as the Seminoles defeated rival Florida behind a stifling defense and then beat No. 14 Louisville in the ACC championship game despite using a freshman third-string quarterback. Alabama's three-point upset of Georgia in the SEC title game in Atlanta created the dilemma of which conference champion to leave out of the top four—undefeated Michigan? Undefeated Washington? One-loss[5] Texas? One-loss[6] Alabama? Or undefeated Florida State?

The CFP decided that FSU was the odd team out. The Seminoles did have the weakest schedule of all the contenders but still had marquee wins over No. 5 LSU and No. 16 Duke in addition to Louisville. Not surprisingly, the decision proved highly controversial, eliciting demands from FSU fans and also Florida politicians, who yet again could not resist meddling with national-title picking, for an explanation and change. The attorney general of the Sunshine State even opened an antitrust investigation. In response to this pressure, the CFP's executive director, Bill Hancock, issued a statement:

> The protocol requires the Committee to take into consideration the unavailability of key players that may affect a team's performance during the postseason. Simply put, Florida State is not the same team without its star quarterback. That caused the Committee to believe that there were indeed four teams that should rank higher than FSU. FSU's strength of schedule was not as strong as the four teams that were ranked ahead of them. As I'm sure you are aware, strength of schedule is a key metric the Committee takes into consideration. If being undefeated without regard to a team's strength of schedule was part of our protocol, other universities with undefeated records would have routinely been considered for the Playoff. There have been eight, counting Florida State, undefeated teams that did not make the Playoff. While this is the first year such a team was from a so-called P5 conference, strength of schedule remains a crucial factor.

The challenge with the CFP, unlike its BCS predecessor, is that the weight of criteria is unclear. Seemingly subjective measures (availability of key personal, for example) are cited, but their exact weight is not explained. This is an "oracle" approach, whereby the leaders ask everyone else to take their word for it in terms of determining who are the best teams. So Florida State was out, as was Georgia, while Alabama moved on to the playoff to potentially confront a team (Texas) that had already beat the Tide in Tuscaloosa. And when the Seminoles arrived in Miami, depleted by opt-outs, they were ripped to shreds by UGA—a result pointed to by critics as evidence that they shouldn't have been considered for the CFP final four.

Over at the NCAA, Baker weighed in, noting that the playoff committee was outside his control. Indeed, the foundation of the CFP was created in litigation with the NCAA four decades ago precisely to limit the NCAA's influence over the business of football. If the litigation in *NCAA v. Board of Regents* fails, or is not brought, the NCAA remains in control of the TV money, and the status continues along unmolested. Freeing the control of TV rights from the NCAA opened the door to negotiating lucrative TV deals more directly, which in turn opened the door for more football on TV.

It led to first the SEC and then other conferences creating championship games for more money. It led the independents to join conferences and to be able to participate in revenue sharing. It led to the creation of the BCS and then CFP. The line is direct, known, and unimpeachable. The same NCAA vulnerability (antitrust) that led to big TV money also opened the door to players getting money for cost of attendance, name-image-likeness compensation, and direct payments from universities. It led to unlimited transfer portals and potentially unlimited eligibility. Every rule the NCAA erected in the name of "sanity" had been felled by antitrust.

But finally something was broken, and it didn't find its roots in the NCAA's antitrust vulnerabilities. Baker's comments drip with relish that, for once, something screwed up in college football was not the association's fault.

"It's up to them," Baker responded when questioned by the *Tampa Bay Times* about the CFP leaving FSU out of the playoff. "The teams that are involved in this, the schools that are involved in it, they make their own rules, right? And they should decide what they think makes the most sense."

Baker also echoed a caution advanced previously by other critics of playoff reform (including this writer) about the expansion to twelve teams. "I'm glad they're going to twelve teams next year. I'm hoping when they go to twelve, we won't have that kind of challenge. We'll probably have something that happens between twelve and fifteen or whatever."

Because, put simply, no matter where you put the decision point for keeping someone out of the playoff, fans, journalists, and politicians are going to nitpick the decision, criticize the process, and try to discredit the outcome. It is their way.

With the Florida State controversy resolved, then came the actual playoff. Michigan confronted Alabama in "The Granddaddy of Them All,"[7] the Rose Bowl. The Wolverines' controversial 2023 campaign had been tainted by allegations of sign stealing that resulted in the Big Ten suspending head coach Jim Harbaugh for the final three regular-season contests. Still, they came into the game with back-to-back one-score wins over Maryland and Ohio State and a solid 26–0 victory against Iowa in the conference title game.[8]

The Tide, meanwhile, had lost early on at home to Texas before running the rest of the table and beating Georgia by three in the SEC title game. In Pasadena, Alabama gave Michigan all it could handle and actually led in the fourth quarter, threatening to upset the Wolverines. However, Michigan tied the game with only 1:34 left on the clock. Alabama nearly capitalized when the Wolverines muffed an attempted punt return in the final seconds of regulation, which seemed like a safety at first glance. Instead, Michigan was able to recover the ball on its own one-yard line. Harbaugh opted to kneel-out the clock, sending the game to overtime. In the extra frame, Michigan scored first and then stopped Alabama on fourth and goal at the Wolverines' three-yard line for a 27–20 victory, earning a trip to Houston.

Down in New Orleans, the Sugar Bowl hosted Texas and Washington, the latter of whom had finished with three straight victories decided by no more than three points each and five wins overall during the regular season against ranked opponents. The Superdome witnessed an epic battle, as the Huskies' Michael Penix shredded the Longhorns' secondary with 430 passing yards and two touchdowns in a 37–31 win.

The championship game in Houston nicely legitimated the selection committee's decisions. Top-seed Michigan soundly beat second-seed Washington, 34–13, in a solid effort, a mechanical blowout in little need of elaboration. One might argue that the CFP dodged a potential bullet. The controversy behind the selection of playoff finalists arose in part from rankings that disagreed with the sports reporters and coaches. Florida State was ranked No. 4 by the writers (AP poll) and No. 3 by the coaches (AFCA), in both instances ahead of Alabama.

Suppose instead of being abandoned by the talent on the team, the Seminoles had stuck together. And suppose they had displayed the stingy defense they'd shown all season and beaten Georgia solidly on the field. Then suppose one-loss Texas and one-loss Alabama had advanced in the CFP and played an uninspired, messy championship game narrowly won by either team. What would prevent the AP writers from doing what they had done in the past, which is vote FSU No. 1 and poke the CFP committee in the eye, as they did to the BCS in January 2004?

This did not happen. As we know, Georgia destroyed Florida State. This happened in part because of the departure of key FSU players who entered the transfer portal or wanted to prepare for the NFL Scouting Combine. But UGA had key players out too. Something else was amiss with the Seminoles. Perhaps history will say Florida State was overrated or that Georgia should have been in the playoff over Alabama or Texas. But on paper, looking back in time, the CFP appears to have gotten it right in regard to FSU.

But there are scenarios far worse than the hypothetical described above involving Florida State. Now with a twelve-team playoff, the likelihood is heightened that a combination of the following happens: (1) an undefeated one-seed narrowly loses in the first round of the playoff; and (2) a three-loss team from the nine through twelve seeds wins out, claiming the CFP title. The reporters could easily pick the higher-ranked team with one narrow loss over a three-loss team that otherwise wouldn't have been playing in a New Year's Six bowl game under the BCS two-team and CFP four-team playoff systems.

And so the bar argument continues.

THE 2024 COLLEGE FOOTBALL PLAYOFF

When I started this little book in 2018, an expanded college football playoff was a remote possibility. The NCAA had been using playoffs at all other levels of college football for decades, and the journey to a satisfying playoff in FBS had been underway for nearly thirty years. In 2020, we had speculated about expansion in sports-strategy meetings at my university. If the pandemic didn't kill sports, the possibility of an expanded playoff would have to wait until after the expiration of the current playoff media deal in 2025.

Realignment followed the pandemic, an earthquake set off by Oklahoma and Texas leaving the Big 12 for the SEC. The wheel of change rolled through every conference, ending in the destruction of the PAC-12 as we know it and radical reconstitutions of the Big 12 and the ACC.[9] In the midst of these moves, which ultimately impacted over half of the FBS programs, the decision was made to move to a twelve-team playoff, starting in 2024. The top five ranked conference champions, and whomever else was lucky enough to crack the top twelve of the CFP's rankings, would make the postseason. This guaranteed at least one spot in the playoff for a Group of 5 champion.

The CFP was designed to fix everything. Picking the top two (BCS era) or top four (initial CFP era) teams had its share of controversies. Formulas for ranking schools were scrutinized, criticized, and revised. The unwillingness of the sportswriters of the AP poll to play along in 2003 resulted in a split title in year six of the BCS.

In the CFP era (post-2013), the polls twice disagreed with the CFP on the top four teams at the end of the regular season; the very last year of the CFP saw both an undefeated squad (Florida State) and arguably the best team in the country (Georgia, who lost the 2023 SEC title game on a controversial pass-reception call) left out of the four-team playoff pod. The Bulldogs then destroyed FSU, 63–3, in the Orange Bowl, as was described above. However, this wouldn't be a problem in an expanded playoff.

Yeah, right. It was a problem. Critics moved the goalposts, resulting in three related storylines of controversy. The first contrived dispute involved the relative rankings of conference champions. The top five conference winners made the Playoff; the top four were guaranteed a bye to the second round. The implicit assumption was that all four of the major conferences would be able to contend in the top twelve and also be the top four seeds. Through most of November, the Mountain West Conference's Boise State was ranked as a likely bye, due to the circular firing-squad behavior of the Big 12, which entered Thanksgiving weekend with seven contenders for the conference title game.

The result was a seeding that defied the logic of team quality. All four power conference champions made the playoff field, along with Boise State. But the low ranking of two-loss Arizona State, the Big 12 winner, and even lower ranking of three-loss ACC champion Clemson led to the Broncos being the third-seeded champion (with a bye) while Arizona State got the fourth seed, holding the last bye. Clemson (the lowest-ranked team participating) was consigned to the twelfth seed and would meet fifth-seeded Texas in the first round. SMU, who lost to Clemson in the ACC championship, was seeded eleventh, ahead of Clemson, and would take on Penn State, the sixth seed.

The second controversy was that of who was a "deserving loser." Among teams with one, two, or even three losses, how did one know which should be among the seven at-large bids in the CFP? This narrative emerged because of the high-powered quality and relative parity of the SEC. Two-loss schools were expected to make the playoff field, but the SEC raised the specter of very high-quality teams having three conference losses. Would they make the Playoff?

The committee telegraphed a "yes" to this question by releasing potential seedings for a postseason with Texas as the SEC representative and an SEC runner-up in the Playoff. This could have only happened with a three-loss runner-up. We might describe this problem as the "Alabama Paradox."[10]

The Crimson Tide were proud owners of three SEC losses, which included falling to Vanderbilt in the greatest upset of the twenty-first century and also a defeat at the hands of a mediocre Oklahoma squad. A variety of secondary factors and subjective comparisons were advanced to justify including Alabama instead of SMU. The Tide did have one of the tougher schedules in the FBS but not one substantially stronger than other three-loss teams.

The difference was, of course, that this is *Alabama*. And the CFP did not grow up with the 11th Commandment of SEC Football, that Bear Bryant gets what Bear Bryant wants and, by inheritance, so too does Alabama. The Tide lost two games it should have won, pointed at its logo, blamed the committee (and also scheduling), and then sulked off to demand that all the rules be changed before accepting their bowl game bid.[11]

The committee put together a pretty efficient, relatively closed subsystem of teams that were independently successful at a high level. An in-depth look at the potential participants and their schedules reveals that Clemson and Michigan were the most efficient common-comparator opponents on either side of the bracket with a "clasp" running through Texas, linking what was basically the SEC-Georgia dominant orbit to the Big Ten–Oregon dominant orbit.

This takes us to the third narrative, which was querying exactly what was in the secret sauce of the mysterious CFP Selection Committee. The committee itself was no mystery and was indeed far more qualified to pick a field than its critics. For the 2024–25 CFP season, the selection committee members were four former FBS coaches (Chris Ault, Jim Grobe, Gary Pinkel, and Mark Riley), seven current or former athletic directors (Chet Gladchuck, Warde Manuel, Mack Rhoades, David Sayler, Carla Williams, Hunter Yurachek, and the aforementioned Ault), two former NFL players (Randall McDaniel, Will Shields), and a former college football reporter (Kelly Whiteside). Pairs of committee members acted as information gatherers on each conference to keep the committee informed. Despite the noise of talking heads and some sports journalists, these are people who do know the sport of football and know it better than most media members and fans. But because they made the critical mistake of trying to explain themselves, they immediately became suspect.

The CFP Selection Committee, as policy, considers the following principles: strength of schedule, head-to-head competition, comparative outcomes versus common opponents (but not margin of victory), and "other relevant factors" such as the absence of players or coaches who impacted the team's regular-season performance (henceforth the Jordan Travis Rule). Each round of rankings is data- and information-intensive, leading to a top-twenty-five list. The details of the voting processes are at CollegeFootballPlayoff.com.

Oddly enough, despite considering all these factors, critics of the result doubled down when all of the higher-seeded teams in the first round won, decisively so, at home. The most curious comment might have come from Kirk Herbstreit of ESPN, who suggested incorporating strength of schedule into a committee selection plan that already included strength of schedule.

The committee did not consider media polls or power ratings. However, there's remarkable agreement between the committee rankings and the media poll rankings; the respective teams and CFP regular-season rankings appear in the table below. For each week of the season in November and December, I ran a linear regression analysis[12] of the relationship between the CFP rankings and the AP writers poll, the Coaches Poll, and also the SRS power rating formula, which is based on performance versus strength of schedule as discussed in the appendix of this book. The SRS system accounted for about 80 percent of the variance in the CFP rankings while the AP writers and Coaches were 97 percent correlated from week to week and always agreed generally on who would be in the top five and top ten. The particular order sometimes varied, but the final rankings and seedings were almost perfectly correlated with the AP poll. So somewhat surprisingly, the committee and the reporters generally agreed on who was strong and perhaps even why.

The CFP did its job of driving interest and generating durable controversy every week, allowing fans, podcasts, talk radio, and the sports networks to all speculate. Wins and losses among the top contenders late in the season created a revolving door in the top twelve and also among the seeded conference champions (see the table below).

As for the Playoff itself, every better-seeded team won in the first round. There were no upsets. Then all four of the seeded conference champions who earned byes were defeated in the round of eight—Oregon (the No. 1 seed), Georgia (No. 2), Boise State (No. 3), and Arizona State (No. 4). None of the top-seeded conference champions were favored by Las Vegas oddsmakers, though, so these are not really upsets on outcome so much as on the magnitude of victory by the wild-card contestants. The favored teams in Vegas also won in the semifinals. Notre Dame (No. 7) edged Penn State (No. 6), 27–24, in the Orange Bowl at Hard Rock Stadium in Miami, while Big Ten runner-up Ohio State (No. 8) beat Texas (No. 5), 28–14, in the Cotton Bowl Classic, played at JerryWorld (AT&T Stadium) in Arlington, Texas.

Notre Dame had finished the regular season ranked No. 3 in the AP and Coaches polls, while Ohio State was No. 6 in the AP poll and No. 7 in the Coaches Poll.[13] When Ohio State prevailed and covered the spread, they were ranked as the top team not just by the contractually bound Coaches Poll, but also by the AP writers. The benefit of having an inclusive playoff is that it settles the matter on the field. Which it did. And it also defies the precedent and opinions of expert-based judgments. Which it also did.

Neither Ohio State nor Notre Dame was the choice as "best" at the end of regular season among the consensus experts (writers and coaches). And neither would have made the Playoff in the previous four-team system (nor would have Alabama).

Of course, the intriguing point is about observer expertise. The Vegas oddsmakers are better judges of the relative rank and quality of college football teams than the sportswriters and the CFP committee. Every single game in the CFP shows this to be the case. Perhaps we ought to just hand them the job of ranking, picking, and seeding, and be done with it?

For now, the deed is done. Demands will be made to change the system, but we also know that even when the process changes, the process will still have flaws. And it is there, in the flaws, where the bar argument thrives in college football.

COLLEGE FOOTBALL PLAYOFF SELECTION COMMITTEE RANKINGS,
NOVEMBER 5–DECEMBER 8, 2024

CFP	Nov. 5	Nov. 12	Nov. 19	Nov. 26	Dec. 3	Dec. 8
1	*OREGON*	*OREGON*	*OREGON*	*OREGON*	*OREGON*	*OREGON*
2	Ohio State	Ohio State	Ohio State	Ohio State	*TEXAS*	*GEORGIA*
3	*GEORGIA*	*TEXAS*	*TEXAS*	*TEXAS*	Penn State	Texas
4	*MIAMI*	Penn State	Penn State	Penn State	Notre Dame	Penn State
5	Texas	Indiana	Indiana	Notre Dame	Georgia	Notre Dame
6	Penn State	BYU	Notre Dame	*MIAMI*	Ohio State	Ohio State
7	Tennessee	Tennessee	Alabama	Georgia	Tennessee	Tennessee
8	Indiana	Notre Dame	*MIAMI*	Tennessee	*SMU*	Indiana
9	BYU	*MIAMI*	Ole Miss	SMU	Indiana	*BOISE STATE*
10	Notre Dame	Alabama	Georgia	Indiana	*BOISE STATE*	SMU
11	Alabama	Ole Miss	Tennessee	*BOISE STATE*	Alabama	Alabama
12	Boise State	Georgia	*BOISE STATE*	Clemson	Miami	*ARIZONA STATE*
13	SMU	Boise State	SMU	Alabama	Ole Miss	Miami
14	Texas A&M	SMU	BYU	Ole Miss	South Carolina	Ole Miss
15	LSU	Texas A&M	Texas A&M	South Carolina	Arizona State	South Carolina
16	Ole Miss	Kansas State	Colorado	Arizona State	Iowa State	Clemson
17	Iowa State	Colorado	Clemson	Tulane	Clemson	BYU
18	Pittsburgh	Washington State	South Carolina	Iowa State	BYU	Iowa State
19	Kansas State	Louisville	Army	BYU	Missouri	Missouri
20	Colorado	Clemson	Tulane	Texas A&M	UNLV	Illinois
21	Washington State	South Carolina	Arizona State	Missouri	Illinois	Syracuse
22	Louisville	LSU	Iowa State	UNLV	Syracuse	Army
23	Clemson	Missouri	Missouri	Illinois	Colorado	Colorado
24	Missouri	Army	UNLV	Kansas State	Army	UNLV
25	Army	Tulane	Illinois	Colorado	Memphis	Memphis

Teams that would receive a CFP bid are in **bold**.
Teams that would receive a first-round bye are *CAPITALIZED and in italics*.

CLAIMING CHAMPIONSHIPS:
ONE FAN'S TAKE

So if we go back and look at all the title claims from this book, who has valid claims in my opinion? The list below doesn't elaborate on the reasoning but indicates my championship picks and sometimes a brief rationale.[1]

MY PICKS:

1936	Minnesota, although Alabama has a great case at 8–0–1.
1937	Pitt
1938	TCU in a very close decision.
1939	Cornell on the Tale of the Tape.
1940	Minnesota
1941	Minnesota
1942	Ohio State, it pains me to say.
1945	Army
1946	Army and Notre Dame are absolutely tied.
1947	Michigan
1950	Princeton was the last undefeated. Tennessee wins the bar argument.
1951	Michigan State
1952	Michigan State
1954	Ohio State
1955	Oklahoma
1956	Oklahoma
1957	Auburn, even though they were on probation.
1958	LSU
1959	Syracuse

1960	Ole Miss
1961	Alabama
1962	USC
1964	Arkansas won it on the field.
1965	Michigan State
1966	Notre Dame—tougher schedule, stronger power rating.
1967	USC
1970	Texas
1973	Notre Dame
1974	Oklahoma, even though they were on probation.
1978	USC on the head-to-head.
1981	Clemson
1982	Penn State
1990	Georgia Tech—no losses, no controversy.
1991	Washington
1997	Nebraska—based on power rating.
2003	USC
2017	Alabama—UCF is undefeated but against nominal competition.

CONSENSUS MAJOR SELECTOR CHAMPIONS BY SEASON

AP ERA

Season	AP
1936	Minnesota
1937	Pitt
1938	TCU
1939	TAMU
1940	Minnesota
1941	Minnesota
1942	Ohio State
1943	Notre Dame
1944	Army
1945	Army
1946	Notre Dame
1947	Notre Dame
1948	Michigan
1949	Notre Dame

WIRE-SERVICES ERA

Season	AP*	UP/UPI Coaches**	INS	FWAA	NFF
1950	Oklahoma	Oklahoma			
1951	Tennessee	Tennessee			
1952	Michigan State	Michigan State	Georgia Tech		
1953	Maryland	Maryland	Maryland		
1954	Ohio State	UCLA	Ohio State	UCLA	
1955	Oklahoma	Oklahoma	Oklahoma	Oklahoma	
1956	Oklahoma	Oklahoma	Oklahoma	Oklahoma	
1957	Auburn	Ohio State	Ohio State	Ohio State	
1958	LSU	LSU		Iowa	
1959	Syracuse	Syracuse		Syracuse	Syracuse
1960	Minnesota	Minnesota		Ole Miss	Minnesota
1961	Alabama	Alabama		Ohio State	Alabama
1962	USC	USC		USC	USC
1963	Texas	Texas		Texas	Texas
1964	Alabama	Alabama		Arkansas	Notre Dame
1965	Alabama	Michigan State		Alabama/ Michigan State	Michigan State
1966	Notre Dame	Notre Dame		Notre Dame	Michigan State/ Notre Dame
1967	USC	USC		USC	USC
1968	Ohio State	Ohio State		Ohio State	Ohio State
1969	Texas	Texas		Texas	Texas
1970	Nebraska	Texas		Nebraska	Texas/Ohio State
1971	Nebraska	Nebraska		Nebraska	Nebraska

Season	AP*	UP/UPI Coaches** INS	FWAA	NFF
1972	USC	USC	USC	USC
1973	Notre Dame	Alabama	Notre Dame	Notre Dame
1974	Oklahoma	USC	USC	USC
1975	Oklahoma	Oklahoma	Oklahoma	Oklahoma
1976	Pitt	Pitt	Pitt	Pitt
1977	Notre Dame	Notre Dame	Notre Dame	Notre Dame
1978	Alabama	USC	Alabama	Alabama
1979	Alabama	Alabama	Alabama	Alabama
1980	Georgia	Georgia	Georgia	Georgia
1981	Clemson	Clemson	Clemson	Clemson
1982	Penn State	Penn State	Penn State	Penn State
1983	Miami	Miami	Miami	Miami
1984	BYU	BYU	BYU	BYU
1985	Oklahoma	Oklahoma	Oklahoma	Oklahoma
1986	Penn State	Penn State	Penn State	Penn State
1987	Miami	Miami	Miami	Miami
1988	Notre Dame	Notre Dame	Notre Dame	Notre Dame
1989	Miami	Miami	Miami	Miami
1990	Colorado	Georgia Tech	Colorado	Colorado
1991	Miami	Washington	Washington	Washington

*Voted before bowl games until 1968.
**Voted before bowl games until 1974.

BOWL COALITION/BOWL ALLIANCE/BCS/CFP ERA

Season	AP	Coaches*	FWAA**	NFF*	BCS/CFP***
1992	Alabama	Alabama	Alabama	Alabama	
1993	Florida State	Florida State	Florida State	Florida State	
1994	Nebraska	Nebraska	Nebraska	Nebraska	
1995	Nebraska	Nebraska	Nebraska	Nebraska	
1996	Florida	Florida	Florida	Florida	
1997	Michigan	Nebraska	Michigan	Michigan	
1998	Tennessee	Tennessee	Tennessee	Tennessee	Tennessee
1999	Florida State	Florida State	Florida State	Florida State	Florida State
2000	Oklahoma	Oklahoma	Oklahoma	Oklahoma	Oklahoma
2001	Miami	Miami	Miami	Miami	Miami
2002	Ohio State	Ohio State	Ohio State	Ohio State	Ohio State
2003	USC	LSU	USC	LSU	LSU
2004	USC	USC	USC	USC	USC
2005	Texas	Texas	Texas	Texas	Texas
2006	Florida	Florida	Florida	Florida	Florida
2007	LSU	LSU	LSU	LSU	LSU
2008	Florida	Florida	Florida	Florida	Florida
2009	Alabama	Alabama	Alabama	Alabama	Alabama
2010	Auburn	Auburn	Auburn	Auburn	Auburn
2011	Alabama	Alabama	Alabama	Alabama	Alabama
2012	Alabama	Alabama	Alabama	Alabama	Alabama
2013	Florida State	Florida State	Florida State	Florida State	Florida State
2014	Ohio State	Ohio State		Ohio State	Ohio State
2015	Alabama	Alabama		Alabama	Alabama
2016	Clemson	Clemson		Clemson	Clemson
2017	Alabama	Alabama		Alabama	Alabama
2018	Clemson	Clemson		Clemson	Clemson
2019	LSU	LSU		LSU	LSU
2020	Alabama	Alabama		Alabama	Alabama
2021	Georgia	Georgia		Georgia	Georgia
2022	Georgia	Georgia		Georgia	Georgia
2023	Michigan	Michigan		Michigan	Michigan

*Automatically awarded to the BCS/CFP winner.
**Retired the Grantland Rice Trophy after 2013 and merged voting with the NFF/CFH.
***Technically the BCS/CFP winner is not a Major Consensus Selector champion according to the NCAA.

A NOTE ON POWER RATINGS

One of the thorny thickets of American sports is the problem of ranking and rating college football teams. Ranking teams in college sports has always proved controversial. There are basically three types of systems: expert, poll, and mathematical. There are many mathematical systems, now more commonly known as computer rankings, but there's nothing new about them—they caught on with people because people caught on to computers with the microcomputing and internet revolutions of the 1980s and 1990s.

Surprisingly, computer-style systems have actually been around since the 1920s, including the Dickinson system (1926), Houlgate (1927), the long-running Dunkel System (1929), Boand (1930), Williamson (1932), the Litkenhous Rankings (1934), and Poling (1935). Many of these persisted into the 1980s and 1990s and were regularly naming champions that were recorded by the NCAA, although not sanctioned as official titles. These systems and more modern computer systems, which were developed and actually used to create the BCS standings, considered much of the same information to rank teams. But unlike human polls or expert opinion, they sought to drive out subjective bias in favor of data that measured performance *on the field*.

Most every computer-ranking system considers the most basic outcome, wins and losses. Teams with no losses or very few losses are deemed better than teams with more losses. The quality of the opponents played is considered, usually reflected in a strength-of-schedule measure and sometimes also by accounting for "quality wins" against well-regarded opponents.

Some systems also incorporate margin of victory in order to account for not just wins but the decisiveness of victories. However, margin of victory is problematic to many critics of the computers, especially if the metric is not contextualized to account for the quality of the opposition. A related approach to dealing with margin of victory is to account for performance against expectations, such as covering the Las Vegas betting line. Still other systems incorporate a variety of different measures to judge performance, such as passing, rushing, and total offense statistics.

And many systems consider past performance, since games are often episodic while team qualities are seasonal. A small number of games and limited overlap of competition creates problems for estimating who is "best" from week to week—130 Division I FBS teams playing a dozen regular-season games provides limited information from which to draw statistical power.

A visit to one of the most thorough aggregators of computer-generated rankings, the Massey Ratings website, provides college football data from over eighty computer ratings available to the public. While the variables for all these rankings differ, they commonly overlap in two areas: wins and losses, and strength of schedule/strength of opposition. Otherwise, they consider some, all, or none of the other measurements noted above.

If we look at end-of-year rankings and polls, we get really good data to understand the similarities. Once a season is over is when both the computers and humans have the most information to render judgments. When reviewing the data provided by Massey for the final polls and computer rankings since 1998, we can learn a lot. These rankings use a bunch of different statistical estimation and weighting techniques to arrive at a cardinal ranking of the 130 Division I teams in FBS.

The dozens and dozens of computer systems generate remarkably similar results. How do we know this? The data tell the story. The numbers reveal that the use of computers produces high agreement on which teams are the very best and the order they should fall in, as well as high agreement on which teams are the very worst and the order they should fall in. There is also high agreement regarding who is in the vast middle of mediocrity but little agreement on how to order those mediocre teams. There's a lot of "noise" in the middle.

1. **All the computer rankings are generally the same.** If we correlate the ranking values of every team in FBS, across every poll, in every year, all of the rankings are highly correlated from week to week. Most of the statistical power in computer rankings comes from the common elements of wins and losses and strength of schedule. The computer rankings have correlation coefficients with each other ranging from .750 to .999, where the maximum correlation is 1.000, meaning that two indices produce exactly the same outcome in terms of relative ranking.

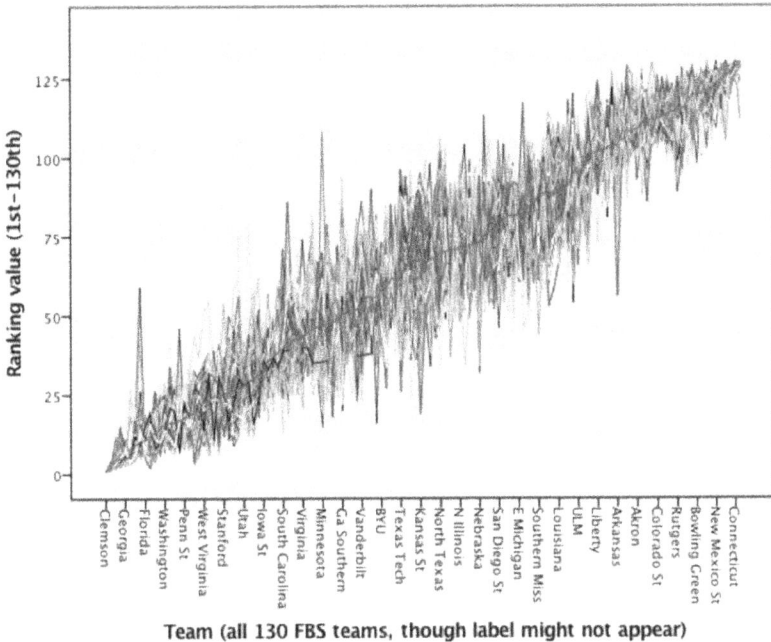

Correlated rankings for every algorithm, 2018. IMAGE BY AUTHOR

2. **There's more agreement about who is best and who is worst.** The graphic with the crescent-shaped plot below takes the average rank of every FBS team, in every computer poll, at the end of every season since 1998—over two thousand team-ranking events across more than eighty ranking systems (the mean value). And it also looks at how similar all those individual rankings are for each team, compared to the mean—what's called the dispersion or standard deviation around the average score for all rankings. The average value for each team is

plotted on the horizontal axis, running from top-ranked (closer to No. 1) on the left, to bottom-ranked (closer to No. 130) on the right. Then, for each team the size of the standard deviation is plotted. The bigger the value of the standard deviation, the less agreement there is on where to rank a team.

3. For the two decades of the BCS/CFP era, **the relationship between average team ranking and the level of agreement across ranking systems is curvilinear** (shaped like a crescent). There is high agreement across computer systems on which teams are in the top twenty-five and where they rank within the top twenty-five. And at the bottom of the FBS, the same pattern emerges. The computers generally handle the very best teams and the very worst teams the same way as each other.

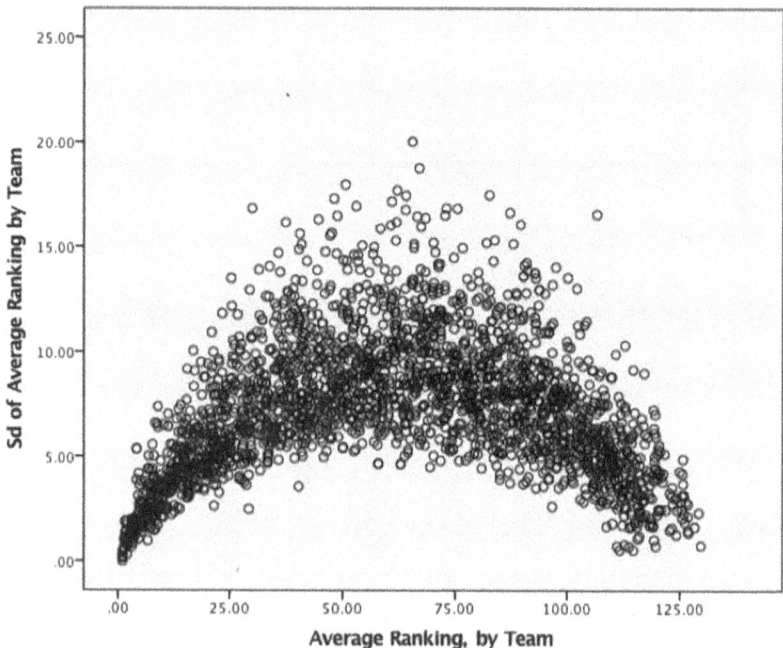

Plotted standard deviations of every team's average algorithm ranking. IMAGE BY AUTHOR

4. **. . . but not who is in the middle.** The middle is the muddle for the ranking systems. There is far less agreement across algorithms regarding how to rank the teams between No. 26 and No. 105. Standard deviations around the average ranking are far larger for the middling

teams. Across the dozens of ratings, teams often rank ten to twenty positions above or below their average rank in any given ranking system. These patterns—stronger agreement at the top and bottom and lots of disagreement in the middle—are repeated across all years. The same crescent of a larger and smaller dispersion of rankings is consistently shown season after season.

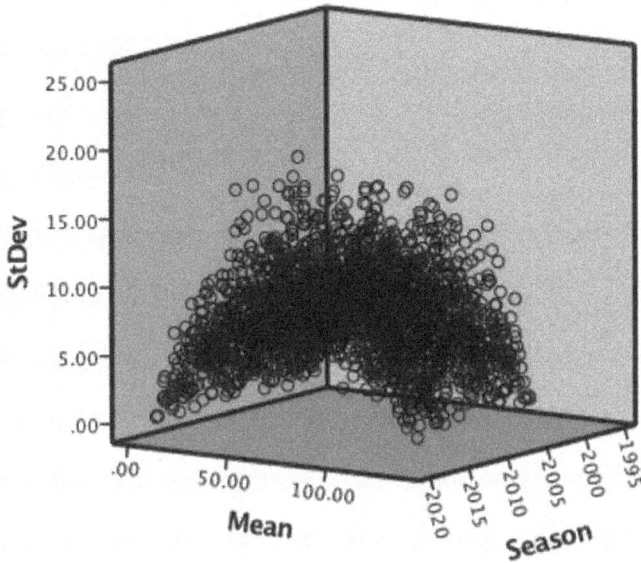

Plotted standard deviations of every team's average algorithm ranking by year, 1995–2020.
IMAGE BY AUTHOR

5. **Also, the computers generally correlate with the human-poll rankings.** A statistical test of the similarity of the Associated Press poll and the *USA Today* Coaches poll to the average computer result shows strong similarity.[1] And the human beings and the computers converge with each other as we try to determine the very best teams.[2]

6. **Humans have biases.**[3] There's research that's been done by people who study decision-making and also by those who study sports marketing about whether there is bias in the human football polls. Studies of this sort are conducted using powerful statistics, the same sort of statistics we use to figure out where to put money in the stock market or to understand the outbreaks of epidemics. Coaches and sportswriters exhibit biases when voting for the college football top twenty-five.

Once you control for various indicators of a team's strength, writers are biased toward teams in their state, teams that play in conferences in their state, Power 5 teams, and teams that get on TV more often. In addition, they penalize teams when they lose in the week before the poll. Coaches, meanwhile, will rank recent opponents an average of 4.3 places higher and opponents of where the coach played football himself 3.2 places higher than other coaches. Coaches are also more responsive to margin of victory and will rank teams higher if they have big wins. Coaches also tended to rank Big Ten, Big 12, and SEC teams generally higher.[4]

7. **Computers pick winners, but not perfectly.** Presumably, a computer-ranking system, if objective, would have a high level of predictive validity—the higher-ranked teams would beat the lower-ranked teams. One test of this, the Perron–Frobenius theorem, produced a ranking that, when tested in 1989, had 110 upsets in 1,166 games for that season. That worked out to about 9 percent of cases, or about one upset per team in Division I-A.[5]

NOTES

INTRODUCTION

1. The loss stung, as did the pepper spray used by OSU security on both teams (as well as journalists and others on the field) in an attempt to break up a postgame scuffle over an attempted flag planting by Michigan.

2. Russo has great credibility to engage this issue. He ran the AP poll for twenty years.

3. A few years back, the noted *Atlanta Journal-Constitution* writer Jim Galloway observed before the 2018 Georgia vs. Alabama CFP final, held on January 8, 2018, what he called "a lesson in Southern tribalism." Jim was "standing next to a [Georgia] Tech grad at last night's Wild Hog [Supper]. He's a prominent GOPer and sick of the Bulldogging. If UGA were playing ISIS, he said, he'd be on the sidelines with his wife. And she'd be wearing a burqa." I am a fan of Jim for his years as a political reporter, but he also has a permanent place in my heart for appearing in the best courtroom procedural ever, the comedy *My Cousin Vinny*. Jim sits just behind Joe Pesci in the trial scenes, appearing as a journalist in a nonspeaking role. I photograph and write about old southern courthouses, and that's just cool. And as for the stakes of Stalingrad, I'd recommend William Craig's *Enemy at the Gates*, which was published by *Reader's Digest* in 1973 and Penguin in 1974.

CHAPTER 1

1. The phrase "mythical national champion" was coined by reporter Henry Farrell in 1920. See Henry L. Farrell, "Season Fails to Develop Real Gridiron Champion." *The Post-Crescent* (Appleton, WI). November 29, 1920, 8.

2. My friend Paul Musgrave at UMass says that academic writing is bad because academics spend so much time citing prior authorities and precedent. I've heeded Paul's observation and only provide footnotes to inform, or which are kindly distracting, like hijacking a conversation among friends. If the writing is bad, it's not because of the citations. It's just me.

3. Michael Pinto, "The 20 Most Undeserving National Champions in College Football History," Bleacher Report, November 15, 2010, accessed at https://bleacherreport.com/articles/518058-the-15-most-undeserving-national-champions-in-college-football-history; Pinto's column had great comments on the most egregious cases of claimed titles that are bogus. I'll note those in here so you have them at your fingertips but leave it to the reader to decide the matter.

4. Christopher Klein has a great essay about Roosevelt's intervention to save and rehabilitate football on The History Channel's website, "How Teddy Roosevelt Saved Football" at https://www.history.com/news/how-teddy-roosevelt-saved -football

5. The NCAA had started holding championship playoffs in football at the Division II and III levels in 1973 and in Division I-AA starting in 1978 when the major college division was split; Division I-AA is now the Football Championship Subdivision.

6. Striving for what political scientists call a Condorcet winner, a winner who will beat anyone else in a pair-wise contest.

7. The transitive property is one of the foundational assumptions of logic, that if A > B and B > C, then it follows that A > C. The problem in football is proving that in instances where A > B > C, there's not also a C > D > A, which ends up creating what's called a "cycling problem." Even when doing this with mathematics, the relatively small number of games played by participants means any attempt at reconciling differences is troubling because of the "any given day" problem—that on any given day a weak team might upset a strong team, while if they played one hundred times, in ninety-nine the stronger team would prevail. Statistically, this is the one superior dimension of baseball and its 162-game schedule.

8. I was on faculty at OU at the time, in the middle of a twenty-seven-year tour that would end with my retirement in 2023 (before taking a new position at TCU). Contrary to the beliefs of some in Sooner Nation, faculty membership brings neither discount football tickets nor an obligation to root for one's paycheck. But I like good football, and I like Bob Stoops. He's bought me a drink or two, and he remembers that I worked for UGA football, serving seven rungs below former head coach Vince Dooley as a grad student. Go Dawgs.

9. Stoops at this point had one national title as a head coach (2000) and had previously collected a ring with Florida as defensive coordinator in 1996 (both of Stoops's titles were won over Florida State). Saban had yet to collect a ring before this January night in New Orleans. Twenty-odd years later, he retired with seven—one from LSU (2003) and six at Alabama (2009, 2011, 2012, 2015, 2017, 2020).

10. In the history of the AP poll, only eleven teams have successfully started the season ranked No. 1 and then emerged in January as national champions.

11. On the Monday after the 2003 Big 12 title game, center Vince Carter walked into my classroom in the Physical Sciences Center at OU, the Blender to Sooner alums. For all appearances, he was a man who had labored hard and mighty ("rode hard and put up wet" as we used to say in horse country). I gave him a knowing look and said, "Vince, what happened?" He sat down on the front row, pulled down his sunglasses, and said, "Dr. Gaddie, it was way too cold, and K-State was way too fast."

12. Venables later left OU to run the outstanding Clemson defenses for Dabo Swinney's national title teams. He then returned to OU as head coach in 2022.

13. I'm a Georgia alumnus. I had no notion that the January 2004 Sugar Bowl was the beginning of a two-decade reign of frustration with Nick Saban. At that point in time, we Dawgs were also absolutely convinced that Mark Richt, who had coordinated offenses for none other than Bobby Bowden at FSU, would surely find a way to win a title. This proved wrong, as Richt's Dawgs always seemed to instead find a way to lose one game they should have won. "Georgia's gonna Georgia, right?" Taken together, these are the reasons why this book is informally dedicated to Kirby Smart, the Baron of Bainbridge, for finally breaking Georgia's title drought in the 2021 season and then winning it again in 2022.

14. Say what you might about Ron Zook, but in 2007 he did the seemingly impossible and took Illinois to the Rose Bowl.

15. USC never recovered to the sustained level of performance enjoyed under Pete Carroll. Coaches who followed him included Lane Kiffin, Ed Orgeron, Clay Helton, and Steve Sarkisian. The great irony is that one of the guys they fired, Orgeron, would later win a national title at LSU. In 2013, USC basically had four coaches. Kiffin was fired during his fourth season after coming to USC from Tennessee and going 25–13. But he then started the year 3–2. Orgeron was named the interim head coach and went 6–2 but then quit at the end of the regular season when Sarkisian was named the new coach. Clay Helton took over the team as interim for the bowl game. And USC struggled for nearly a decade. We'll see how things go for Lincoln Riley, who was hired in 2022. His tenure looked kind of rocky at the time of this writing (early 2024). Meanwhile, Orgeron went back to his roots in Louisiana and became the third different LSU head coach in a sixteen-year stretch to bring home all the hardware—in addition to Saban, the other one was Les Miles in 2007.

16. The reaction of writers over the prospect of losing to computers carries faint echoes of John Henry, the Steel Driving Man, whose heart exploded during a contest against a steam-powered rock-drilling machine. The BCS formula was subsequently revised to diminish the role of the computers and their algorithms and to increase the weight of human polls. Nonetheless, the system continued to break hearts.

17. Other than the football and rhetorical genius that is John McKay, the reader will find that this writer isn't much of a fan of USC football. This condition existed long before the midnight flight of Lincoln Riley from Norman to the bright lights and easy recruiting grounds of Southern California (swimming pools, movie stars).

18. Living in Norman, there's rarely a month that goes by where, in some bar surrounded by highly knowledgeable Sooners fans, one of two questions is posed: (1) With USC losing the title, is it ours? And (2) would OU have defeated the No. 3 team in the rankings, Auburn? The WarDamnPlainsTigerEagleMen had gone

undefeated in the regular season under Tommy Tuberville with wins over four ranked opponents. They were No. 3 in both human polls and the (revised) BCS algorithm, thereby missing the title game. Auburn would beat No. 9 Virginia Tech in the Sugar Bowl, garnering Auburn a second undefeated season since 1993 without a national title.

19. I finished the initial draft of this book in fall 2022. Looking out my office window from the Gibbs College of Architecture, I could see the practice field across the street to the south of Owen Field. Rookie coach Brent Venables and his Sooners were in the midst of the toughest start to a season in nearly six decades, or at least since the worst three-year period from 1995–97 when Howard Schnellenberger and John Blake definitively wrecked the program. The Sooners finished the season out of CFP contention for the first time since 2014, going 6–7 with a 35–32 loss to No. 13 Florida State in the Cheez-It Bowl. The next season was a bit better, as Oklahoma went 10–2 in the regular season before losing in the Alamo Bowl to No. 14 Arizona, 38–24.

20. Bob Stoops was never fired, despite a couple of down years, which in Oklahoma is defined as losing more than one game in the regular season. When he retired in summer 2017 and was succeeded by Lincoln Riley, he did some other things, including business deals, XFL football, a tequila business, and Fox Sports. When Riley bolted for the exits to USC after a loss to Oklahoma State in the 2021 Bedlam game, earning the Twitter nickname "TBOW," Bob Stoops cemented his legacy. Already in the employ of OU athletics, he helped halt the hemorrhage of players and commitments, stabilized recruiting until Brent Venables was hired, and then took over the headset and prowled the sidelines as interim head coach in the Alamo Bowl, coaching a 47–32 win over Oregon. As he observed to the press, "This is about the program." For the classically educated individual, the closest comparison would be Cincinnatus laying down his plow to save Rome. My only regret is that Bob didn't bring Barry Switzer with him as interim offensive coordinator, if only to run the wishbone just one more time. And if you're curious about Cincinnatus, take a look at Michele Valerie Ronnick, 2021, *How, When, and Why to Surrender Power: The Case of Lucius Quinctius Cincinnatus before and after the Plough*. Thousand Oaks, CA: Sage.

21. Up in Oklahoma they still refer to Texas as "Baja Oklahoma," thanks in no small part to the writing of Dan Jenkins and the crooning of Karla Bonoff.

22. OU and USC indirectly collide often in this book. The Sooners are 2–6–1 all-time against the Trojans, which is part of why Lincoln Riley's departure in 2021 was so painful in its execution. The Sooners and Trojans are also contestants in two split-title controversies.

23. Alabama does get a bit of a bum rap regarding made up titles. One of their titles is simply not credible, truly. But a couple of their titles that might be called into question are the fault of the system, not the Crimson Tide.

24. This is said with respect—I pity Auburn in this book. In addition to the two titles they've claimed since World War II (1957, 2010), they've also had three legitimate misses where they probably had the best team in football but couldn't get to the table. And let me reiterate, this book resides in my SEC-addled brain, and it's all about respect. Respect, Auburn. You deserved better.

25. An expanded playoff will doubtlessly democratize things a bit. Only one team not in the Autonomy 65 (the Power 5 conferences plus Notre Dame) made the CFP throughout the four-team format—Cincinnati in 2021. Six of thirty-two qualifiers through 2021 were not conference champions.

26. Arcane is sometimes misunderstood as "ancient" or "old" or "lost to history," but it just means "understood by few." Mathematical selectors have varied in their transparency about their math and methods. Several of them were promoted in the media as national selectors before the writers and coaches polls came along, and their championships are legitimated in the record books of the NCAA. The math across most selectors is basically power-rating/strength-of-schedule based and produces similar but not identical results. I deal with the arcane math at the back of the book.

27. The most legitimate titles were conferred by the consensus major selectors: Associated Press (AP writers), United Press/UPI (later *USA Today*) Coaches Poll, the Football Writers Association of America (founded in 1941), and the National Football Foundation (expert panel). Why? In part because, in the opinion of this writer, as much as sportswriters might write about algorithms, algorithms can't write about the opinions of sportswriters and coaches. But a sportswriter can easily write about the opinions of other writers or coaches, especially when those opinions are aggregated by the folks who distribute stories. There's a vested interest in trusting expertise that extends beyond metrics. There's also a vested interest in trashing math that inconveniently disputes expert opinion, which is often impressionistic, intuitive, and conveniently discards inconvenient history.

28. The National Football Foundation (NFF) split with all the other selectors on three occasions.

29. In addition to being a great video game designed by Alexey Pajitnov (creator of *Tetris*), Pandora's box is a Greek mythological artifact. Pandora, the first human woman, opened a jar left in her care that released all the ills of the world.

30. Except for UCF. They were never in the argument.

CHAPTER 2

1. There is an obligation to mention that Rutgers is the birthplace of college football in any work that also mentions Rutgers or New Jersey. Rutgers and Princeton played in the first intercollegiate American football game on November 6, 1869, on the Rutgers New Brunswick campus. Rutgers wore scarlet kerchiefs atop their heads (hence the Scarlet Knights) and won the first game before losing a week later

at Princeton. Both were named co–national champions six decades later in what has been described thus: "more of a satirical selection than anything else, Rutgers and Princeton are recognized [as national champions] for having played the first ever intercollegiate football game." See Michael Pinto, "The 20 Most Undeserving National Champions in College Football History," Bleacher Report, November 15, 2010, accessed at https://bleacherreport.com/articles/518058-the-15-most -undeserving-national-champions-in-college-football-history. But give the Scarlet Knights their due—in the BCS/CFP era they are 7–4 in postseason bowl games.

2. For the purpose of this book, Herschel Walker only exists from 1980 to 1983. It's safer that way. Go Dawgs.

3. No doubt he'd hate this book.

4. This Lafayette team was great, battling Princeton (also undefeated) to a scoreless tie. The Princeton Tigers played a far tougher schedule, giving them a higher power rating and therefore more support as champion in nearly all of the algorithmic rankings.

5. The basic SRS for all teams and seasons can be obtained from Sports-Reference's website. Most of the computer selection algorithms are variants of this basic formula. Some readers will wonder why I didn't use ESPN's Football Power Index. The FPI is highly similar to the SRS and enjoys the same basic assumptions and root math. But it is only available for a limited time frame, which makes consistent evaluation and analysis across ninety years of football impossible. The SRS data is publicly available, generally consistent with the FPI and other algorithms, and therefore as good as anyone else's measure for the purpose of this exercise. After all, this book doesn't declare champions. It just debates them. You pick. (See https:// www.espn.com/blog/statsinfo/post/_/id/122612/an-inside-look-at-college-fpi.)

6. The details of SRS power rankings and its relationship to the one hundred–plus other existing algorithm ratings is in Appendix A.

7. Applying the SRS algorithm reveals that, instead of the Parke Davis champion, there are several southern teams that had better title claims, including four Georgia Tech squads, two from Vanderbilt, two from Auburn, and one each from Alabama, Georgia, and Sewanee (University of the South). From the West, a list would include two Michigan teams, two Minnesota teams, and one each from Chicago, Nebraska, Notre Dame, USC, and Wisconsin.

8. Years Parke Davis has no backing by any retrospective or algorithm: 1872, 1874, 1875, 1879, 1893, 1894, 1895, 1897, 1898, 1901, 1902, 1915, 1916, 1924, 1926, 1928, 1929, 1931, 1932, 1933. Years Davis is backed by one retrospective or algorithm: 1877, 1881, 1884, 1886, 1896, 1899, 1905, 1914, 1920, 1922, 1925. Years Davis is backed by two retrospectives or algorithms: 1880, 1882, 1883, 1906.

9. Looking at you, Oklahoma State.

10. I understand that I do not have this authority, but I figure I've had better luck in federal court than the NCAA, so perhaps my opinion is at least as good.

11. The not-for-profit Associated Press was created in 1846 by five newspapers in New York City as a cooperative venture to cover the war with Mexico.

12. Found at https://www.sports-reference.com/cfb/.

13. In the bowl-saturated modern era of the game, it is hard to imagine why the AP wouldn't wait for the bowl games. But there were very few bowls until after World War II. Not all institutions would participate in bowls (such as Notre Dame), and conferences sometimes had rules that precluded teams from, for example, going to a bowl in back-to-back seasons. By the 1960s, bowl participation was more regularized, and with bowl participation came the prospect of upsetting poll champions.

14. Three trophies have been awarded to the final AP poll No. 1 selectee at various points in time. From 1941 to 1947, the Dr. Henry L. Williams Trophy, sponsored by the M Club of Minnesota, was awarded to the national champ. It was subsequently retired by Notre Dame upon their victory in 1947. It was succeeded by the Reverend J. Hugh O'Donnell Memorial Trophy, which was then retired by Oklahoma in 1956. It was replaced by the AP Trophy, which was rechristened the Paul W. "Bear" Bryant Trophy in 1983 following the death of the legendary Alabama coach.

15. It is true that the father of an Alabama player accidentally broke the 2011 national title crystal trophy. The 2006 Florida trophy was also shattered. And the 1993 and 1999 Florida State crystal trophies were stolen.

16. The AFCA also engaged in some acts of retrospective award giving, identifying teams from before 1950 (the first year of the Coaches Poll) that could potentially be designated a champion. Schools so identified were then told they could apply for the honor officially. Three have so far: TCU (1935, 1938), Texas A&M (1939), and Oklahoma State (then called Oklahoma A&M, 1945). We'll discuss this last title a bit later.

17. According to the FWAA website, members also get a discount at Hertz rental cars.

18. There's really no good football anecdote for William Randolph Hearst, even though he was the inspiration for the greatest black-and-white movie of all time, *Citizen Kane*.

19. Conferences and conference strength play into this problem, making realignment relevant. And in the end, the realignment dance isn't just about competition or opportunity. It is about prestige and money. Prestige leads to money, and money makes athletics go round. Absent the lucre of college football television contracts, most other Division I sports might not be funded at all.

20. This conversation conveniently forgets that the NCAA has successfully run a decades-long experiment with postseason college football playoffs at the Division I-AA/FCS, Division II, and Division III levels.

21. A complete list of these and other NCAA-recognized selectors, as well as some historical information about them, can be found in the NCAA's football bowl

subdivision online record book. Accessible at https://www.ncaa.org/sports/2013 /11/19/ncaa-football-statistics.aspx.

22. According to a story by the Associated Press in 1927, scores were computed for ninety-six teams across conferences, awarding "30 points for a victory over a strong team, and 20 for victory over a weak team. Defeats count half as much as victories [15 points vs. strong team, 10 points vs. weak team], and ties are considered as games half won and half lost [22.5 points vs. strong, 15 vs. weak]. Dividing this total by the number of games played gives the final rating."

23. Internet-based critiques of the Dickinson System argue that (a) it got a lot less attention after the AP poll came along, and (b) once the AP poll started up, Dickinson disagreed with the wire-service results and reporter opinions in print. These arguments are not persuasive for the simple reason that this criticism is leveled at every algorithm when it disagrees with reporters. The only validity test of human opinion versus algorithms is through actual "trial by combat"—play on the field.

24. Azzi Ratem. As I Rate 'Em. Get it?

25. Knute Rockne was the legendary Notre Dame head coach (105–12–5 lifetime) who made regular use of the forward pass and was immortalized by actor Pat O'Brien in the 1940 movie *Knute Rockne, All-American*. Notre Dame claims three national titles for Rockne in a career cut tragically short by his death in an airplane crash. Glenn Scobey "Pop" Warner, whose legacy lives on in the youth football league that bears his name, coached the legendary Jim Thorpe at the Carlisle Indian Industrial School, then went on to a collegiate career coaching at Georgia, Iowa State, Cornell, Pitt, Stanford, and Temple, winning national titles at Pitt and Stanford. He created the single-wing and double-wing offensive formations, which were precursors to the spread and shotgun offenses. A less commonly known name, Howard Jones coached at Syracuse, Yale, Ohio State, Iowa, Trinity College (now Duke), and USC, and titles are claimed in his name at Yale, Iowa, and USC. One of his USC players was Marion Robert Morrison, better known as John Wayne.

26. Georgia had finished the regular season 8–0–2 and ranked No. 4 in the AP poll, then lost to Arkansas in the Sugar Bowl, 16–2. The Bulldogs do not claim the Litkenhous title.

27. UCF also enjoys the distinction of being declared national champions by the Florida legislature in a peculiar exercise of states' rights over a national question.

28. Loosely translated from Latin to English: "After this, therefore it was this," or even more loosely, "We decided later that this is what happened, so it must have happened that way back then."

29. Accessed at https://nutshellratings.blogspot.com/.

30. Thomas Bayes was an eighteenth-century Presbyterian minister and mathematician who posited a theorem that bears his name: the probability of an event or circumstance is related to previous events or conditions that might be related to the event.

31. Washington & Jefferson College is located just outside of Pittsburgh in Washington, Pennsylvania. Founded in the eighteenth century, W&J is one of the oldest institutions of higher learning in the United States. According to William F. Boand, creator of the 1930s Boand Azzi Ratem system, the Presidents were the best football team of 1921. Boand's algorithm named contemporary champions from 1930 to 1960 but also assigned retrospective championships from 1919 to 1929. The 1921 Washington & Jefferson team was 10–0 in the regular season with wins over Bucknell, Syracuse, Pitt, and West Virginia. As the Eastern Independent champion, the Presidents participated in the 1922 Rose Bowl and tied Cal, 0–0.

32. All of the SRS data for college football and some other sports are available at Sports-Reference.com.

33. https://www.sports-reference.com/cfb/about/glossary.html.

34. In the Pearson correlation coefficient, r is a measure of linear correlation between two variables. If the absolute value of r = 0, there's no relationship. As a value approaches one, there's a nearly perfect relationship. And a value above .75 indicates a relationship that eliminates most of the error in guessing. The two r's presented here indicate very strong, linear relationships.

35. A guy stood near me and my buddy David Wrobel in Section 3 of Oklahoma Memorial Stadium a couple of seasons back. This fellow wanted to make absolutely sure all of us knew that he was calling a better game than Lincoln Riley for sixty minutes of play in every game.

36. Noam Chomsky, personal correspondence to the author, October 8, 2013. Chomsky is referred to as "the father of modern linguistics" and seems to be quoted or is quotable on most any topic. I'm not a Chomskyite, but I do think he nailed this point, and he has my thanks for writing back.

37. During the pandemic, I was still on the faculty at OU. When the bars and restaurants initially reopened in Norman, there were still no live sports on TV. The bar I hung out at, El Toro Chino Latin+Asian Kitchen, was populated with guys who loved to bet sports and who had all flocked back to our hangout as soon as it reopened. The city was requiring temperature checks to admit people to hospitality businesses. Within an hour of reopening, we were betting on people's temperatures when they came in and got scanned.

CHAPTER 3

1. Red Sanders, who coined the phrase, "Winning isn't everything; it's the only thing" (no, it wasn't Vince Lombardi), spent six seasons at Vanderbilt before taking the helm at UCLA in 1949. He was 102–41–3 in his career and 66–19–1 at UCLA. Sanders invented the 4–4 defense (four down linemen, four linebackers), albeit as a spread/prevent defense rather than an attacking/rush defense. He also was the father of the squib kick. The 1954 UCLA title was his only one.

2. Terry Brennan's 1954 Irish team went 9–1, with only an early-season loss to nineteenth-ranked Purdue as a blemish on its record (the Irish were ranked No. 1 at the time). They beat four ranked opponents (Texas, Navy, Iowa, and USC). Brennan succeeded Frank Leahy, who had coached the Irish to a 9–0–1 record the season before. Brennan would last five seasons, going 32–18–0 with four ranked teams in five years. He was fired at the end of the 1958 season. Over the next five years, his successors went 19–30–0, and the Irish looked doomed to mediocrity until Ara Parseghian was hired in 1964.

3. Ole Miss went to the Sugar Bowl for the SEC and defeated Texas, 39–7.

4. Abe Martin's Horned Frogs were slightly better than mediocre, going 5–4–1.

5. "Split the baby" refers to the story of the Judgment of Solomon, recounted in 1 Kings 3:16–28, in which two women dispute who is actually the mother of an infant child. When Solomon, lacking other evidence, orders the child to be split in half with a sword for the mothers to then share, the true mother reacts with anguish and asks Solomon to give the child to her rival rather than kill it. Thus Solomon knows to whom to grant the child. Most "split the baby" scenarios are, in fact, mediocre solutions granting neither party a full, satisfying outcome.

6. In thirteen seasons coaching at Boston College and Notre Dame, Frank Leahy was 107–13–9. Of his thirteen losses, eight were by a single score, but only five were to ranked opponents. In eleven seasons at Notre Dame, there were just thirteen weeks where the Irish were not ranked, and those were mainly in 1950. Leahy played on two of Knute Rockne's teams that won mythical national titles, and he coached four national champion teams at Notre Dame.

7. In an era where live college football is available four nights a week and for about fourteen hours a day on Saturday, it is hard to imagine that, until the 1980s, the number of televised games and also the number of national and regional TV appearances for each team was constrained. In order to comply with this rule and not show Notre Dame nationally twice, the game was blacked out in the Dakotas.

8. Ties—and officiating—have often served the Irish well. As USC's John McKay observed two years later of an officiating call that allowed Notre Dame to tie his Trojans, "I'm not surprised. The referee is a fine Catholic fellow by the name of Patrick Murphy."

9. See Keith Dunnavant. *The Missing Ring: How Bear Bryant and the 1966 Alabama Crimson Tide Were Denied College Football's Most Elusive Prize.* New York: Macmillan, 2007.

10. The game, nationally televised on CBS, was nearly postponed in a moment of weirdness when vandals broke into the stadium the night before and set fire to part of Virginia's Astroturf field.

11. In thirteen seasons at Colorado, McCartney was 93–55–5 with three Big Eight conference titles. He started his career coaching high school in Detroit and then

was hired as an assistant by Michigan head coach Bo Schembechler. McCartney was the only high school coach Schembechler ever hired, which taken together with the fifth-down game at Missouri, gives him two miracles. The same fall as Colorado's national title run, McCartney founded Promise Keepers ministry. He stepped aside from the organization in 2003, returned in 2008, and eventually retired for good in 2018.

12. The officiating crew was suspended for one week by the Big Eight 8 Conference.

13. Michael Pinto, "The 20 Most Undeserving National Champions in College Football History," Bleacher Report, November 15, 2010, accessed at https:// bleacherreport.com/articles/518058-the-15-most-undeserving-national -champions-in-college-football-history.

14. After retiring, Tom Osborne was a US Representative for Nebraska's 3rd Congressional District from 2001 to 2007. He also made an unsuccessful run for governor in 2006 and served as athletics director at the University of Nebraska from 2007 to 2013.

15. Lloyd Carr went 122–40 as the head coach at Michigan and won the Big Ten five times. And having suffered a split title, it is fitting that Carr has had the chance to work on the solution by serving on the CFP Selection Committee.

16. Brian Griese's father, Pro Football Hall of Fame quarterback Bob Griese of the Miami Dolphins, called the game for the ABC television broadcast.

CHAPTER 4

1. There are six consensus major titles claimed by someone in disagreement with both the AP writers and the Coaches Poll. FWAA titles are claimed by Iowa (1958), Ole Miss (1960), Ohio State (1961), and Arkansas (1964). National Football Foundation titles (MacArthur Bowl) are claimed by Michigan State (1966) and Ohio State (1970).

2. Until World War II, college football was historically played with highly limited substitution. Players were expected to play iron-man football, and once a man left the game, he couldn't come back in. When unlimited substitution was introduced in 1941, this led to the invention of the two-platoon system (one for offense, one for defense) by Fritz Crisler at Michigan. The innovation soon diffused throughout the game. By 1954, though, the NCAA reversed itself on the rule, effecting limited substitution—one player between plays—and not allowing a player who left the game back on the field until the next quarter. This change would remain in effect until 1964, subject to annual tweaking and changing, when unlimited substitution returned to football to stay. In the meantime, platooning and increased specialization was taking hold in the game, leading eventually to formal offensive and defensive units and the existence of special teams. One innovator was Paul Dietzel, whose advances in platooning were key to LSU's success in 1958.

3. LSU has an amazing marching band and music tradition associated with football. The song "Tiger Bandits" is still played by the LSU marching band after a third-down defensive stop or when a turnover is forced.

4. The 1961 Rose Bowl is best remembered for the Great Rose Bowl Hoax. At this point in American football, crowds would hold up giant cards (numbered on the back) in what are called card stunts. They would spell out their team's name or, for example, the words "go," or "touchdown." At the Rose Bowl this particular year, a group of students from the California Institute of Technology had renumbered the cards to be used during halftime, causing the Washington Huskies card stunt to spell out "CALTECH" instead of "HUSKIES."

5. Michael Pinto, "The 20 Most Undeserving National Champions in College Football History," Bleacher Report, November 15, 2010, accessed at https://bleacherreport.com/articles/518058-the-15-most-undeserving-national-champions-in-college-football-history.

6. In tribute to my old friend and TCU colleague Jim Riddlesperger, and my friend and TCU alumnus Eddie Weller, I'll note that TCU's cheer, "Riff, Ram, Bah Zoo, Lickety, Lickety, Zoo, Zoo, Who, Wah, Wah, Who, Give 'Em Hell, TCU" is one of the oldest cheers in college football and goes back to the 1920s. It was termed by, of all outlets, *The Dallas Morning News* as one of college sports coolest traditions (see Adam Grosbard, 2019, "TCU Fans' Singing of 'Riff Ram' One of Texas' Coolest College Football Traditions," *The Dallas Morning News*, April 20). For those who've not spent time in Fort Worth, there's not much regard for Dallas over here. Legendary Fort Worth newspaper founder and TCU booster Amon G. Carter once referred to Dallas as "where the East peters out," while thirty miles away in Fort Worth is "where the West begins." He supposedly always packed a sack lunch for meetings in Dallas to avoid spending money over there.

7. Associated Press. "Buckeyes Finally Lose, 28–25 in Bowl Debate," *Toledo Blade*, Nov. 29, 1961, 48.

8. The Colorado Buffaloes, 9–1 in the regular season with a nonconference loss to Utah, had won the Big Eight and would go to the Orange Bowl as the seventh-ranked team in the AP poll. There, they lost to No. 4 LSU, who had also defeated Ole Miss.

9. Namath was selected by the New York Jets with the No. 1 pick in the 1965 AFL Draft, one of twelve members of the Tide who were drafted into the AFL or NFL.

10. Abe Lincoln never played football, but there's no doubt he would have been an outstanding quarterback or tight end. He is, among all presidents, the best candidate to play iron-man ball.

CHAPTER 5

1. Georgia Tech 1952 and Michigan State 1957 are discussed in chapter 3. Iowa 1960 is discussed in chapter 4.

2. Kimbrough was later inducted into the College Football Hall of Fame.

3. The 1939 Trojans were his last great team. Jones would drop dead of a heart attack at age fifty-five in the summer of 1941.

4. It took sixty-five years for the Trojans to recognize this team and claim the Dickinson title. As stated by USC athletic director Mike Garrett to the press on July 26, 2004, "It was brought to our attention by various individuals that we should be claiming the 1939 Trojans among our national champions in football. We took this matter seriously, did significant research and determined this to be true. That 1939 team was one of the greatest in our history."

5. Critics were not persuaded. Pop Warner observed, "If Stanford wins a single game with that crazy formation, you can throw all the football I ever knew into the Pacific Ocean." See College Football Hall of Fame "Clark Shaughnessy," accessed at https://footballfoundation.org/.

6. Again, Pop Warner: "Shaughnessy has taken that T formation we used when I played at Cornell in 1892 and made it work as it has never worked before. This is because he has added his own ideas. There is no mystery about Shaughnessy's success at Stanford, as I see it. The only mystery is where the ball is on some of those tricky plays of his." See Harold Parrott, "Out of the Frying Pan, Into the Rose Bowl," *The Milwaukee Journal*, Dec. 29, 1940, 10. The T became the foundation for most modern set formations, including the option veer, the wishbone, the pro set formation, and the power I.

7. Yes, this is the same Frank Leahy who was the legendary coach of Notre Dame. And it is also fun to note, BC played most of their home games at Fenway Park in Boston. The field was laid out with end zones on the third base line and in right field.

8. This footnote will be interesting to perhaps three people, but I've been on faculty at both Centre and Tulane. Centre won a national title in 1919. The Colonels are also the vaunted national football power that Texas A&M defeated in the legendary 12th Man Game. Tulane is Tulane, and they're fine with that. It's a great place, and they hosted three Super Bowls on their home field.

9. Leahy's departure was controversial. He tried to get a release from his newly extended contract at BC to take the Notre Dame job. Failing in his appeals, he called a press conference anyway to announce he had been released and would be going to Notre Dame.

10. Michael Pinto, "The 20 Most Undeserving National Champions in College Football History," Bleacher Report, November 15, 2010, accessed at https://bleacherreport.com/articles/518058-the-15-most-undeserving-national-champions-in-college-football-history.

11. Tulsa was led by second-year head coach Henry Frnka, who had come out of the high school coaching ranks in West Texas to become freshman coach at Vanderbilt before taking the head job with the Golden Hurricanes in 1941. Frnka went 40–9–1 in five seasons, guiding Tulsa to five straight bowl games and three

Missouri Valley Conference titles while establishing himself as the greatest coach in school history. He left Tulsa in 1946 to take over the Tulane Green Wave, winning the SEC in 1949 and compiling an overall 31–23–4 record before leaving Tulane following the 1951 season.

12. If you want to torture an Aggie-now-Cowboy, you *might* point out that not only is the 1945 Oklahoma A&M team not on Connelly's top-fifty list, but no Oklahoma A&M or Oklahoma State team is on the list at all, while three University of Oklahoma squads made it (1972, 1973, and 1986). You might also note that Barry Switzer was the offensive coordinator for one of these squads and the head coach of the other two.

13. Jim Lookabaugh was an Oklahoma A&M alumnus born in the Oklahoma Territory. After a fourteen-year career coaching high school football in Jet and Oklahoma City, he became head coach at Oklahoma A&M in 1939. Leading that program for eleven years, Lookabaugh won three conference titles in the MVC and went 58–41–6.

14. Yes, you read that right. Sixteenth-ranked Rice.

15. This was the Bear's second head coaching job (if you don't count one game at Vanderbilt). He coached at Maryland for one season (1945), going 6–2–1, but developed a rift with the university president. Bryant went to Kentucky in 1946, and Maryland eventually hired Jim Tatum away from Oklahoma in 1947 (where he'd been for a single season), who in turn elevated Bud Wilkinson. The three men would win a combined ten national titles.

16. The Jeweled Shillelagh trophy would be introduced in 1952.

17. He was later commissioner of the NFL. Same guy.

18. Quarterback Billy Vessels led the Sooner offense, and while he didn't get his day in Tulane Stadium, he would win Oklahoma's first Heisman Trophy in 1952. Vessels scored fifteen touchdowns for OU's 1950 national champs. The high school football stadium in Cleveland, Oklahoma, is named for him.

19. Michael Pinto, "The 20 Most Undeserving National Champions in College Football History," Bleacher Report, November 15, 2010, accessed at https:// bleacherreport.com/articles/518058-the-15-most-undeserving-national -champions-in-college-football-history.

20. Michael Pinto, "The 20 Most Undeserving National Champions in College Football History," Bleacher Report, November 15, 2010, accessed at https:// bleacherreport.com/articles/518058-the-15-most-undeserving-national -champions-in-college-football-history.

21. McKay had played at Purdue and Oregon and then served as an assistant at Oregon for several years before joining Don Clark's staff at USC in 1959, a staff that also included Al Davis, future head coach and owner of the Oakland Raiders. McKay became head coach for the Trojans in 1960 when Clark resigned after losing his final two games of the 1959 season to rivals UCLA and Notre Dame, with USC suffering as part of a conference-wide recruiting scandal in the late 1950s.

22. McKay had an interesting perspective on losing. Six years later, in 1966, after USC lost 51–0 loss to Notre Dame, he shared with the press that he told his Trojans, "It doesn't matter. There are 750 million people in China who don't even know this game was played," but that, "The next day, a guy called me from China and asked, 'What happened, Coach?'"

23. The ESPN *30 for 30* documentary *Ghosts of Ole Miss* does an excellent job of examining the contrast between the segregated-Rebels' 1962 championship season and the conflict surrounding the efforts to integrate Ole Miss during the civil rights era, which resulted in the breakthrough enrollment of James Meredith.

24. It seems like every other year since 1970 Oklahoma has been eligible for a title from an algorithm. If we only look back before 1967, Oklahoma declined titles from Billingsley (1915, 1949), the College Football Researchers Association (1949, 1953), Berryman (1953, 1957), and Poling (1967).

25. Purdue (8–2) also has a higher power ranking (18.3) than Tennessee, although the Boilermakers have no selector offering them a trophy.

26. Meyer would leave SMU after the 1981 season to become head coach of the New England Patriots and was at the helm for the infamous "Snowplow Game" in 1982. During a December regular-season game in Foxborough, Massachusetts, against Miami, with just over four minutes left in a scoreless tie game, Meyer had a stadium worker drive a snowplow onto the field and clear a small square for the holder to place the ball on a field goal attempt. It succeeded for a 3–0 Patriots win. The Dolphins unsuccessfully protested.

27. Arkansas was coached by Lou Holtz, by then in his sixth season. He went 9–2–1 in 1982 with the Razorbacks, wandered off to Minnesota for 1984 and 1985, and then had an eleven-year run at Notre Dame, where he orchestrated the Irish's last truly successful season in 1988. Notre Dame went 12–0 that year and beat head coach Don Nehlen's West Virginia Mountaineers in the Fiesta Bowl to secure the national title.

28. Odds are, if you're reading this, you've seen the ESPN *30 for 30* documentary *Pony Excess*. If not, do. It's excellent.

CHAPTER 6

1. The American Athletic Conference was created in 2013 once the Big East evolved into a basketball-only conference and an FBS conference was needed for the remaining football-playing members. Realignments since 2005 had caused several football-traditional programs to depart, culminating in Louisville and Rutgers staying in The American for one season before joining the Power 5 ACC and Big Ten conferences, respectively. As realignment has continued, The American has captured pass-through memberships from schools that were once major eastern independents, many of which also were with Conference USA at some point in time.

2. How a game between Penn State and Nebraska would have played out is one of the great unknowns of college football history.

3. This was the second rematch of Florida-Florida State in three seasons. In 1994, the Gators had blown a 31–3 lead in the fourth quarter with thirteen minutes left, as FSU scored four unanswered touchdowns to tie the game for a final score of 31–31, forever known as the "Choke at the Doak." Florida was knocked out of the No. 2 spot in the bowl coalition rankings, making room for Miami to go to the title game. Florida would win the SEC championship game over Alabama, then face Florida State again in the Sugar Bowl on January 2. Nicknamed "The Fifth Quarter in the French Quarter," the pregame scoreboard in the Superdome read 31–31. The Seminoles jumped out to a 17–3 lead in the second quarter and never looked back, winning 23–17.

4. See "The Essential Guide to Predictive College Football Rankings," accessed at https://thepowerrank.com/guide-cfb-rankings/).

5. After No. 1 Ohio State lost, 28–24, to unranked Michigan State on November 7, the Buckeyes then finished the season with wins at Iowa, over No. 11 Michigan, and in the Sugar Bowl against No. 8 Texas A&M, the vanquisher of Kansas State in the Big 12 Championship.

6. Check out https://bleacherreport.com/articles/1886736-bcs-years-in-review -1998-new-beginning-for-college-football.

7. Having spent a few years in New Orleans teaching at Tulane, I'd wager there are no complaints in Uptown about the 1998 season.

8. Bob Stoops played for Hayden Fry at Iowa, then was mentored by Kansas State's Bill Snyder, and was a coordinator for Steve Spurrier at Florida before becoming Oklahoma's head coach in 1999. With a record of 191–48, he has the most wins of any coach in OU history and owns a national title and ten Big 12 titles. His last victory came as interim coach in the 2021 Alamo Bowl when he stepped in for a recently departed head coach. When Stoops showed up on campus in spring 1999, I had a few football players in my survey research seminar. One day, after spring practice had started, they came limping in. One of them looked at me and said, "Dr. Gaddie, we see why Florida is so good. Coach, he's *tough*." Twenty-five games later, they had rings on their fingers that read "National Champions."

9. Heupel became the head coach at the University of Central Florida in 2018 following the departure of Scott Frost and then took over Tennessee in 2021. Within two seasons of leading the Volunteers, he duplicated his mentor's trick of immediately creating a national title contender from the ashes of a program in disarray.

10. Losing to Miami by a field goal or because of a missed field goal as time runs out are both FSU traditions dating back to at least 1987. I've seen them all as a student or a Seminole alum.

11. Go see https://bleacherreport.com/articles/1892503-bcs-years-in-review-2000 -fsu-miami-sows-seeds-of-controversy.

12. Jere Longman, "Stanford Rallies and Spoils Another Oregon Season," *New York Times*, October 21, 2001.

13. In 2002, the final BCS standings ratified the clear primacy of the undefeated. Georgia (No. 4 in the AP) and USC (No. 5) each got bumped up one slot in the final BCS standings due to the computer rankings. Iowa's (No. 3) loss and weak schedule (forty-first, compared to Georgia's twenty-fourth toughest and USC's No. 1-toughest) shone through in the algorithms and also the BCS formula.

14. Bayes Theorem is named for Thomas Bayes, an English theologian and statistician. He posited that any probability A given B is true is conditioned as the probability of B given A is true, times the probability of A (given no conditions), in turn divided by the probability of B (given no conditions). This is the basis of conditional probability, which itself is foundational to understanding most of the algorithms used in sports-ranking algorithms.

15. It also helped that LSU beat high-quality opponent Georgia *twice*.

16. One half expected Captain Kirk to come beaming down to destroy the dehumanizing computers, sort of like in the *Star Trek* episode "A Taste of Armageddon."

17. Go check out https://www.thewareaglereader.com/2014/07/the-story-behind -the-2004-auburn-teams-national-championship-rings/ for more.

18. Michael Pinto, "The 20 Most Undeserving National Champions in College Football History," Bleacher Report, November 15, 2010, accessed at https:// bleacherreport.com/articles/518058-the-15-most-undeserving-national -champions-in-college-football-history.

19. https://bleacherreport.com/articles/1917815-bcs-years-in-review-2006-the -dawn-of-secs-reign-in-college-football.

20. A look at the final SRS power rankings places USC and Louisville as the two strongest programs in college football, ahead of Florida.

21. Check out https://bleacherreport.com/articles/541-florida-beats-ohio-state -odds-for-bcs-title.

CHAPTER 7

1. **2014**: The AP and CFP top four diverge; the AP ranked Baylor fourth, while the CFP ranked the Bears fifth and Ohio State fourth; however, all eight of the CFP top eight are in AP top eight. **2015**: The AP and CFP top four are exactly the same; all eight of the CFP top eight are in AP top eight. **2016**: Aside from Ohio State and Clemson being flip-flopped at Nos. 2 and 3, the AP and CFP top eight are the same. **2017**: The AP and CFP top eight are exactly the same. **2018**: The AP and CFP top four are exactly the same; all eight of the CFP top eight are in AP top eight. **2019**: The AP and CFP top five are exactly the same; seven of CFP top eight are also AP top eight; only Florida (AP No. 6, CFP No. 9) is not. **2020**: The AP and CFP top five are exactly the same; seven of the CFP top eight are also AP top eight; only Indiana (AP No. 7, CFP No. 11) is not. **2021**: The AP and CFP top five are exactly

the same; all eight of the CFP top eight are in AP top eight. **2022:** The AP and CFP top six are exactly the same; seven of the CFP top eight are also AP top eight; only USC (AP No. 8, CFP No. 10) is not. **2023:** The AP and CFP top four diverge; the AP ranked Florida State fourth, while the CFP ranked the Seminoles fifth and Alabama fourth; however, all eight of the CFP top eight are in AP top eight.

2. Grigory *Potemkin* was a Russian prince and confidant of Empress Catherine the Great. His name has become synonymous with setting up a deliberate ruse.

3. Stewart Mandel, "Mandel: CFP Expansion Arrives Just in Time for Everyone Outside the Big Ten, SEC," *The Athletic*, Sept. 2, 2022, accessed at https://theathletic.com/3562607/2022/09/02/college-football-playoff-expansion-conference-bids/.

4. Oregon State and Washington State, left in the dust when everyone else left the party, entered into a scheduling agreement with the Mountain West conference and also went to court to seize control of the PAC-12 and its assets.

5. Texas lost to Oklahoma, 34–30, on a neutral field in Dallas.

6. Alabama lost at home to Texas, 34–24.

7. I respectfully request that you read that name for the game in the voice of the late, great Keith Jackson.

8. After the season, Harbaugh would bolt to the NFL with a title in his pocket to take on the challenge of coaching the Los Angeles Chargers.

9. USC and UCLA first left for the Big Ten, followed by Arizona, Arizona State, Colorado, and Utah going to the Big 12, Oregon and Washington also joining the Big Ten, and then Cal and Stanford heading to the ACC while picking up SMU on the way.

10. The original Alabama Paradox has to do with congressional seat apportionments and a quirk of the 1880 Hamilton formula for distributing seats to states after a census. In this paradox, if the US House had 299 seats, then Alabama would get eight seats under the Hamilton formula. But if the House had 300 seats, Alabama would only get seven seats. Making the US House bigger by one seat caused Alabama to lose a seat. See Frances Robinson, "The Alabama Paradox," *Teaching Mathematics and Its Applications: International Journal of the IMA* 1, no. 2 (1982): 69–72.

11. The Tide did everyone the favor of losing the ReliaQuest Bowl on New Year's Eve to a 7-5 Michigan team that finished seventh in the Big Ten and had defeated eventual national champion Ohio State.

12. Linear regression estimates how strong and tight a straight-line relationship is between two things. Imagine you're tracking how many hot wings you eat and how many beers you drink at a party. You notice a pattern: the more wings you eat, the more beers you tend to drink. If you plot this on a graph (wings on one axis, beers on the other) for several parties you attend, linear regression helps find the straight line that best shows this relationship. That line can predict how many beers you'll drink based on the wings you eat. The slope shows how much your beer intake increases for every extra wing—thus, your "hot wings-to-beer" ratio!

13. The last time a team ranked so low in the final regular-season wire-service polls then won the national title was in the 1983 season, when No. 5 Miami (11–1) beat No. 1 Nebraska (then 11–0) in the Orange Bowl, 31–30, on January 2, 1984. That same day, the second-ranked Texas Longhorns and fourth-ranked Illinois Fighting Illini both lost. The Hurricanes vaulted over one-loss Auburn, ranked No. 3, for the AP writers and UPI coaches national titles. This was an unavoidable circumstance. All of the top-four teams were locked in to bowl games as conference champions, precluding a one-two matchup between Miami and Texas. The WarDamnPlainsTigerEagleMen cried foul. Various NCAA-recognized minor selectors, largely relying on algorithms, picked either Nebraska or Auburn as national champion, but the Cornhuskers and Tigers declined to claim those titles, averting a direct claimant conflict. The title was conceded to the wire-service champs.

APPENDIX A

1. My running buddy Zach Allen wants a Beer Goggle Test for each claim for each season. The Beer Goggle Test asks, "How many beers do you need to drink before the argument makes sense?" The more beer steins by the pick, the more beers you need to drink to agree with the argument.

APPENDIX C

1. The technique used, linear regression, shows that about 84 percent of the value of the AP ranking and 82 percent of the Coaches Poll ranking can be guessed from knowing the computer-ranking average. The Coaches and AP polls explain 98 percent of the value in each other. People are people . . . and they are also nearly computers.

2. There are sixty-eight cases where a team ranked in one of the top twenty-five human polls but had a computer average above twenty-five and also a dispersal measure greater than five. Of the sixty-eight teams in this group, twenty-seven came from Power 5 conferences and another eight came from the Big East. So roughly half of the teams with problematic computer ratings relative to human judgment were from the elite FBS conferences, which is consistent with the proportion of teams in the Power 5 appearing in BCS or CFP bowl games over these two decades.

3. Computers have biases too. The biases are programmed into them by the people who create their algorithms, based on the assumptions underlying the programming. Computers are consistent with their math and their decision criteria, which makes them more reliable over time (biases and all) than the more subjective human polls. However, human polls have a critical strategic advantage. The writers and coaches can argue unfiltered for their preferences when they disagree with the computers. Computers don't have that privilege.

4. B. Jay Coleman, Andres Gallo, Paul M. Mason, and Jeffrey W. Steagall, "Voter Bias in the Associated Press College Football Poll," *Journal of Sports Economics* 11, no. 4 (2019): 397–417; Mark David Witte and McDonald Paul Mirabile, "Not So Fast, My Friend: Biases in College Football Polls," *Journal of Sports Economics* 11, no. 4: 443–55.

5. James Keener, "The Perron–Frobenius Theorem and the Ranking of Football Teams," *SIAM Review* 35, no. 1 (1993): 80–93. The theorem deals with the problem of creating rankings under a positive matrix, where pairings across ranked competitors are not equal or uniform—that you are ranking absent the presence of a round-robin. This is not a problem in pro basketball or pro baseball, where long seasons ensure that rankings arise from competition involving all potential contenders.

INDEX

243

ABOUT THE AUTHOR

KEITH GÅDDIE is Hoffman Chair in the American Ideal and professor at TCU. Author of over 20 books, he is a graduate of FSU and a 'Double-Dawg' graduate of University of Georgia. He wrote this book under the careful supervision of his English bulldog Winston.